The Little
Mac iApps Book

The Little Mac iApps Book

A guide to Apple's applications, Mac.com, and more

John Tollett

with Robin Williams

Peachpit Press • Berkeley • California

The Little Mac iApps Book

©2003 John Tollet with Robin Williams

Cover design: John Tollett
Production: John Tollett and Robin Williams
Index: Laura Egley-Taylor and Robin Williams
Editing: Nancy Davis
Prepress: Hilal Sala
All interior illustrations and photographs ©2003 John Tollett

Peachpit Press

1249 Eighth Street
Berkeley, California 94710
800.283.9444
510.524.2178 voice
510.524.2221 fax

Find us on the World Wide Web at **www.peachpit.com**
To report errors, please send a note to errata@peachpit.com
Peachpit Press is a division of Pearson Education

ISBN 0-321-18747-4

10 9 8 7 6 5 4 3 2
Printed and bound in the United States of America

Contents

iLife

1 iPhoto   3

2 iTunes

3 iMovie

4 iDVD

5 Mail

Address Book

6 iCal

7 iChat and Rendezvous

.Mac apps

More Cool apps

AppleWorks: Spreadsheet

AppleWorks: Painting

AppleWorks: Drawing

AppleWorks: Presentation

18 OmniGraffle

19 FAXstf

20 Inkwell

Index

Index

A Book is Born

The Little Mac iApps Book was conceived late one November night as Robin worked feverishly to finish her *Mac OS X Book, Jaguar edition,* that was scheduled to be at the upcoming Macworld Expo in San Francisco. "Do you realize this book is going to be over 1500 pages if I include chapters for all of the iApps that come with OS X?" she asked as I clicked the Photoshop icon in my Dock. "Who wants a fifteen-hundred page book? You'll get a back ache just taking it to the checkout counter," she fumed as I chose "Save As" from the File menu. "There's so much OS X information to write about that we're going to have to put all the iApps in a separate companion book," she decided. "Good idea," I replied, as I set a radius of six pixels in Photoshop's Gaussian Blur window. "And you can write it cuz you like all that iMovie stuff," I heard through the cloud of Dust & Scratches I was removing from the image of the high desert.

That initial creative brainstorming session has resulted in this book, *The Little Mac iApps Book.* We've covered all the main applications that come with a Mac, and a few that may not be on every Mac but can be downloaded from the Internet. If there's a Mac application or utility that's not covered here, it's in the *Robin Williams Mac OS X Book, Jaguar edition.*

Some of the applications we explain in this book are available as part of a .Mac membership (pronounced "dot Mac," also referred to as a "Mac.com" account). The .Mac section tells all about the great software, features, and services it provides.

Enjoy your iApps and the other very cool applications that are designed exclusively for your Mac.

John

Section one

iLife

What is **iLife** and what does the "i" mean?

When the iMac was originally introduced, the "i" was explained as symbolizing both *innovation* and the computer's built-in *Internet* capabilities. But that was many millions of web pages ago. Now the "i" represents the concept of a digital lifestyle and the software applications that can enhance that lifestyle. Your Mac is meant to be a *digital hub* that enables the various iApps to work together as powerful, creative tools. At the core of the digital hub concept are four separate applications: iMovie, iPhoto, iTunes, and iDVD. As stand-alone applications, they're amazing—add the feature of built-in integration between them and the result is an increase in creativity and productivity that can only be described as *inspirational*. This special collection of applications is what's called **iLife.**

If you have a digital still camera, digital video camera, or a CD collection gathering dust, iLife will turn them into your most important creative tools. It's unofficial, but think of the "i" as a symbol for **inspiration** in your digital lifestyle. You're certain to find yourself thinking "iAppsolutely love iLife!"

iPhoto

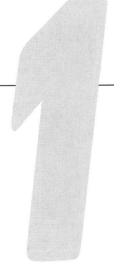

iPhoto

iPhoto is an application made exclusively for Mac OS X. It makes managing, sharing, and enhancing your digital photos both easy and fun. You can effortlessly import photos straight from most digital cameras, as well as from other sources, such as a digital card reader, CD, Zip disk, or from a location on your iMac's hard disk. Use iPhoto to organize and edit your photos, then share them with friends, relatives, or business associates in a number of different ways.

iPhoto's integration with iTunes and iDVD takes all the extra work and confusion out of potentially complex tasks, such as adding music to slideshows or creating DVD slideshows.

If you have a .Mac account (see page 271), you can use iPhoto to effortlessly create web photo albums and screensaver slideshows. iPhoto works with .Mac so you can order custom prints online. You can even create and order hard-cover photo albums of your own digital photos.

iPhoto's editing tools enable you to expertly retouch blemishes, adjust contrast and brightness, and make other adjustments.

If you don't own a digital camera, you can send your exposed film to companies that offer digital film service, then import those image files into iPhoto. These companies can process your film and put your photos on a CD or post them on the web for you to download. Visit **www.ofoto.com** or **www.shutterfly.com** to see what services are available.

For a list of **compatible** cameras, printers, and digital card readers check the iPhoto web site (**www.apple.com/iphoto**). If your digital device is not listed as compatible, there is still a chance that it may work—try it before you buy a new one.

iPhoto

Open iPhoto

Go to the Applications folder (click on the Applications icon in the Toolbar of any open Finder window), then double-click the "iPhoto" icon. The iPhoto window (below) opens, although yours will be empty if this is the first time you've used it.

The **Library** (top-left item in the window below) stores all the photos you ever import. Create separate **Albums** (pages 12–13) to store customized selections from the Library.

The Library:
Click here to
see your entire
collection of photos.

Viewing area.

Albums.

Resize button (drag).

Album pane.

File Information
area.

Play Slideshow.

Add new Album.

File information:
click to show Info,
click again to show
Comments pane.

Rotate.

Lower pane.

View buttons.

Size slider.

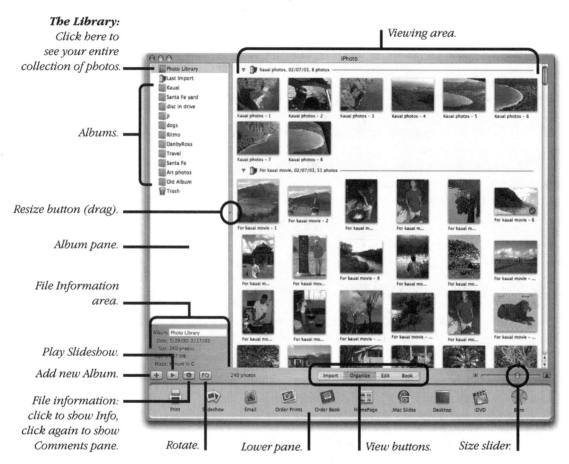

The iPhoto Main Window

Before you can use iPhoto's various features, you first have to **import** the photos into the Photo Library, as explained on the following pages. When you import photos, iPhoto considers each import a "Film Roll." That's why iPhoto automatically names each photo with a "Roll" number and an "image" number. A photo named "Roll 1 – 6" indicates that in "Film Roll" number one, this photo is the sixth image. You can **rename** any photo with a name that makes more sense, as shown below: Just select a photo, click on the photo's *Title* text field to highlight it, then type in the new name.

The photo Title: Click here, then type a new name.

Selected photo.

Import Your Photos to iPhoto

When a digital camera or a memory card reader is connected to the computer with a USB cable and recognized by iPhoto, the "Import" view button is automatically selected. The next few pages explain how to import your photos directly from a camera, a digital card reader, a CD, or a location on your hard disk.

Import photos from a digital camera

You can transfer photos directly into iPhoto if your camera has a USB port and if it is compatible with iPhoto (see page 3 regarding compatibility).

1. Turn your camera off.

2. To conserve your camera's battery power, we suggest you connect the camera's AC power adapter to the camera, then plug the adapter into a power outlet.

VIKINGFLASH

When you connect a digital camera to your Mac, an icon appears on your Desktop named with the brand of memory card that's in the camera.

3. Use the USB cable that came with the camera to connect the camera to your Mac's USB port. **Turn on your camera.** These things happen:

   ▼ An icon representing the digital card in your camera (shown to the left) appears on the Desktop, indicating it has been mounted.

   ▼ The Mac automatically recognizes the camera and opens iPhoto.

   ▼ iPhoto opens with the Import pane showing at the bottom of the main window (shown below).

   ▼ A camera icon and the name of the attached camera appears on the left side of the Import pane.

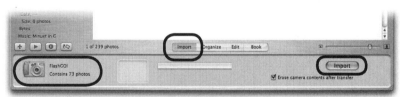

4. **To delete all the images from your camera** after they've been imported to iPhoto, select "Erase camera contents after transfer" in the lower-right corner of the Import pane.

5. Click the "Import" button on the right side of the Import pane (shown on previous page). To stop an import, click the "Stop" button.

6. After the photos have been imported, drag the digital card icon on the Desktop to the Trash to unmount it. **If you do not unmount the card before disconnecting the camera, you'll get an error message warning that you could possibly damage any images left on the memory card.**

7. Turn the camera off and disconnect it from your computer.

Thumbnail preview of imported images.

If there are images in your camera (or on your digital memory card) from the last import, iPhoto asks if you want to import the duplicate photo.

The imported photos are placed in the Photo Library. All of your newly imported photos will **always** go to the Photo Library. From there you can organize them, as described on pages 14–16.

Import photos from a digital card reader

You can import your photos from a **digital memory card reader,** even if your digital camera is not directly supported by iPhoto.

VIKINGFLASH

This icon appears on your Desktop, named for the card that's in the reader.

The most common types of memory cards are CompactFlash,™ SmartMedia,™ and Memory Stick.™ Some card readers can read only one type of memory card, while others can read two or more types of cards.

1. Make sure the card reader is connected to your iMac using the proper cable.

2. Take the digital memory card (CompactFlash, SmartMedia, or Memory Stick, etc.) out of your camera and insert it into the card reader.

   The card's icon appears on your Desktop, as shown to the left, indicating it has mounted.

3. iPhoto automatically recognizes the digital card and opens; if iPhoto is already open, it switches to "Import" view. The card reader, instead of a camera, is identified on the left side of the "Import" panel, shown below.

4. **To erase the contents of your digital card** after importing the photos, select "Erase camera contents after transfer" in the "Import" pane.

5. Click the "Import" button in the bottom-right. After you click "Import," it becomes a "Stop" button, as shown above. The lower pane of the iPhoto window shows the import in progress, plus a thumbnail (small version) of the current image being copied to iPhoto.

6. Unmount the digital card when all is done: drag its icon from the Desktop to the Trash.

   Or Control-click on the digital card icon and choose "Eject" from the contextual menu that pops up.

The imported photos are placed in the Photo Library. (They are also temporarily available through the "Last Import" icon in the Album pane, explained on page 10, until the next import session when another batch of photos becomes the "last" import.)

Import photos from a location on your hard disk or from a CD

You can import any photos that you already have stored on your hard disk or any that might be on a CD.

1. Press the Eject Media key on the upper-right corner of your keyboard to open the CD tray. If your keyboard does not have an Eject Media key, try pressing the F12 key.

2. Place the CD that contains photos you want to import into the tray, and press the Eject Media key to close the CD tray. If your CD drive is slot-loading, insert the CD into the slot.

3. Open iPhoto if it is not already open.

4. From the File menu, select "Import..." to open the "Import Photos" window, shown below. In the window, find the CD you inserted, or choose a location somewhere on your hard disk where photos are stored that you want to import.

5. Select an entire folder of photos, an individual photo, or multiple photos, then click the "Import" button.

The selected photos are placed in the iPhoto Library. They also appear in the "Last Import" roll shown in the Album pane, as explained on page 10.

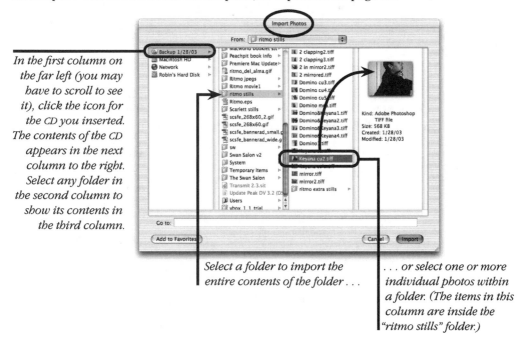

In the first column on the far left (you may have to scroll to see it), click the icon for the CD you inserted. The contents of the CD appears in the next column to the right. Select any folder in the second column to show its contents in the third column.

Select a folder to import the entire contents of the folder . . .

. . . or select one or more individual photos within a folder. (The items in this column are inside the "ritmo stills" folder.)

Viewing Your Photos

Once you've imported photos to iPhoto, there are several ways to view them within the main viewing area.

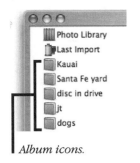

Album icons.

▼ Single-click the **Photo Library** icon (upper-left) to view all photos that have been imported into iPhoto during your various Import sessions.

▼ Single-click the **Last Import** icon in the Album pane (the white pane on the left) to show only the photos from the most recent Import session.

▼ Single-click an **Album** icon in the Album pane (the white pane on the left) to show only photos that have been placed in that specific Album (how to create and use Albums is explained on pages 12–13).

▼ From the View menu, choose "Arrange Photos."

By Film Roll arranges photos into the groups in which they were originally imported.

By Date arranges photos by the date they were taken in the camera, **if** you set the date in your camera before you took pictures.

By Title arranges photos alphabetically.

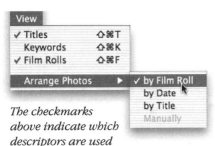

The checkmarks above indicate which descriptors are used with photos in the main View area.

Manually lets you drag photos to rearrange them, but only in Albums, not the Photo Library.

The "View mode" Buttons

Each **View button** beneath the viewing area gives you various options and tools to use (the tools for each button are displayed in the lower pane). Each of these views is explained in detail on the following pages.

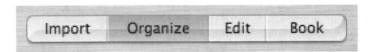

Import view: Supplies information and options for importing photos.

Organize view: Provides tools for organizing and sharing photos.

Edit view: Displays a larger version of the selected photo in the upper viewing area, and the lower pane switches to editing tools.

Book view: Provides tools for creating a hard-bound book.

File Information and Comments

iPhoto gives you file information about selected photos, such as date created, size in pixels (dimensions) and size in bytes (how much space it takes up on your hard disk), and what music is currently selected for slideshows. Comments you type in will be used in albums, books, or web pages created by iPhoto.

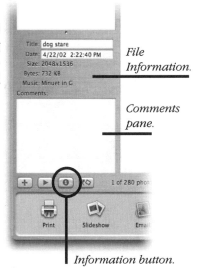

File Information.

Comments pane.

1. Single-click on a photo to select it.

2. Click the "Information" button to show File Information.

3. Click the "Information" button again to show the Comments pane. Type any comments you want in here.

4. Click the "Information button" once more to hide both the File Information and Comments pane.

Information button.

iPhoto Preferences

You can set basic characteristics that affect how you view your photos. Go to the iPhoto menu and choose "Preferences...."

Appearance:

> **Drop Shadow:** Shows photos in the viewing area with a drop shadow effect against a white background.
>
> **Border:** Places a white border around photos.
>
> **No Border:** Eliminates a border around photos.
>
> **Background:** Use the slider to adjust the background shade of the viewing area.
>
> **Align to grid:** Keeps photos neatly arranged by aligning them to an invisible grid.
>
> **Place most recent photos at the top:** Shows most recent photos taken, or imported, at the top of the viewing area.

Double-click:

> **Opens in Edit view:** Double-click a photo to open it in Edit view.
>
> **Open in separate window:** Double-click a photo to open it in a separate iPhoto window with a customizable Edit toolbar.
>
> **Opens in other:** Double-click a photo to open it in another application, such as Photoshop. Click "Select" to choose an application.

Rotate:

> Choose the direction photos will rotate when you use the Rotate tool.

Mail:

> Choose the email application you want to use with iPhoto's email feature.

Create an Album and Add Photos to It

Create **Albums** to help organize your photos, make them easier to find, and sort them in any order you wish.

You can put the same photo in any number of Albums because iPhoto just "points" to the original photo stored in the Library (like aliases on your Desktop), which means you don't end up with sixteen copies of the same photo taking up space on your hard disk.

1. **To create a new Album,** click the "Add" button in the lower-left corner of the iPhoto window, circled below.

The Photo Library is currently selected, which displays photos from all Import sessions. Each "Roll" in the Viewing area represents a separate Import session.

2. In the "New Album" dialog box that appears, enter a name for the Album and click OK. Your new Album appears in the Album panel.

3. **To add photos to the Album,** drag images from the viewing area and drop them on an Album icon.

After you click the "Add" button (below) and name an Album, the new Album appears here.

Photos that you delete from the Photo Library go to the Trash. They remain there until you empty the Trash. Go to the File menu and choose "Empty Trash."

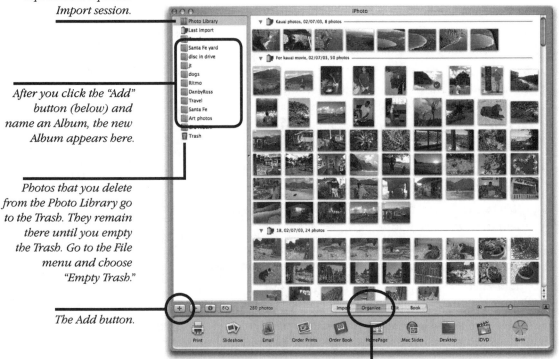

The Add button.

Use the "Organize" view to arrange, name, organize, or delete photos, as well as assign keywords and conduct searches for photos. See the following pages for details.

To rename an existing Album:

Double-click the Album name and type a new name.

To delete photos from an Album:

If you delete a photo from an Album, this will *not* delete it from the Photo Library—remember, the image in the Album "points" to the stored image in the Library. **But** if you delete a photo from the Photo Library, it *will* disappear from every Album that contained it.

1. Select an Album from which you want to delete one or more photos.

2. Select one or more photos to delete.

3. Press the Delete key.

To duplicate an Album:

You may want to experiment with different arrangements of photos for a book project or a slideshow. You can duplicate an entire Album. In the duplicate, you can rearrange the photos, delete some, add others, and it won't affect the original Album.

1. Single-click an Album in the Album pane to select it.

2. From the File menu, choose "Duplicate," **or** press Command D.

3. Double-click the new Album icon in the pane, then type a new name over the default name assigned by iPhoto.

The Organize View

After you've imported all the photos from the camera to iPhoto, you can begin organizing, arranging, and sharing them. The **Organize view** lets you see and select many photos at once, and provides all the tools you need to share your photos in many different ways.

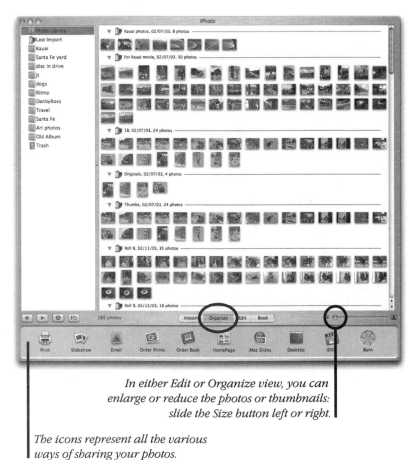

Double-click a thumbnail to display a large version of that photo in the Viewing area. This automatically switches iPhoto to the Edit view (depending on your Preferences settings).

To return to the Organize view, click the Organize button.

In either Edit or Organize view, you can enlarge or reduce the photos or thumbnails: slide the Size button left or right.

The icons represent all the various ways of sharing your photos.

Organize into Albums

At this point, for the sake of organization, you may choose to place selected images into an existing Album or create a new Album, as explained on the previous pages. (Briefly, to create a new Album, click the "Add" button [the plus sign], name the new Album, then drag photos into it.)

To delete unwanted photos from the Photo Library:

Note: If you delete a photo from the Photo Library, it *will* disappear from every Album that contained it, and from iPhoto itself.

Tip: When you delete a photo from an Album, it **will not** be deleted from the Photo Library.

▾ **To delete multiple photos that are next to each other** (contiguous), click on an image, then Shift-click on another image. All images between the two clicks are automatically selected. Press the Delete key to put all of the selected photos in the Trash.

▾ **To delete multiple photos that are NOT next to each other** (non-contiguous), Command-click on the images you want to select, then press the Delete key to put all selected photos in the Trash.

Photos deleted from the Photo Library are moved to the Trash icon in the Album pane. They are stored there until you go to the File menu and choose "Empty Trash." Or Control-click on the Trash icon and choose "Empty Trash" from the contextual menu.

To retrieve a photo from the Trash, click the Trash icon to display the images that are in it, then drag the photo from the viewing area to the Photo Library.

The Trash icon appears below the Albums in the Album pane.

To arrange the order of the photos:

When you create a Slideshow, Book, or HomePage (in the Share pane) iPhoto builds your project with your photos in the order they appear in the Album's viewing pane. So you might want to rearrange the photos in an Album or in the Library. There are a couple of ways to do this.

▼ **To change the order of photos in an Album** (this doesn't work in the Library), drag one or more images to the location desired. As you drag, a black vertical bar indicates where the photos will be placed when you release the mouse button.

▼ **In the Library,** you can arrange the photos by the date they were taken (if you set your camera's date before you took the pictures), by Title, or by import session ("Film Roll"): From the View menu, choose "Arrange Photos," then from that submenu, choose "by Film Roll," "by Date," or "by Title," as described on page 10.

Add titles and comments

The titles and comments that you type in the Information pane are used by the Book and Homepage features to add headlines and captions. When you create a web page or a book from these photos, you'll want them to have a meaningful name instead of something like DSCN0715.jpg. Meaningful titles also make it easier to conduct a search for photos.

1. Single-click a photo to select it.

2. Click the "Info" button (the "**i**" beneath the Album pane) to show that photo's Info area.

3. Click in the "Title" text field, then press Command A to select any existing text, that might be in that field, such as "Roll 1 - 6."

4. Type a new title into the "Title" text field.

5. Click the "Info" button again to show the "Comments" field. Click inside that field, then type a caption for the photo.

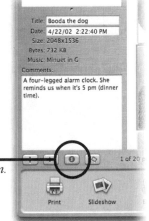

Information button.

Keywords and Searching

Searching for photos in iPhoto is fast and easy, especially if you previously assigned keywords or gave meaningful titles to your photos. You can create as many different keywords as you need and put them in the Keywords list.

To assign keywords to photos:

By assigning keywords to photos, you make it possible to search for photos based on those words. If you take the time now to assign keywords, you'll save a lot of time later when you're trying to find a certain photo.

1. From the Edit menu, choose "Keywords" to open the "Keywords/ Search" pane, or press Command K.

2. Select a photo or multiple photos in an album or in the Photo Library. (To select multiple photos, drag across a group of them, or hold down the Command key and click on individual photos.)

3. Single-click one of the preset keywords in the Keywords pane ("Family," for instance).

4. Click the "Assign" button. That keyword is now attached to the selected photos.

The checkmark (see below).

To assign multiple keywords: Select the photo in the viewer, hold down the Command key to select multiple keywords, then click "Assign."

To remove keywords from a photo: Select the photo in the viewer, select the keyword in the Keywords list, then click the "Remove" button.

To add, rename, or delete keywords from the list, including the ones that Apple has already provided: Select a keyword in the list, then click on the pop-up menu in the "Keywords/Search" pane (shown above, right), and make your choice. Of course, deleting a keyword from the list will also remove it from any photo.

The Keywords/Search window shows the keywords you can assign to your photos. Use the pop-up menu to edit existing keywords or create new ones.

To display the keywords in the viewer pane, go to the View menu and choose "Keywords." They will display next to each photo that has them.

The checkmark

The checkmark acts as a temporary keyword, useful for marking photos for which you haven't decided on a keyword or category. You can search for all photos that have a checkmark.

Photos that have been assigned a "checkmark" have a checkmark in the bottom-right corner.

To search for photos by using keywords:

1. From the "Edit" menu, choose "Keywords" to open the "Keywords/ Search" window.

2. Click on the Album you want to search, or click "Photo Library" to search your entire collection.

3. Single-click one of the keywords in the Keywords/Search window.

4. Click the "Search" button.

iPhoto displays all the photos that have been assigned that keyword.

This search of the Photo Library found all photos with the keyword "DVD project." Some of the photos have also been assigned a checkmark.

To search for titles and comments:

You can search for photos by typing a word or phrase that you remember as part of the photo's title, or words that you typed into the photo's "Comments" pane.

1. Select an album to search, or select the Photo Library to search all photos.

2. From the Edit menu, choose "Keywords" to open the "Keywords/ Search" window.

3. In the "Search" edit box, type a word you might have used in the photo's Title or Comments. As you type, only those photos that match your text appear in the viewing area.

4. To show all of the photos in the selected album again, click the "Show All" button.

The photos in the viewing area were found in this search because they all had the word "Kauai" in their title.

The Edit View

In the Edit view you can perform basic image-editing operations, such as adjusting brightness and contrast, cropping, reducing red-eye, and converting an image from color to black-and-white. The new Enhance wand and Retouch brush make image adjustment and retouching incredibly easy.

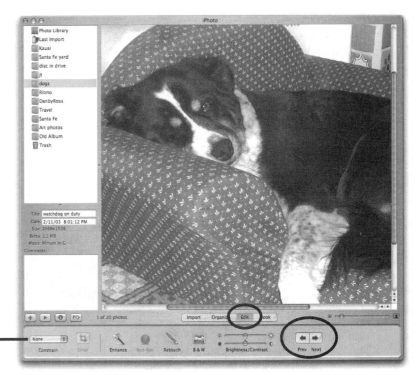

Editing tools

To view a photo for editing:

Select a photo, then click the "Edit" view button (beneath the viewing area). Two things happen:

▾ The selected photo fills the entire viewing area.

▾ The lower pane displays iPhoto's editing tools.

To choose the previous or next photo in the collection without leaving Edit view, click the "Prev" or "Next" buttons in the bottom-right.

To undo editing changes:

As you make the changes described on the following pages, you can use the Undo command (Command Z, or "Undo" from the Edit menu) to undo your steps, one at a time.

Once you quit iPhoto, you cannot use Command Z to undo any changes you made last time you used iPhoto. But you can go to the File menu and choose "Revert to Original" and the original photo will reappear.

Create a duplicate photo before you do anything drastic

When you drag a photo from the Library into an Album, iPhoto doesn't make a separate *copy* of that photo—it puts a "link" from the Album to the original photo that's still stored in the Library. This prevents your hard disk from getting full of multiple copies of the same photo.

So when you edit a photo, you affect its appearance not only in the Photo Library *but in all other Albums in which that photo appears.* To avoid changing the photo's appearance in every instance, create a *duplicate* of the photo and edit the duplicate.

1. Select a photo in the Photo Library. You can duplicate a photo in an Album, and it will appear in both the Album *and* the Library; any changes you make will apply to both duplicates, since they're actually the same photo.

2. From the File menu, choose "Duplicate," **or** press Command D.

3. Rename the duplicate photo: select it, then enter a new name in the Title field of the Information area (click the "Info" button beneath the Album pane to show the Title field, as shown below).

4. Edit the duplicate photo.

Warning: It's possible to duplicate an entire Album (select the Album name, then press Command D), but any editing changes you make to photos in the duplicate Album will apply to the original photos!

Original photo.   *Duplicate photo.*

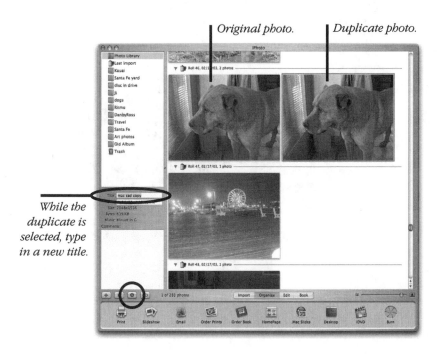

While the duplicate is selected, type in a new title.

Cropping this photo brings more attention to Booda's alertness.

Crop an image

The Crop tool lets you select the most important part of a picture and delete the rest of it. Thoughtful cropping makes your photos stronger and more visually interesting.

1. Select a photo.
2. Click the "Edit" view button.
3. Select an option (explained below) from the Constrain pop-up menu, which is on the left side of the Edit pane (bottom of the window).

   The Constrain menu gives you common proportion ratios to apply to the Crop tool. Choose "None" if you want no restraints on your cropping. Choose one of the other options to limit your cropping area to a specific ratio. For instance, if you plan to use the photo in an iPhoto book, select the "4 x 3 (Book, DVD)" option.

4. Position the pointer at one corner of the desired cropping area, then press-and-drag diagonally to select a cropping area, as shown below. Let go of the mouse.

   To move the crop selection, *press* inside the cropping area and drag.

   To resize the crop selection, position the tip of the pointer in any corner of the cropping selection; when the pointer changes to a "pointing finger," press-and-drag the selection to the desired size.

5. Single-click the "Crop" button.

Limit the shape and proportion of the cropped area by selecting an option from the Constrain pop-up menu.

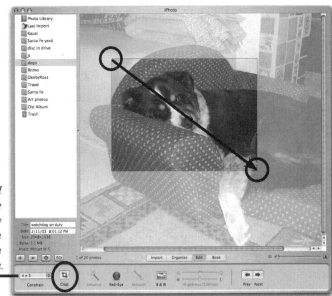

Drag the arrow pointer diagonally to draw a cropping area within the selected photo. The "faded out" area will be deleted when you click the "Crop" button.

Click the "Crop" button after you draw a selection.

Jazz up photos with the Enhance wand

Sometimes images look pretty good because you don't have anything to compare them to. Colors may be dull and the contrast may be flat, but who notices? The Enhance wand analyzes an image and automatically adjusts the color and contrast. You will not always prefer the enhanced version, but it often makes dramatic improvements to photos.

To compare the "enhanced" photo to the original version, press the Control key. Release the Control key to show the current effect.

To use the Enhance wand:

1. Select a photo from an Album or from the Photo Library.

2. Click the "Edit" button to fill the viewing area with the photo.

3. Click the "Enhance" wand once. Check the photo in the viewing area to see if you like the changes.

    If you don't like the new version, undo the operation by pressing Command Z. Or, from the Edit menu, choose "Undo Enhance Photo."

    If the enhancement is not dramatic enough, click the Enhance wand again.

To return to the original after several adjustments, press Command Z several times, or, from the File menu, choose "Revert to Original."

Experiment with a combination of adjustments to find the best results. I often use the Enhance wand, then adjust the contrast with the Brightness/Contrast sliders (see page 26).

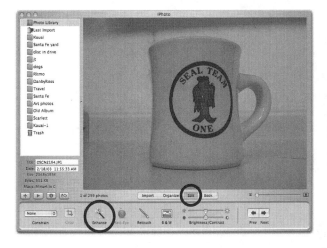

The Enhance wand can often make dramatic improvements in your photos.

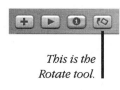

*This is the
Rotate tool.*

Rotate an image

You can rotate a photo from any view mode. Just select a photo and click the "Rotate" tool to rotate the image 90 degrees counterclockwise (if counter-clockwise is what you chose in Preferences, page 11). Additional clicks will continue to rotate the image in 90-degree increments.

Option-click the Rotate tool to rotate the photo in the opposite direction indicated by the Rotate icon.

Reduce red-eye

Use the Red-Eye tool to eliminate or reduce the red glare in a subject's eyes caused by the flash. The results may vary with different photos.

1. Select a photo that needs red-eye reduction.
2. Click the "Edit" view button (if you're not already there).
3. In the Edit pane, choose "None" from the Constrain menu so you will be able to draw freely.
4. Press-and-drag a selection around the area of one eye. Select as small an area as possible. If necessary, zoom in on the photo before making your selection: drag the Size control toward the right.
5. Single-click the Red-Eye tool. iPhoto will remove all red from the selected area. Repeat steps 4 and 5 for the other eye.

If you're not satisfied with the results, press Command Z (Undo), or from the File menu choose "Revert to Original."

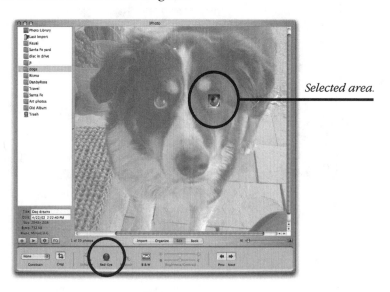

Selected area.

Touch-up photos with the Retouch brush

Even your best photos usually have some imperfections in them. If you scanned a photo, dust or scratches on the scanner glass may be visible, and digital images straight from a camera contain artifacts or digital "noise" that appears as oddly colored pixels in the image. There's also the possibility that the model or the background could have a blemish you want to remove.

The Retouch brush does an excellent job of fixing minor problems. Acting like a combination blur and smudge brush, it blends the pixels under the brush into the surrounding area.

Any retouching changes you make are applied to the original photo in the Photo Library, even if you selected the photo from an Album instead of from the Photo Library. **The retouched version will replace all occurrences of the photo in all Albums in which it appears.** If you want to prevent this, make a duplicate of the photo *before* you make changes.

To use the Retouch brush:

1. Select a photo to retouch.
2. Click the "Edit" button to fill the viewing area with the photo. Use the "Size" slider to enlarge the area you want to retouch.
3. Click the "Retouch" icon in the "Edit tools" pane.
4. Press and drag the brush cursor (cross-hairs) on top of blemishes, using short strokes.

The retouched photo, above, shows how expertly you can make repairs to an image.

Retouch brush cursor.

Convert a photo to black & white

To convert a photo to black and white, select it and click the "Edit" button. In the Edit pane, click the "B & W" button.

Remember, this will affect how this photo looks in every Album it appears in. If you don't want to affect other occurrences, make a duplicate of the photo, rename it, and convert the duplicate to black and white.

Adjust the brightness and/or contrast

When a photo is a little too dark or too light, you can adjust the brightness and contrast. It's an easy way to juice up a flat photo.

To adjust the brightness and/or contrast, open a photo in Edit view. Drag the "Brightness/Contrast" sliders left or right until you're satisfied with the results.

The settings for this photo have not been altered.

While in Edit view, you can move from one photo to another with the "Prev" and "Next" buttons.

In this photo, I increased the brightness (moved the Brightness slider to the right) and increased the contrast (moved the Contrast slider to the right).

Even photos that don't need brightness and contrast adjustments can be manipulated to create different and unusual effects.

Open photos directly into another image-editing application

iPhoto's editing tools are fairly limited. For additional image editing, you might want to open a photo in another program, such as Adobe Photoshop (for professionals) or Adobe Photoshop Elements (for home users).

1. From the iPhoto menu, choose "Preferences...."

2. In the Preferences window, find the "Double-click" option.
   Click the button "Opens in other," circled below.

3. Click the "Select..." button to get an "Open" dialog box.
   Find and select the application you want to use for more advanced image editing. Click "Open" (bottom-right corner).

4. Close the Preferences window.

Select the "Opens in other" button, then click "Select..." so you can choose another application in the "Open" window (shown below).

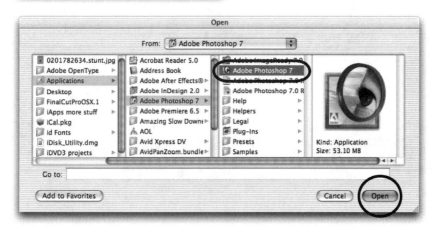

5. Double-click on a photo in iPhoto's viewing area. iPhoto will open the photo in the image-editing application you selected.

Tip: If you want photos to open into individual windows every time you double-click, choose that option in the Preferences; see the previous page.

Edit a photo in a separate window

You can choose to edit a photo in its own, separate window rather than in the iPhoto window. This lets you customize the window Toolbar to display the tools you use most.

To open a photo in a separate window, hold down the Option key and double-click a photo.

Click this icon to display the Customize Toolbar sheet, shown below.

This separate window lets you edit the photo without losing the entire window view of thumbnails. You can open a number of separate windows— just Option-double-click on any number of thumbnails.

Drag an item to any location in the toolbar.

If you use a certain cropping constraint often, such as 8 x 10, drag one of the Portrait (P) or Landscape (L) Constrain icons to the toolbar. Before you crop a photo, click the constrain icon in the toolbar and the Crop tool will be constrained to that proportion.

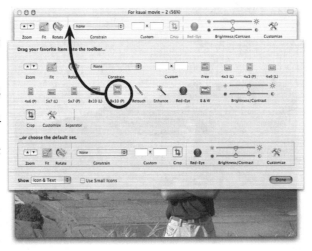

Drag toolbar items sideways to rearrange them.

Command-drag items off the toolbar.

Click the Hide/Show button in the upper-right to hide or show the toolbar.

Change how the buttons are displayed in the toolbar (use the Show menu, bottom-left).

The Book View

Through iPhoto, you can create a professionally printed hard-bound copy of a Book you design with your photos and captions. It might be a catalog, picture book, story book, portfolio, or any other sort of Book you dream up. After you create it, you can order it with the click of a button and your beautiful Book will be delivered to your door. A ten-page book costs $30, and it's about $3 for each additional page.

Create a Book with your own photographs

1. First create a new Album (as explained on pages 12–13), *or* select an existing Album. The order that photos appear in an Album is the order in which they will appear in the book that you create, so rearrange the photos before you start building your Book. The first page in the Album will be the cover of your Book.

2. With your Album open, click the "Book" button to show the layout in the large viewing area, a scrolling thumbnails pane, and the Book layout tools in the lower pane.

3. Choose one of the design themes from the "Theme" pop-up menu. *—continued*

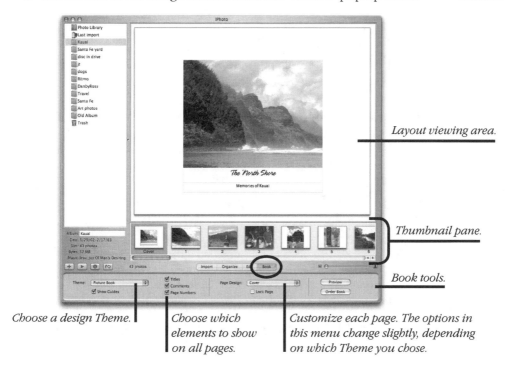

Layout viewing area.

Thumbnail pane.

Book tools.

Choose a design Theme.

Choose which elements to show on all pages.

Customize each page. The options in this menu change slightly, depending on which Theme you chose.

4. Select a thumbnail page in the Thumbnails pane, then from the "Page Design" pop-up menu, choose a page layout style.

5. You can add titles and comments to most photo pages, depending on the theme style or page design you choose.

   To edit the text on a Book page, select the text in the text box and type your changes.

   To add text directly to a Book page, click inside any text box and it will enlarge so you can see your text as you type.

   To choose a font, go to the Edit menu and choose "Font...."

   If you need to **rearrange photos, add or delete photos, or edit** individual photos, click the "Organize" button to go back to your Album. Your Book for this Album will stay as you left it; when you return to the Book, it will reflect the changes you made in the Album.

6. Choose to show or hide "Titles," "Comments," and/or "Page Numbers" on the Album pages by clicking (or not clicking) their checkboxes. These options affect the entire Book, not individual pages.

7. Click the "Preview" button to see how your finished Book will look.

Yellow triangle?

When you create a Book, some images may display a low-resolution warning (a yellow triangle containing an exclamation mark). iPhoto warns you if a photo has a resolution that is lower than that recommended for quality printing. Such photos will still print, but they may look pixelated and jaggy or appear to be of lower quality. If you plan to shoot photos for a Book, set your camera to at least a medium-quality setting or even high-quality. You can often salvage a low-resolution photo by choosing a page layout that shows two or three photos on a page, making the photo smaller and its resolution less problematical.

If a caution sign appears on a photo in Book view,
it means the photo will print at a very low quality.

Congratulations! You've designed and built a great looking coffee-table Book. To order copies of this Book with a single click, see the opposite page.

To order your Book:

After you create a Book (as explained on the previous pages), you can order hard-bound copies of it using your Internet connection.

1. With the Book open on your screen, click the "Order Book" button.

2. Your Mac will connect to the Internet (if it isn't already) and open the "Order Book" window, shown below. A "Progress" window opens on the Desktop as the "Assembling Book…" process takes place.

Click here to order your book.

3. If the button in the lower-right says, "Enable 1-Click Ordering," click it. You will be asked to start an Apple account and provide your name, address, and credit card information (don't worry—this is safer than giving your card to an unknown waiter who takes it to the back room), as well as your shipping preferences. If you already have an Apple account, you will be asked to turn on "1-Click Ordering." Click OK.

4. In the "Order Book" window, choose a color for the cover, the quantity of Books (they will all be copies of this one Book), and the shipping options.

5. Click "Buy Now."

6. You'll see a "Transferring book …" progress window that indicates the files for your Book are being transferred via the Internet to the publisher. Your Book will arrive on your doorstep in about a week.

If this button says "Enable 1-Click Ordering," you must click it to set up an Apple account before you can order a Book.

You'll receive a notice when the ordering process is finished.

The Organize Pane

The Organize pane is visible when you are in the "Organize" view and contains tools that let you share your photos with others in a variety of ways. You can print your photos in various formats, create a slideshow to play on your computer, export a QuickTime slideshow for others, order professional prints over the Internet, order a professionally bound, hard-cover book, create a web site and publish it with blinding speed, burn your photos to a CD or DVD, and more.

Print

Print your photos to your desktop printer

1. Select a single photo or multiple photos from an Album or from the Photo Library.

The "Style" pop-up menu offers these options.

2. Click the "Print" icon in the Organize pane.

3. In the Print window, click the "Style" pop-up menu and choose one of the print Style options. Each option will display different parameters; check it out.

4. Enter the number of copies to print.

5. Put photo-quality paper in your printer and click "Print."

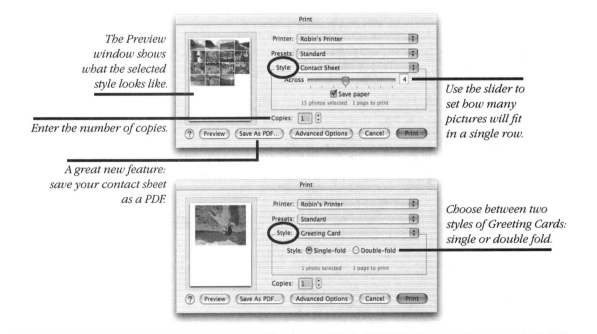

The Preview window shows what the selected style looks like.

Enter the number of copies.

Use the slider to set how many pictures will fit in a single row.

A great new feature: save your contact sheet as a PDF.

Choose between two styles of Greeting Cards: single or double fold.

Create a slideshow to view on your iMac

With the Slideshow tool in the Organize pane you can quickly create a slide-show with a sound track that will play full-screen on your monitor.

1. Select an Album, the Photo Library, or a group of photos within either collection.

2. Click the "Slideshow" icon. The "Slideshow Settings" window will open, as shown below.

An advantage of creating a separate Album for a slideshow (or for any project) is that you can rearrange the photos in an Album in the order you want them to appear.

3. Enter the number of seconds for each photo to display.

4. Choose if you want the photos to display in random order.

5. Select the music you want to use for a sound track: From the "Music" pop-up menu, select "iTunes Library." Choose any song that you've imported into iTunes.

   Select "Sample Music" to play one of the songs that Apple has provided for you, in case you haven't had time yet to import any of your own music.

6. Click "Play Slideshow" to start the slideshow.

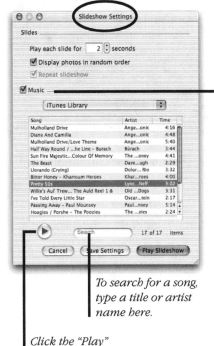

If your computer is in an office, you may prefer that your slideshow be silent. In this case, uncheck the "Music" checkbox.

To search for a song, type a title or artist name here.

Click the "Play" button to preview your song selection.

Slideshow quick-play

You don't have to go through the Settings window to play a slideshow: Just select an Album or a group of photos, then click the "Play" button. You might have to wait a few seconds while iPhoto prepares the show.

Play Slideshow.

Slideshow keyboard commands

Use keyboard commands to control the playback of your iPhoto slideshow:

- ▼ **Up arrow:** Speeds up the slideshow.
- ▼ **Down arrow:** Slows down the slideshow.
- ▼ **Spacebar:** Toggles the slideshow between Play and Pause.
- ▼ **Left and right arrow keys:** Shows the previous slide or next slide.
- ▼ **Mouse:** Stops the slideshow.

Send your photos through email

One way to share your photos is to send them to someone through email.
iPhoto makes it incredibly easy to do just that.

1. Select one or more photos in the viewing area; you can choose
   photos from any Album or from the Photo Library.

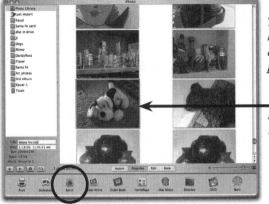

*To select multiple photos,
hold the Command key
as you click on your
photo selections.*

*Selected photos
show blue borders.*

Note: If you use AOL, go
to the Preferences and
choose "America Online"
as your email application.
The "Email" button in the
lower pane will turn into
an AOL button and you can
send photos to anyone.

**Note: If you use any other
email program,** people
receiving your photos
who use older versions of
America Online may have
trouble seeing the iPhotos
you send this way.

2. Click the "Email" icon in the Organize pane to open the "Mail Photo"
   window (shown below).

3. In the "Mail Photo" window, choose a photo size from the pop-up
   menu, and choose whether to include titles and comments that
   you may have added to photos (as explained on page 5). Click
   the "Compose" button.

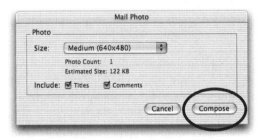

4. Compose your email message in the "New
   Message" window that opens (as shown to the
   right). Your photos are already sized and placed
   in the message area.

5. Click the "Send" icon in the email window
   Toolbar. Your Mac will connect to the Internet
   (if it isn't already) and send the photos along
   with your email. Amazing.

Order traditional prints of your photos

You can order regular, real, hold-in-your-hand prints of any photo or collection of photos. Your first **ten** 4x6 prints are **free!**

1. Make sure you're connected to the Internet.

2. Select an Album or a group of photos within an Album or in the Photo Library.

3. Click the "Order Prints" button in the Organize pane.

4. If the button in the lower right says, "Enable 1-Click Ordering," click it. You will be asked to start an Apple account and provide your name, address, and credit card information, as well as your shipping preferences.

   If necessary, click the "Order Prints" button again in the Organize pane to reopen the Order Prints window.

5. Select the size and quantity you want of each photo in the "Order Prints" window:

   In the top-right corner you can "Quick Order" 4x6 prints. Click the top arrow button to order one 4x6 of each photo in the list. Click again to change the order to two 4x6 prints of each photo. Every click adds to the order. To lower the quantity, click the bottom arrow button.

   In addition to **or** instead of the above, you can select individual photos and buy separate prints, like a 16x20 or a collection of four wallet-sized.

   As you enter a number to order each photo, the amount is instantly calculated in the window. You can always type in "0" to change your mind.

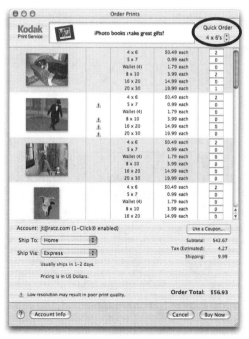

6. Click the "Buy Now" button. Depending on the shipping option you chose in the "Ship Via" pop-up window, you should have your prints in several days. Wow.

If you see yellow triangle warnings next to certain print sizes in the "Order Prints" window, it indicates that the photo's resolution is not suitable for a quality print at that size. A smaller size may be available without a warning.

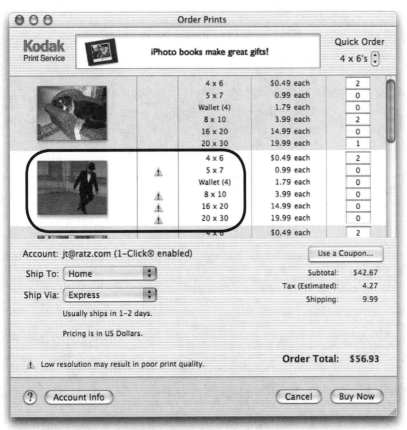

The photo above was originally captured from a single frame of video, then imported into iPhoto. Because video resolution is low (72 pixels per inch), this image is not suitable for printing at larger sizes, but should be fine printed as wallet size or as a 4x6 print.

HomePage

Build a HomePage Photo Album and publish it to the web

If you signed up for a .Mac account (as explained on page 271), iPhoto will automatically create and publish a web site of your selected photos and store it on Apple's Internet servers. It's really incredible.

Tip: To create a web page with your photos that you can upload to a site you already own, see pages 46–47.

1. Select an Album or a group of photos within an Album. The order in which photos appear in the Album determines the order in which they appear on the web page that iPhoto creates. To rearrange photos, drag them into new positions in the Album.

2. Click the "HomePage" button in the Oganize pane. Your Mac will connect to the Internet and open the "Publish HomePage" window, as shown below. Your selected images are displayed on a web page template that you can customize.

If your web page appears with only one photo on it, perhaps you accidentally had one photo selected in the Album. Click "Cancel" and go check.

All text in this window is editable.

Publish HomePage

Kauai's North Shore

There's a place... I recall... not very big... in fact in kinda small...

Two locals   The Napali Coast   Josh

Hanalei River   Hanalei morning   Sunset

Click a framestyle to apply it to the page.

From the pop-up menu, choose your .Mac account name.

Publish to: roadrat   Include: ☑ "Send Me a Message"

Layout: ○ 2 Columns   ◉ 3 Columns   ☑ Counter

Click "Publish."

Cancel   Publish

3. Click one of the thumbnail images at the bottom of the window to choose a style for the frames that will border your photos. The same frame will border every photo on the page.

Tip: To remove a HomePage Photo Album, log in to your .Mac account, then click the "HomePage" button. You'll see a list of the Albums you have posted. Single-click on the name, then click the minus sign right below the list.

4. Select the existing captions on the page (press-and-drag over the text) and replace them with your own words. If you have given titles to photos (as explained on page 5), those titles appear as captions on your HomePage.

5. From the "Publish to" pop-up menu at the bottom of the window (shown above, bottom-left), select your .Mac account name.

6. Click the "Publish" button. After the files have been transferred to Apple's .Mac server, a notice will appear telling you the web address of your new web site; this notice has a button called "Visit Page Now." Click it to open your brand-new HomePage Photo Album.

This notice gives you the web address for your HomePage Photo Album. Click "Visit Page Now" to see it online.

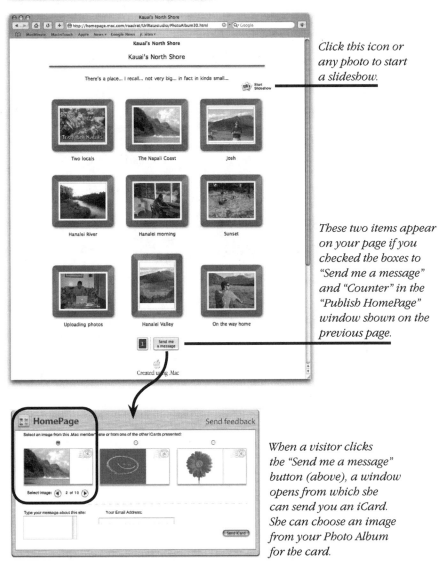

Click this icon or any photo to start a slideshow.

These two items appear on your page if you checked the boxes to "Send me a message" and "Counter" in the "Publish HomePage" window shown on the previous page.

When a visitor clicks the "Send me a message" button (above), a window opens from which she can send you an iCard. She can choose an image from your Photo Album for the card.

.Mac Slides

Publish your slideshow on the Internet with .Mac Slides

If you have a .Mac (pronounced "dot Mac") account, .Mac Slides lets you publish a slideshow to your iDisk (storage space on Apple's servers) and anyone who uses Mac OS X version 10.2 (Jaguar) or later can view the slideshow on the Internet.

To create a .Mac slideshow:

1. Click the "Organize" button.

2. Select photos to use in the .Mac slideshow.
   Photos must be selected *individually,* not by clicking on an Album in the Album list. You can either Command-click on individual photos in the viewing area, or drag a selection around the desired photos.

3. Click the ".Mac Slides" button.

4. In the window that opens, click the "Publish" button.

When you publish a .Mac slideshow, it replaces any other slideshow you may have previously published to that .Mac account name.

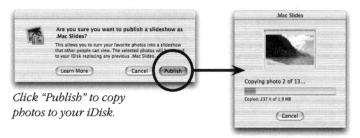

Click "Publish" to copy photos to your iDisk.

5. After your photos have been copied to your iDisk, click the "Announce Slideshow" button to send an email announcement. The automatically generated email contains instructions for viewing your .Mac slideshow. Address the email to one or more friends, then click "Send."

See Chapter 15 for more information about .Mac Slides Publisher. See Chapter 9 for information about iDisk.

Use a photo as your Desktop background

Select one of your photos to use as a Desktop image. It's a great way to personalize the appearance of your Mac. Any photo you choose will fill the Desktop space.

1. Single-click **one** photo in any Album or from the Photo Library.

2. Click the "Desktop" icon in the Share pane. The selected photo displays instantly on your Desktop.

This is a picture of Mac The Dog as a Mac Desktop image.
Notice I selected a photo that won't interfere with the visibility
of the Desktop icons in the upper-right corner of the screen.

Send photos to iDVD

If you have a SuperDrive in your Mac (a drive that can read *or write* DVDs), you can send a selection of photos to the iDVD application to make a DVD slideshow, which you can then burn to a DVD. In iDVD you can add music to play with the slideshow. To learn more more about iDVD, see Chapter 4.

To send photos to iDVD:

1. Click the "Organize" button.

2. Select an entire Album, or a group of photos from an Album or from the Photo Library.

3. Click the iDVD icon in the Organize pane. (The iDVD icon will not appear unless your Mac has a SuperDrive.)

4. iDVD opens and automatically creates a menu with a title and a "text button" that links to a slideshow of your photos. You can customize the iDVD menu in all sorts of ways, change the design theme, the font style, the music, the slide duration, and more (see Chapter 4 for details).

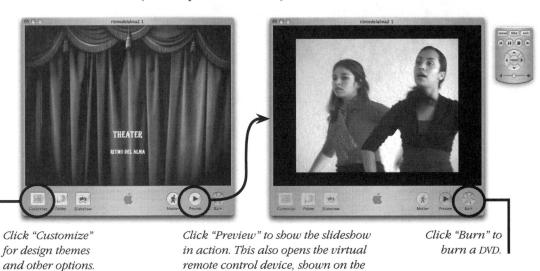

Click "Customize" for design themes and other options.

Click "Preview" to show the slideshow in action. This also opens the virtual remote control device, shown on the right. Use it to test the slideshow.

Click "Burn" to burn a DVD.

5. Click the "Burn" icon in the lower-right corner of the iDVD window to burn the slideshow to a DVD. *Or* just save the project so you can work on it later.

Burn a CD or DVD-R disc from selected photos

To burn your photo collections onto a CD or DVD, your computer must have an Apple-supported CD or DVD drive. If your computer has a SuperDrive, it can burn CDs or DVDs. The advantage of burning a DVD-R disc is that it holds much more that a CD (4.7 gigabytes of data, compared to 650 megabytes).

The "Burn" button looks like this before you click it.

To burn photos onto a disc:

1. Select a collection of photos to burn to a disc (one or more Albums, individually selected photos, or the entire Photo Library).

2. Click the "Burn" icon in the Organize pane.

3. Insert a blank disc. Depending on the kind of drive in your computer, the disc can be a CD-R (CD recordable), a CD-RW (CD rewritable), or a DVD-R (DVD recordable).Click OK.

The "Burn" button looks like this after you click it.

A disc icon appears in iPhoto's information panel. The green color on the disc icon shows how much of the disc space is required to burn your photo selection (shown on the right).

4. After you insert a disc, click the "Burn" icon in the Organize pane again.

5. In the "Burn Disc" window that opens, click the "Burn" button.

The darker color on the disc shows how much disc space the selected photos take.

6. The disc ejects when the burning is finished.

This process does not allow multiple burning sessions. After you burn a disc, the disc is "closed" and you can't put additional data onto it.

Export Photos in Various Formats

There are still more ways to share your photos with iPhoto. You can save photos into various file formats, export them as a web page, or use them to create a QuickTime slideshow.

Export copies or convert photos to other file formats

You might want to export photos to a different project folder or convert them to another file format. This does *not* remove the photos from the Photo Library. The converted or exported photos will be *copies* of the originals; any changes you make to those copies will not affect the originals.

To export or convert photos:

1. Select a single photo, an Album, or a group of photos within an Album or the Photo Library.

2. From the File menu, choose "Export...."

3. In the "Export Photos" window that appears, click the "File Export" tab.

4. From the **Format** pop-up menu, select a file format in which to save photos: "Original" saves photos in whatever format they currently use. The other options are "JPG," TIF," and "PNG." If you're not familiar with file formats, "JPG" is a safe choice that anyone can use. Most digital cameras create photos in this format. If you plan to place the exported image in a page layout application for a printed project, TIF would be the correct format.

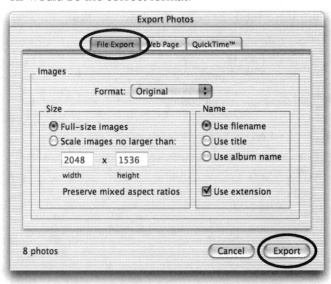

5. **Size:** "Full-size images" exports photos the same size as the original. *Or* you can enter specific dimensions in pixels.

6. **Name:**

   Use filename: The exported photos will have the default names your digital camera assigned (such as "DSCN0715.jpg"), unless you've renamed them.

   Use title: The photos will display the titles you gave them in iPhoto.

   Use album name: The photos will display the Album name and a number for each image ("Kauai-07," for example).

   Use extension: The file format extension will appear at the end of the file name ("Kauai-07.jpg," for example).

7. Click "Export." In the "Export Images" dialog box (below), iPhoto automatically chooses the "Pictures" folder. If you want to put your copied photos into another, separate folder, click the "New Folder" button, and name the new folder. The pictures will be saved into that folder, which you can find in the Pictures folder. And, of course, you can save the exported files anywhere on your computer.

8. Click OK to export the photos.

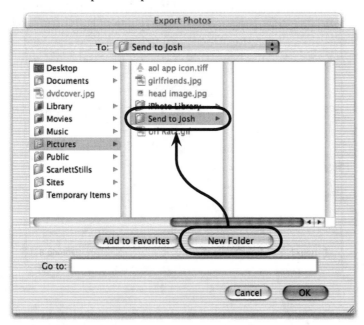

Save exported files into any folder on your computer or create a new folder in any location.

Export your photos as a web site

The Web Page option of the "Export Images" window is very different from the HomePage feature as explained on pages 38–39. This Web Page tool creates a slightly plainer web site and saves it on your computer—it does not post this site on Apple's server. You can upload this site yourself to a server of your choice, or you may want to burn the site to a CD to share with others.

To export your photos as a web site:

1. Select an Album or a group of photos within an Album. The order the photos appear in an Album is the order they will appear in the Web Page you create.

2. From the File menu, choose "Export...."

3. In the "Export Photos" window that opens, click the "Web Page" tab.

4. Make the following choices:

   Title: Enter a title for the Web Page.

   Columns and Rows: Choose how many columns and rows of thumbnail photographs to create on the start page (the first page of the web site).

   Background: To choose a background color, click the **Color** radio button, then click the color box for the palette. To choose a background image for the page, click the **Image** radio button, click "Set...," then from the "Open" dialog box, choose an image.

   Text Color: Click the box to choose a color for the text on the page.

See item #6 on the next page to learn why we named our new folder "index" (see the bottom-right example).

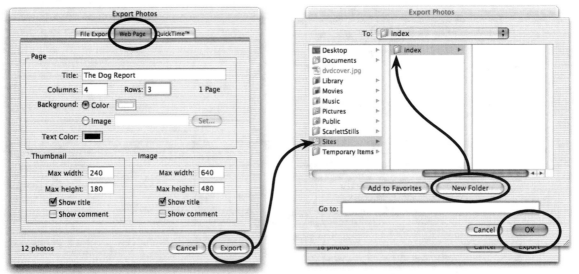

Thumbnail: Set maximum widths and heights for thumbnail images (the small photos on the start page) and for full-size images (the large photos that will appear on individual pages).

Show title: Place the title you assigned to photos under the thumbnail version on the start page.

Show comment: Show comments associated with photos.

Image: Same as "Thumbnail" settings but applies to the large photo pages to which the thumbnail images are linked.

5. Click "Export," shown on the previous page.

6. iPhoto automatically chooses the "Sites" folder in which to store your Web Page. You really need to create a new folder so all of these files will be nicely contained, and so you can create another Web Page someday without overwriting this one.

   So click the "New Folder" button (previous page) and name it **index**. Why? Because, unfortunately, Web Page export names the start page the same as the folder into which it's saved. For a web page to work correctly on the Internet, the start page needs to be named "index." After the photos are exported to the new folder, you should manually change the name of the folder to something unique.

   Click "OK," as shown on the previous page. Your new Web Page and all of its related files will be stored in this folder.

To see your new Web Page (which is really a web *site,* not an individual web *page*), find the new folder you just made (it's in the Sites folder in your Home window, unless you put it somewhere else).

Double-click the file named **index.html.** It will open in your default web browser, *but it's not online!* You're actually just opening files on your own hard disk. That is, if you want other people around the world to see this web

page, you'll have to invite them to your house. This Web Page feature just builds the site for you—it's your responsibility to upload it to a server if you want it online.

The finished Web Page shown in a browser.

Web Page creates a "start page" that contains thumbnail versions of your selected photos. Single-click any thumbnail to open a page that displays a full-sized version of that photo and navigation links for "Previous," "Up," and "Next" ("Up" means back to the start page).

Export your photos as a QuickTime slideshow you can give to friends

You can export photos as a QuickTime slideshow that plays in the QuickTime player or in a program that supports QuickTime, such as a web browser. The QuickTime slideshow can be put on a CD and sent to friends, posted on a web page, inserted into a PDF, or placed in other software that recognizes QuickTime (such as the presentation module in AppleWorks).

To export as a QuickTime slideshow:

1. Select an Album, a group of photos within an Album, or photos in the Photo Library. (The order that photos appear in an Album is the order they will appear in the QuickTime movie.)

2. From the File menu, choose "Export."

3. In the "Export Photos" window that opens, click the "QuickTime" tab.

4. **Images:** Set the maximum width and height for the slideshow images; 640 by 480 pixels is a standard measurement that works well (it's rather large). In the "Display image for" box, set the amount of time that each image will stay on the screen.

5. **Background:** Choose a background color or a background image. If some of your photos have unusual dimensions, the empty background area will be filled with the color or image you choose.

6. **Music:** Click "Add currently selected music to movie." The slideshow will play whatever piece of music is chosen in the "Slideshow Settings" window (click the Slideshow icon in the iPhoto Organize pane, select a song, then click the "Save Settings" button).

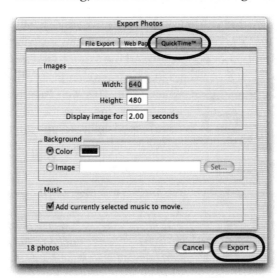

7. Click "Export."

8. In the "Export Photos" dialog box, name the file. iPhoto automatically selects the "Movies" folder to save the slideshow in, but you can choose any location; click the "disclosure" button (the down arrow) next to the "Where" pop-up menu.

9. Click "Save."

To open your QuickTime movie, click the "Home" icon in the Toolbar of any Finder window, then double-click the folder named "Movies." Double-click the QuickTime movie file that you just named and saved.

To play your QuickTime movie, click the "Play" button (the big triangle) on the QuickTime Player.

A QuickTime slideshow plays in the QuickTime Player.
Click the "Play" button (circled above) to play the movie.

Extra Tips and Information

JPEG and JPG are the same thing.

TIFF and TIF are also the same thing.

Most digital cameras store photos in the **JPEG format,** which combines a high-quality image with effective compression to economize file size. iPhoto works best with JPEG formatted photos, although it recognizes most common formats such as TIFF, PICT, BMP, TARGA, and PNG (but not EPS).

Imported photos are actually located in a folder named **iPhoto Library.** To find this folder, open your Home window, then open the Pictures folder; the iPhoto Library is inside Pictures. The Library folder also contains a folder of the **Albums** you created in iPhoto. But these Albums don't really contain photos, even though you placed photos in them while working in iPhoto. Instead, they contain "references" to photos that have been imported into the Photo Library. This way, you have the same photo in many different Albums without overloading your computer with multiple copies of a photo.

If you plan to have a lot of fun using your digital camera and iPhoto, chances are sooner or later you'll have so many photos in your iPhoto Library that you'll run out of storage space. Plan to back up your iPhoto Library folder regularly by copying it to another disk or burning a CD.

Search the Internet for iPhoto scripts and plugins

You'll find some very interesting freeware and shareware that makes iPhoto even better. Search Google (or any search site) for "iPhoto scripts," or go to VersionTracker.com and search for "iPhoto." Some very useful scripts are:

When you download and use software from freeware and shareware developers, be aware that you're doing so at your own risk and that the developers do not take any responsibility for unexpected hardware or software problems that may occur.

iPhoto Diet: Whenever you edit photos, such as cropping or making color and contrast adjustments, iPhoto keeps a copy of the original in the Photo Library so you can choose to revert back to the original later. A convenient feature, but at the cost of using a lot of storage space. iPhoto Diet is an AppleScript droplet that slims down your Photo Library by moving unwanted duplicates to the Trash. Just drop your iPhoto Library (located in the Pictures folder, in your Home folder) on top of the iPhoto Diet droplet. Find it at www.VersionTracker.com.

BetterHTMLExport: This iPhoto plugin creates web pages, but gives more control over the appearance of the pages than iPhoto's built-in Web Page feature. After installation, the plugin appears as an extra tab in the "Export Photos" window (from the File menu, choose "Export...."). Visit www.droolingcat.com to download.

Last but not least, perhaps even best: Apple's web site has a page dedicated to iPhoto scripts. Go to www.apple.com/applescript/iphoto/ to download an entire collection of truly amazing iPhoto scripts, plus other goodies.

iTunes

iTunes

With the iTunes application, you can create music CDs that will work in just about any regular CD player (and on your Mac), or create digital music files to play while you're working on your Mac. iTunes can convert music files from one format to another (called "encoding"). Using iTunes, you can organize your music files into Playlists and create music CDs of those Playlists. In addition, iTunes can connect to the Internet's CD Database and retrieve information about your CDs, including artist, song titles, album name, and music genre. It can also connect to dozens of Internet radio stations offering a wide variety of music and talk radio. And it can put on a dazzling, live, visual-effects show synchronized to the current music selection. What more could you ask? How about this—if you have an iPod (Apple's MP3 player), iTunes will upload and synchronize the iPod with your iTunes Playlist (up to 4,000 songs on the 20 GB model) using a lightning-fast FireWire connection.

Add to all this the iTunes integration with the other iLife applications, (iDVD, iMovie, and iPhoto), and you've suddenly become part of a modern-day formula for inspiring creativity.

iTunes

Playing CDs

You can play any music CD you stick in your Mac. Make sure your sound is on and turned up.

To play a music CD:

1. Insert a CD into the drive, label side up.

2. Open iTunes, if it isn't already open:

   If the iTunes icon is in your Dock, click once on it.

   If there is no icon in the Dock, open the Applications folder, find the iTunes icon, then double-click it.

3. The CD icon appears in the "Source" pane, as shown below. Click the CD icon to see the song list and other information in the "Song Name" column.

   If you're connected to the Internet, iTunes will automatically go to the CDDB (CD Database) web site, retrieve the song titles, and place them in the Song Name column and other displayed columns.

   If you're NOT connected to the Internet when you insert a CD, song titles will appear as track numbers.

Track number.

Choose which columns to display in a CD's detail window: From the Edit menu, choose "View Options...."

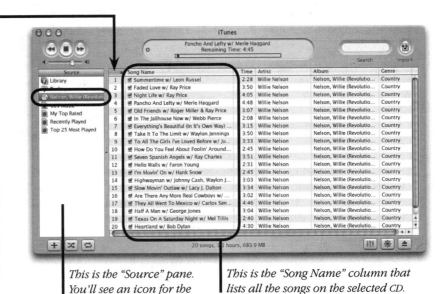

This is the "Source" pane. You'll see an icon for the CD that is in your Mac.

This is the "Song Name" column that lists all the songs on the selected CD.

To see the actual song titles, if they have not appeared:

1. Connect to the Internet (if you're not already).

2. From the Advanced menu, choose "Get CD Track Names."

If you want iTunes to do this automatically every time you put in a CD, see the information about iTunes preferences on page 75.

To choose the songs on the CD you want to play:

When you insert a CD, all of the songs have checkmarks next to them. If the box is checked, the song will play. To customize the list, check only the songs you want to hear. iTunes skips over songs that do not have a checkmark.

1. Click on the CD icon in the "Source" pane.

2. Select a song in the "Song Name" column.

3. Click the Play button (the middle controller button), *or* double-click the title in the "Song Name" column.

Click on the top line to toggle between track name and Album name.

Click on "Remaining Time" to change it to "Elapsed Time."

The Play/Stop/Pause button.

To uncheck all songs at once, Command click on any box.

The Music Collection Summary gives information about items in the "Source" pane.

The iTunes Library

When you import (rip, encode) a music file from a CD, it is automatically encoded as an MP3 file and placed in the iTunes Library. Once a song is in the Library's list, you can add it to a customized Playlist for your personal enjoyment, as explained on the following page. *Simply playing songs from a CD does not add them to the Library.*

Tip: Each song takes up from 3 to 5 megabytes, at least, of hard disk space, so make sure you have plenty of space before you go crazy with your music files!

To add songs to the Library:

1. Insert a music CD into the drive, label-side up.

2. In the CD list that appears, check each song that you want to add to the Library.

3. Click the "Import" button in the upper-right of the window.

You may already have music files somewhere on your computer that you want to add to the iTunes Library. There are two ways to do this:

▼ **Either** go to the File menu and choose "Add to Library...," then find and select your music files.

▼ **Or** drag a file from any location on your hard disk to the Library icon in the iTunes "Source" pane.

Choose which columns to display in the Library window: From the Edit menu, choose "View Options...."

This is the "Source" pane, and you can see that the Library icon is selected. This indicates that the songs you see in the pane to its right are stored in the Library.

For more about this Multi-Function button, see pages 68–69.

To import this AIFF file (.aif), I dragged it from a folder to the Library.

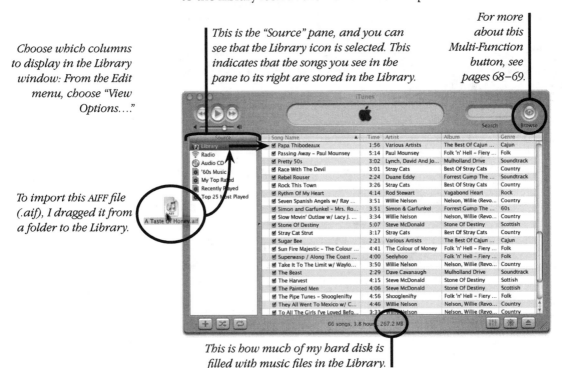

This is how much of my hard disk is filled with music files in the Library.

Create Your Own Playlists

A **Playlist** is your customized collection of audio files. You can create as many Playlists as you like, and you can arrange the songs in any order you prefer by dragging selections up or down in the list. You create Playlists so you can play them on your computer, download them to a portable MP3 player, or burn them onto CDs.

Smart Playlists

Smart Playlists are collections of songs that are generated automatically when imported songs meet certain criteria that you define. iTunes put several Smart Playlists (indicated by the gear symbols) in the "Source" pane that make Playlists based on '60s music, top ratings (see page 72), recently played songs, and your top 25 most-played songs. You can create new Smart Playlists that meet other criteria, such as your favorite Willie Nelson songs.

Smart Playlists display a gear symbol.

To create a new Smart Playlist:

1. From the File menu, choose "New Smart Playlist...."

2. In the Smart Playlist window, set the criteria for the new Playlist. For more criteria options, click the "Advanced" tab.

3. Click OK.

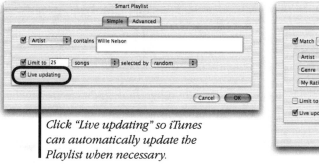

Click "Live updating" so iTunes can automatically update the Playlist when necessary.

To add criteria, click a "plus" button.
To delete criteria, click a "minus" button.

The new Smart Playlist icon appears in the "Source" pane, with all the songs meeting the criteria displayed on the right in the Song Name list. To rename the Playlist, click the name and type a new one.

To create a new Playlist:

You can create dumb Playlists too. The only way to get songs into an ordinary Playlist is to manually put them there, by dragging or by using a menu command. The (dumb) Playlist icon contains a music note.

1. Type Command N, or click the "New Playlist" button at the bottom-left of the iTunes window. A new Playlist icon will appear in the "Source" pane with a generic name of "untitled playlist."

2. Change the name of the new Playlist to something appropriate by typing in the highlighted field.

   You can change a Playlist name at any time: click once on the title, then type a new name in the highlighted field.

When you create a new Playlist, the Mac knows you want to change its name so it highlights the field for you. Just type to replace the existing name.

To add selections to the Playlist from a CD:

1. Insert the CD whose songs you want to add to a customized Playlist.

2. Click the CD icon in the "Source" pane to open its song list.

3. Drag desired selections from the "Song Name" column and drop them on your new Playlist in the "Source" pane, as shown below.

Choose which columns to display in a CD's Playlist window: From the Edit menu, choose "View Options...."

New Playlist.

New Playlist button.

"The Celts" is the name of the CD that is in the Mac and whose songs are showing in the window. "Inspire me" is the name of the new Playlist. You can see song #15 being dragged over to the Playlist name.

Encoding in progress.

When you drag a song directly from a CD to a Playlist, the song is automatically **encoded (imported)** to an "MP3" format, placed in the iTunes Library, and added to the Playlist.

To add a song to a Playlist from the Library:

1. In the "Source" pane, click on the Library icon to display your entire Library collection in the "Song Name" column.

2. Drag a selection from the "Song Name" column to a Playlist icon in the "Source" pane.

There's **another method for creating a new Playlist** that's even easier:

1. In the "Source" pane, click on the Library icon to display your entire Library collection in the "Song Name" column.

2. Select the desired songs in the "Song Name" column (hold down the Command key and click each song).

   Note: The **checkmarks** *do not* indicate whether a file is selected. They indicate two things: songs that will *play* when you click the "Play" button, and songs on a CD that will be *imported* when you click the Import button.

3. From the File menu, select "New Playlist From Selection...." iTunes will automatically create the Playlist and add the selected items to it. You can change the name of the Playlist.

You can drag **multiple selections** all at once to the Playlist:

▾ To make *contiguous* multiple selections (of songs that are next to each other in the list), Shift-click the song names. **Or** click on one song, then Shift-click on another song, and all songs between the click and the Shift-click will be selected.

▾ To make *non-contiguous* multiple selections (of songs that are *not* next to each other in the list), Command-click selections.

Note: When you drag a song file from the Library to a Playlist collection, as shown on the opposite page, the song remains in the Library. *You're not actually moving the digital file*—you're creating a *directory* that tells iTunes which songs are attached to different collections. You can put the same song in as many Playlist collections as you want without bloating your computer with extra copies of large music files.

This shows a non-contiguous selection of songs.

Play the Radio

Click the Radio icon to open the **Radio Tuner,** which you can use to tune into **Internet radio stations** which are built into iTunes (or whose addresses you have entered). These stations play a wide variety of music, news, and talk show programs, and netcast the "streaming MP3" format.

To play the radio in iTunes:

1. Click the Radio icon in the "Source" pane to see the radio options in the "Stream" column (the same column that is labeled "Song Name" when the Source is a CD or your Library).

2. Click the disclosure triangle of a radio category to see the various choices of "streams" (streaming Internet connections).

3. Double-click a stream to begin playing it. iTunes will open the designated URL (web address) and start playing the content.

iTunes uses technology called "Instant On Streaming" that allows content to start playing immediately. It continues to download data as the file plays. If you do not have a full-time Internet connection, iTunes will try to connect to the Internet for you when you double-click your radio selection.

Choose which columns to display in the Radio Tuner window: From the Edit menu, choose "View Options...."

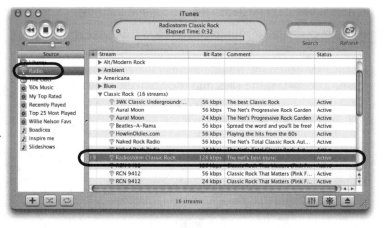

Some radio stations are available in several bit rates (kilobits per second), which affects the size and quality of the stream. If you have a slow connection, choose lower bit rate numbers, such as 24 kbps.

To enter another radio address:

If you know the web address of a streaming MP3 radio station that's not in the iTunes Radio Tuner, you can manually enter it.

1. From the Advanced menu at the top of your screen, choose "Open Stream...."

2. Enter the web address in the text field in the "Open Stream" window. The address must be a complete URL, including the stream file name.

Music File Formats

iTunes works with four common **audio file formats:** MP3, CD-DA, AIFF, and WAV. Using the Import feature, iTunes can encode CD-DA files from a CD to MP3, AIFF, or WAV files. It can also encode MP3, AIFF, and WAV files to CD-DA format when burning a CD. Each file format is suited for a specific purpose.

To select an encoder when importing files, see page 77.

▼ **CD-DA** (Compact Disc Digital Audio) is the file format used on all music CDs. This format is also known as "Red Book" because the specifications were originally published in a book with a red cover, which started a tradition of naming CD specifications by color. When you burn a CD from a Playlist, iTunes automatically encodes the files in the Playlist as CD-DA formatted files so they'll play on CD players.

▼ **MP3** is a highly efficient compression system that reduces music files up to 90 percent, but maintains a very high quality. Because they are so highly compressed, MP3s are ideal for downloading from the Internet or for storing on your computer. The full name of an MP3 is "MPEG-1 audio layer-3" and was developed by the Moving Pictures Experts Group.

When iTunes imports a song from a CD to your computer, it encodes the CD-DA formatted song to an MP3 format. The file size of the Beatles song "I Want To Hold Your Hand" is 24.3 MB as a CD-DA file. The file size changes to 2.7 MB when encoded as an MP3 file. The compression efficiency and high quality of the MP3 format is responsible for the explosion of music file sharing on the Internet and the popularity of digital music. MP3s are also ideal for storing music on your personal computer, requiring 80 to 90 percent less disk space than other formats.

▼ **AIFF** (Audio Interchange File Format) is sometimes referred to as Apple Interchange File Format. It is a music format used by the Macintosh operating system. Web designers use the AIFF format for sound files that can play in web pages on a Macintosh computer. The file size of the Beatles song "I Want To Hold Your Hand" is 24.3 MB as an AIFF file, compared to 2.7 MB as an MP3 file.

▼ **WAV** (Windows waveform format) is a music file format used by the Microsoft Windows operating system. Web designers use the WAV format for sound files that can play in web pages on a Windows computer. The file size of the Beatles song "I Want To Hold Your Hand" is 24.3 MB as a WAV file, compared to 2.7 MB as an MP3 file.

The iTunes Interface

Most of the controls you need are located directly on the **iTunes interface.** Almost every control is explained in detail elsewhere in this chapter.

Detail window,
opposite page.

Controller buttons,
page 62.

Show mini graphic equalizer,
page 66.

Status display,
page 66.

Search field,
page 67.

Multi-Function button,
page 68.

Volume.

Source pane,
page 62.

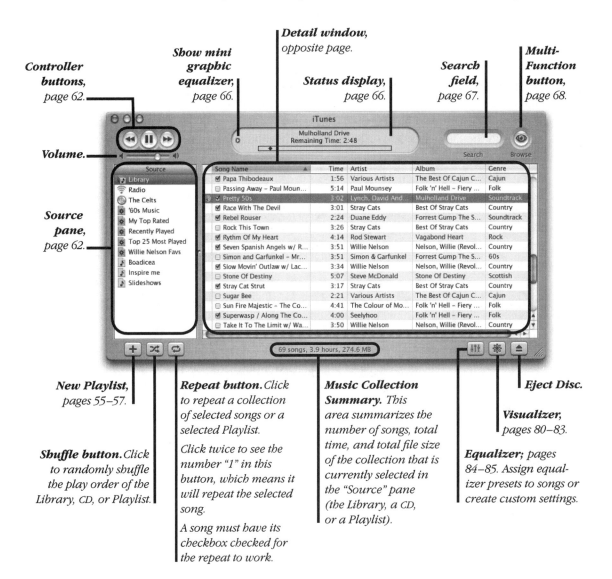

New Playlist,
pages 55–57.

Shuffle button. *Click to randomly shuffle the play order of the Library, CD, or Playlist.*

Repeat button. *Click to repeat a collection of selected songs or a selected Playlist.*

Click twice to see the number "1" in this button, which means it will repeat the selected song.

A song must have its checkbox checked for the repeat to work.

Music Collection Summary. *This area summarizes the number of songs, total time, and total file size of the collection that is currently selected in the "Source" pane (the Library, a CD, or a Playlist).*

Eject Disc.

Visualizer,
pages 80–83.

Equalizer; *pages 84–85. Assign equalizer presets to songs or create custom settings.*

The Detail Window of Songs and Radio Stations

The **Detail window** displays various columns of song information. The visible columns in the Detail window will vary depending on which type of collection you've selected in the "Source" pane and which options you've chosen in View Options (from the Edit menu). The columns typically include Song Name, Time, Artist, Album, and Genre.

Select and play songs

To play any selection in the "Song Name" column, double-click its title. When that selection has finished, iTunes plays the next song in the list *that has a checkmark next to it.*

When you insert a CD, by default *all* the song titles have a checkmark next to them, which means they will all play in order when you click the Play button. The checkmark also determines which songs will be encoded and placed in the iTunes Library when you click the Import button.

> ▾ **To deselect (uncheck) all the songs at once,** Command-click on any song's checkbox.
>
> ▾ **To select (check) all songs at once,** Command-click on any checkbox.
>
> ▾ **To select a group of contiguous songs** in the song list, click on one song, then Shift-click another song. All titles between the two clicks will be automatically added to your selection.
>
> ▾ **To select a group of non-contiguous songs,** Command-click on the songs you want to select.

Resize or rearrange columns

If song titles are cut off by the narrow width of the "Song Name" column, **resize the column.** Place your cursor over the thin, gray, dividing line, then press-and-drag the line to the right as far as necessary to see the song titles.

To rearrange the columns, press on a column's title to select it, then drag the column left or right to a new position.

To resize a column, hover your cursor over the dividing line between columns. The cursor becomes a bi-directional arrow. Drag the divider line left or right.

Organize the column information

The information in the Detail window is always **organized** by the selected column. In the example on the opposite page, the information is organized alphabetically by Song name—you can see that the Song Name column heading is selected.

Click the small triangle to the right of the column name to **reverse the order** in which the column information is displayed.

The three big round buttons are the controller buttons.

Controller Buttons

The **controller buttons** act like the controls on most any CD player.

▼ **To select the Next song,** single-click the Forward button (double arrows pointing to the right).

▼ **To Fast Forward** the current selection, press-and-hold the Forward button.

▼ **To select the Previous song,** single-click the Back button (double arrows pointing to the left).

▼ To **Rapid Rewind** the current selection, press-and-hold the Back button.

▼ The middle button toggles between **Play** and **Pause** when a CD or MP3 file is playing.

The same button toggles between **Play** and **Stop** when the Radio Tuner is active.

The Source Pane

The **Source pane,** on the left side of the iTunes window, displays the iTunes Library, the Radio Tuner, any current CD that is in your CD drive, and any custom Playlists you've created.

*To **resize** the "Source" pane, drag this tiny dot.*

This is the "Source" pane. You can see the Library icon, the Radio icon, an icon for the CD that is currently in the Mac, the default Smart Playlists, and several custom Playlists.

Close, Minimize, and Zoom

As usual for every window in Mac OS X, you see the **three colored buttons** in the upper-left of the window, but they act a little differently in iTunes.

▼ Click the **red button** (the close button) to hide the iTunes window, even while music is playing. It won't affect the music.

To show the player again, from the File menu choose "Show Current Song."

Or use the keyboard shortcut Command 1 (one) to toggle between Hide Player and Show Player while iTunes is active.

▼ Click the **yellow button** to minimize the Player and send it to the Dock. To bring the Player back to the Desktop, click on it in the Dock.

▼ Click the **green button** (the zoom button) to reduce the size of the Player window to its smallest possible size, as shown below. Click the green button again to return to the full window.

The green button collapses the entire iTunes window down to a compact, space-saving, cute little windoid.

Song Information and Options

Get information about song tracks (shown below, left), add comments to songs, and adjust the volume control in the **Song Information** window.

To open the Song Information window:

1. Select one song track or multiple song tracks.

2. Type Command I to open the window.

If you made a single song selection, the Song Information window contains three tabs: "Info," "Tags," and "Options."

The **Info** pane gives some minimal information about the CD track (or other selected music file in your Library or Playlists).

To get information about other songs in the selected Song list without leaving the Song Information window, click the "Prev Song" button or the "Next Song" button, shown below, left.

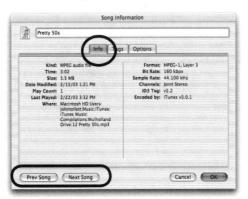 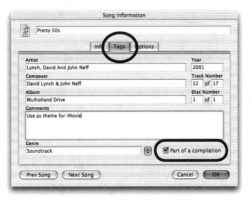

The **Tags** pane provides additional information, plus a Comments field in which you can add your own comments, such as "Use as theme for iMovie."

Mark songs or CDs as a "compilation" to store them together (above, right). When you mark a song as part of a compilation, a new folder is created in the iTunes Music folder named Compilations, and the song is placed in a subfolder named for the album the song came from. When a CD is marked as a compilation CD, a new folder named for the CD is placed in the Compilations folder. This causes any song you import from the CD to be marked as "Part of a compilation."

Compilations can be copied to an iPod, shared with others by copying them to another computer, or burned onto a CD.

The settings in the **Options** pane allow you to set the Volume Adjustment for each individual song. This is helpful if you're a serious rocker and cranking up the other volume controls (the Sound settings in System Preferences, plus the iTunes window volume control) just isn't loud enough. This Volume Adjustment can put your speakers into *Spinal Tap* mode ("Most speakers just go to 'Ten,' but ours go to 'Eleven.'").

The Options tab also lets you set a "Start/Stop Time" for a song. In the event you want to **play or import just a section** of a long song, enter the "Start playback" and "Stop playback" times in a minutes:seconds format (00:00).

To determine which time settings you need, first play the whole song. Watch the Status display at the top of the iTunes window, and write down the beginning and ending "Elapsed Time" of your desired music segment.

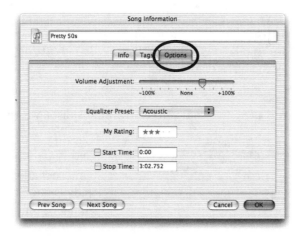

If you selected more than one song, the **Multiple Song Information** window, as shown below, combines all the previous information and options into one window. The Volume Adjustment will affect all selected tracks.

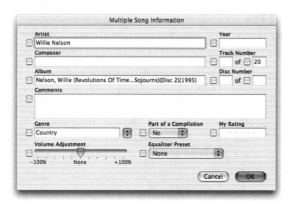

Status Display

When iTunes is playing a song selection from a CD, from the iTunes Library, or from a Playlist, the **Status display** (at the top of the iTunes window) displays three lines of information: music identification, music track time, and an audio track bar.

The **music identification** (top line) in the Status display automatically scrolls through song name, artist name, and album name. Click on the top line to manually cycle through these three bits of song information.

The **time duration** of a song is shown in the middle line. Click on it to cycle between "Remaining Time," "Total Time," and "Elapsed Time."

The **audio track bar** on the bottom line indicates the current location of playback in relation to the entire song. **To move to any point in a song,** drag the black diamond left or right.

When iTunes is playing the **Radio Tuner,** the Status display is similar.

Click the top line to manually toggle between the **URL** (Internet address) of the radio station and its **station name** or call letters.

The middle line shows the **Elapsed Time.**

The bottom line is a **blank audio track** line. You can't drag ahead or back in a streaming file.

No matter what you're listening to, you can turn the Status display into a mini **graphic equalizer:** click the small round/triangle button on the left side of the window. This feature doesn't offer control of any kind, but it's fun.

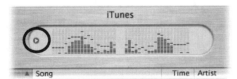

iTunes also includes a real equalizer; see pages 84–85.

iTunes Search

The **Search** field enables you to quickly find songs in the current song list (songs from the Library, a CD, or a custom Playlist).

To search:

▼ In the Search field (circled, below), type one or more key letters or words that are in any part of the artist, song, or album name.

You don't need to hit the Return or Enter key—a list will appear instantly in the "Song Name" list that includes only songs that contain your key words. As you type, the list will change constantly to reflect the matching results.

Type your search in here.

For instance, in the example to the right I'm looking for a song by Roy Orbison called "Almost Eighteen." I start typing the word "almost" into the Search field and the list instantly displays four songs that match the letters typed ("al" so far). The match can be anywhere in the song title, artist name, or album name; capital or lowercase letters don't matter. If I continue to type the word "almost," the list will be narrowed down to a single choice.

Use the iTunes Browser to Search Large Playlists

When you view songs in a large playlist that contains music by many different artists, you can show an overview of the playlist contents by using the iTunes Browser.

The iTunes Browser.

1. From the Edit menu, choose "Show Browser." In the Browser pane that opens, select a genre, artist, or album to show in the song list window.

2. To close the Browser pane, from the Edit menu choose "Hide Browser."

The Multi-Function Button

The button in the upper-right corner of the iTunes Player changes appearance and functionality according to the type of source selected in the "Source" pane and if "Visuals" are turned on. That's why we call it the **Multi-Function button.** Following are its different states.

Browse button: If *Library* is the selected source in the "Source" pane, the Browse button appears. Click Browse and the top section of the iTunes window displays two new panes for browsing: Artist and Album. Click on any item (or multiple items) in these two panes and the display below will show only songs that match the selections above. When you've located the desired song or album, you can drag the selection straight from the Browse section to a Playlist in the "Source" pane.

To add a Genre column to the Browse area: from the iTunes menu, choose "Preferences...." Click the checkbox to "Show Genre When Browsing."

Import: Select a *CD* in the "Source" pane to activate the Import button. Import encodes selected CD audio tracks into the MP3 format and places them in the iTunes Library. See more about importing on page 77.

Refresh: When *Radio* is selected in the "Source" pane, the Multi-Function button becomes the Refresh button. Click the Refresh button to check the Internet for the latest radio listings available through iTunes.

Burn CD: The Burn CD button becomes visible when a ***Playlist*** is selected in the "Source" pane.

To burn a CD:

1. Select a Playlist you've created in the "Source" pane.
2. In the "Song Name" list, uncheck any songs you do not want recorded on the new CD.
3. Click the "Burn CD" button and the button cover opens to reveal the Burn icon.
4. The Status window will instruct you to insert a blank CD.
5. After you've inserted a disc, iTunes flashes a message in the Status window to click the "Burn CD" button again.

6. When finished, a new CD icon will appear on the Desktop.

Options: If ***Visuals*** are turned on, the Multi-Function button becomes the Options button. Click the Options button to present the "Visual Options" window. You can choose to display the animation frame rate, cap the animation frame rate at 30 frames per second, always display the song information, and set a faster display or a better quality display. See pages 80–83 for details about Visuals.

Ripping Music Files to MP3 Format

To **rip** a file is to encode it (convert it) from one format to another. To copy a CD music track **to your computer,** you'll convert it (rip it) from the CD-DA format to MP3.

To rip music files:

1. Insert a music CD and the CD tracks appear in the iTunes Detail window.

   If iTunes does not automatically go to the Internet and get the title names and other track information, go to the Advanced menu and choose "Get CD Track Names." (This will open your Internet connection if you're not already online.) After a few moments, the CD database will fill in the track titles, artist, album, and genre, if they're available online.

2. Select the tracks in the list you want to rip. By default all tracks in the list are checked when you first open a music CD. Uncheck any track that you don't want to rip and save on your computer.

3. Click the "Import" button in the upper-right corner of the iTunes window. The checked tracks will be ripped and added to the iTunes Library in the "Source" pane.

When a song has been ripped, an orange icon with a check mark appears next to the track, indicating that it has already been imported.

An orange icon with an animated wave symbol appears next to a track that is in the process of being ripped.

Rip multiple music files from a CD as one track

If you want to rip (import) two or more *adjacent* songs from a CD "Song Name" list that will play as one track without a pause between the songs, use the "Join CD Tracks" command.

1. Select the songs in the CD Song Name list you want to join.

2. From the Advanced menu, choose "Join CD Tracks."

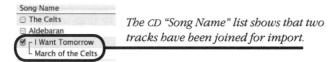 *The CD "Song Name" list shows that two tracks have been joined for import.*

3. Click the Import button in the top-right corner of the iTunes window.

Rip music files to other formats

You may want to **encode a music file to some format other than MP3,** especially if you plan to embed the file in a web page. Encode MP3 files as AIFF or WAV formats by changing the Import settings.

1. From the iTunes menu, choose "Preferences…."

2. Click the Importing tab in the Preferences window.

3. Change the "Import Using…" setting to AIFF or WAV.

iTunes supports Audible.com

Audible (www.audible.com) is a web site that offers downloadable audiobooks, magazines, radio programs, and much more. Their web site tells you how to become a member, how to transfer your audio programs to an iPod or burn them to a CD, and how to listen to them on your Mac.

Rate Your Songs

You can rate songs on a scale of one to five **stars.** The rating can be used to sort songs, create Playlists, or as a criteria in creating Smart Playlists.

1. If the "My Rating" column isn't showing in the iTunes window, Control-click on one of the column heads, then choose "My Rating" from the pop-up menu. **Or** from the Edit menu, choose "View Options…," then click the "My Rating" checkbox.

2. Click on a song you want to rate. Notice that five dots appear in the "My Rating" column.

3. Click on the first dot to add a single star. Click dots further to the right to add more stars to your rating. You can also drag across the dots which adds another star as you drag over additional dots.

To sort the current songs by your rating, click the "My Rating" column heading. The order of songs will be rearranged with the highest-rated songs at the top of the list. **To reverse** the order of the list, click the small triangle on the right side of the column heading.

Export Playlists as Text Files or XML files

iTunes lets you **export Playlists** as text files (.txt) or as XML files (.xml).

Export Playlists as text files if you want to archive the song information, or if you want to import the information into another program, such as a database application.

Export as XML if you want to use the Playlist in iTunes on another computer. When you import the XML file into iTunes on another computer, iTunes looks in its Library for the songs listed in the imported Playlist. Songs that are not in the Library will not show up in the "Song Name" list pane.

1. Select a playlist, then from the File menu, choose "Export Song List…" or "Export Library…."

2. In the Finder panel, name the exported file, set the Format pop-up menu to "Plain Text" or "XML," then choose a location to save it.

The procedure above creates a file that includes information for every column in iTunes, even if some of the columns are not visible in your iTunes window.

To create a text file (.txt) of song information that includes only the columns you have made visible, select one or more songs in the "Song Name" list. Next, from the Edit menu, choose "Copy," then open another program such as TextEdit and paste (from the Edit menu, choose "Paste").

iTunes Preferences

The **iTunes** preferences allow you to adjust a number of settings. From the iTunes application menu, choose "Preferences…."

General preferences

Click the **General** icon to set "Text," "CD Insert," and "Internet" preferences.

- ▼ **Source Text** and **Song Text:** Choose "Small" or "Large" text to display in the "Source" pane and in the Song Name pane. The actual size difference between "Large" and "Small" is not dramatic, so most users will probably choose to leave these settings on the default choice of "Small."

- ▼ The **Show genre when browsing** option can be helpful when using the Browse feature (pages 67 and 68) to search through a large collection of music files—it adds a "Genre" column to the "Artist" and "Album" columns that become visible when you click the "Browse" button.

The **On CD Insert** pop-up menu offers options for what happens when you insert a CD. You can only choose one of the options:

- ▼ **Show Songs** displays the music titles, artist, and album information, but will not play music until you double-click a selection. If you haven't retrieved the CD track names from the CDDB, only the CD track numbers and times will display.

- ▼ **Begin Songs** automatically starts playing a CD when it's inserted.

- ▼ Import Songs automatically begins encoding songs on the CD into MP3 format and placing them in iTunes' Library when a disk is inserted.

- ▼ **Import Songs and Eject** does the same thing as above, then automatically ejects the CD.

If **Connect to Internet when needed** is checked, iTunes will connect to the Internet whenever you insert a CD so it can retrieve song titles and other information from CDDB, an Internet database of CD albums. iTunes will also connect to the Internet when you choose certain items in the iTunes Help window. If you have a modem connection instead of a full-time, broadband Internet connection, you may prefer to uncheck this item to avoid having your modem dial up at unwanted times.

As an alternative, you can manually retrieve CD titles whenever you choose: from the "Advanced" menu in the upper menu bar, choose "Get CD Track Names."

Use iTunes for Internet Music Playback sets iTunes as your default multi-media audio file player when you download an audio file or click an audio file link on the web.

Effects preferences

Click the **Effects** tab to access a couple of extra features.

▼ Check the **Crossfade playback** checkbox to fade music smoothly between songs without a long gap of silence. The slider adjusts the amount of time it takes to fade out of one song and to fade in to the next song. Move the slider all the way to the right for the smoothest transition with the least silence between songs.

▼ Check the **Sound Enhancer** box to add depth and liven the quality of the music. The slider increases or decreases the effect, which is subtle, but noticeable.

▼ Check the **Sound Check** box to make all songs play at the same volume level. Leave this box unchecked if you want to vary the volume level of different songs using the volume control in the iTunes window.

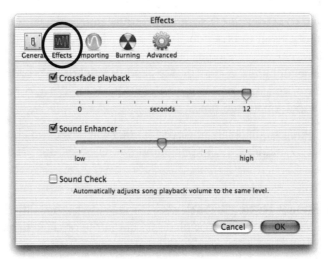

When you burn a CD, these effects do not carry over to the CD.

Importing preferences

Click the **Importing** tab to set encoding and configuration preferences.

▼ **Import Using** lets you choose which format the music files will be encoded into: MP3, AIFF, or WAV (as described on page 59). The default setting of MP3 is ideal for listening to and storing music on your computer. If you want to encode music files for use on the Internet, choose AIFF Encoder (a Macintosh format) or WAV Encoder (Microsoft Windows format).

▼ **Configuration** is a quality setting.

For MP3 encoding, choose between "Good Quality," "Better Quality," and "High Quality." Higher quality settings create larger file sizes.

For AIFF or WAV encoding, choose between "Automatic" or "Custom…." (To learn all about customizing the configurations, see *The Little iTunes Book,* by Bob LeVitus, available from Peachpit Press.)

▼ You can listen to a song as it's being ripped (encoded) by checking the **Play songs while importing** option. Encoding is very fast, usually four to ten times faster than the music plays. The encoding of a song finishes well before the music has finished playing.

▼ Check **Create file names with track number** to force imported songs to be stored in your Music folder in the same order they appear on the CD.

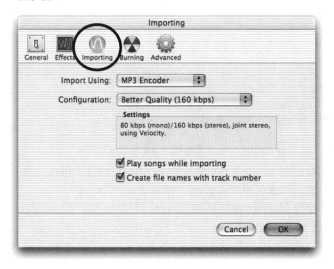

Burning preferences

Click the **Burning** tab to set the speed at which iTunes burns a CD, choose a format for the disc, and determine the amount of time between songs.

- ▾ **Preferred Speed:** From this menu, set the speed at which your CD burner will burn CDs. The default setting of "Maximum" will let iTunes adjust to the speed of your hardware. If you have problems, try setting "Preferred Speed" to a slower speed (a lower number).

- ▾ **Disc Format:** Choose "Audio CD" or "MP3 CD" for burning CDs.

  "Audio CD" uses the standard CD-DA format common to all commercial CD players. You can store approximately 75 minutes of music on a CD using this format.

  You can choose to burn a CD using the MP3 format instead of CD-DA format. An MP3 CD can store over 12 hours of music, but can only be played on computers and some special consumer CD players.

  If you want to store MP3 music files on CDs, choose "MP3 CD" for the most efficient storage solution.

- ▾ **Gap Between Songs** can be set to your own personal preference. Set the amount of pause you want to hear between songs.

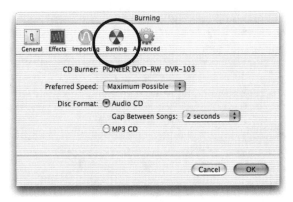

You can burn music CDs using either **CD-RW** discs or **CD-R** discs.

> **CD-RW** (CD-ReWritable, sometimes called Read-Write) discs will play in your computer, but most stereos and commercial CD players don't recognize them.

> **CD-R** (CD-Recordable) discs can play on computers and most CD players.

Discs must be blank to record music on them. You can erase a CD-RW disc and then use it to burn a music CD. A CD-R disc cannot be erased, and it cannot be used if it already has files on it.

Advanced preferences

The **Advanced** tab has settings to designate a location for storing your music files, as well as options for burning CDs.

▼ **iTunes Music Folder Location:** Music files created by iTunes are automatically stored on your startup hard disk. Specifically, they are stored in a folder called "iTunes Music," which is in a folder called iTunes, which is in your Music folder. This folder contains all of the MP3 files you've encoded. You can change this default location to any location you choose. Click the "Change…" button, then navigate to another folder on your hard disk and choose that other folder.

Every user who uses iTunes will have their own iTunes folder inside their Music folder.

▼ **Streaming Buffer Size:** Refers to the Radio Tuner. The buffer size determines how much streaming data is cached (temporarily stored) on your hard disk when you listen to an Internet radio stream. The buffer is like padding that compensates for connection problems that would harm the quality of a direct stream. If you've determined that your connection to the Internet is low-quality, or if your Radio Tuner playback breaks up often, change this setting from the default of "Medium" to the "Large" setting. A large buffer gives iTunes more downloaded streaming data to use for compensation as it deals with slow or faulty connections.

▼ **Shuffle by:** Shuffle the playing order of songs by Song or Album.

▼ **Keep iTunes Music folder organized:** Does just what it says, although we have to admit we're not quite sure exactly what it's doing. We assume it's a good thing to keep this checked.

▼ **Copy files to iTunes Music folder when adding to library:** Puts a *copy* of a song in the iTunes folder if you import songs from other locations on your computer. The song remains in its original location. This is similar to the "Consolidate Library" command in the Advanced menu, which puts a copy of all songs in your Library in your Home folder's Music folder.

iTunes Visualizer

The **iTunes music visualizer** is mesmerizing. Just double-click a song, then click the Visualizer button at the bottom-right corner of the iTunes window, and watch the show. You can also turn Visuals on by pressing Command T, or by choosing "Turn Visuals On" in the Visuals menu.

Play iTunes' Visuals within the iTunes window in three optional **sizes:** from the Visuals menu, choose Small, Medium or Large (shown below).

You can also display iTunes' Visuals in three different sizes while in **Full Screen** mode: From the Visuals menu, choose "Full Screen" to dedicate your entire monitor screen to iTunes' visual effects.

Your previous choice of Small, Medium, or Large will still determine how large the actual visuals appear while in full-screen mode. The Small or Medium option will fill the extra screen space with black.

Toggle between "Full Screen" and "window view" of Visuals with the keyboard shortcut, Command F. When in "Full Screen" mode, click the mouse anywhere on the screen to return to a Song list view without interrupting the music.

"Small" visual effects.   *Visualizer button.*

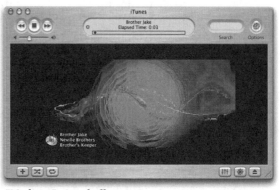

"Medium" visual effects.

"Large" visual effects.

Visualizer configurations

The **iTunes Visualizer** can be even more fun if you know how to interact with it. The Visual Effects Generator uses three different **configurations** to create visuals. You can see these listed at the top-right of the screen if you press the C key while visual effects are playing. The three configurations listed change randomly and morph into one another as music plays. You can change any, or all, of these configurations while music is playing.

The first configuration in the list affects the **foreground** of the visualizer, the primary lines and shapes that modulate and interact with the beat of the music more obviously than the other graphics on the screen. You can cycle through all the built-in effects for this configuration by alternately pressing the Q and W keys (Q for "Previous" selection and W for "Next" selection).

The second configuration in the list affects the **background** graphics, the shapes and patterns that stream from the primary shapes in the top configuration. You can cycle through all the built-in effects for this configuration by alternately pressing the A and S keys (A for "Previous" selection and S for "Next" selection).

The third configuration in the list affects the **color scheme** that is applied to the visuals. You can cycle through all the built-in effects for this configuration by using the Z and X keys (Z for "Previous" selection and X for "Next" selection).

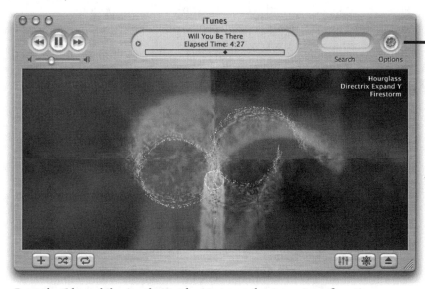

Click this button to set a few options. You can choose to display the animation frame rate, cap the animation frame rate at 30 frames per second, always display the song info, and set a faster display or a better quality display.

Press the C key while visuals are playing to see the current configuation of effects that are generating visuals for iTunes. They're displayed in the upper-right corner of the window, as shown above.

Visualizer modes

Cycle through three different visualizer modes by pressing the M key.

  ▼ **To play the random visual effects** generated by iTunes, press the M key to cycle to "Random slideshow mode."

  ▼ **To force iTunes to play the current configuration** until instructed otherwise, press the M key to cycle to "Freezing current config."

  ▼ **To play only the configurations that have been saved as presets** under the numeric keys, as described below, press the M key to cycle to the "User config slideshow mode."

To manually and randomly change configurations at any time, press the R key. Pressing the R key in beat with the music makes you the conductor of an amazing musical light show.

Save a favorite configuration

When you change an individual configuration (by using the keys mentioned on the previous page), the new effect fades slowly in as the configuration description in the upper-right corner fades out. If you fall in love with an effect, you can save that particular configuration as a preset that can be activated at any time.

To save a favorite configuration as a preset:

1. Press the M key to cycle through the three different options: "Random slideshow mode," "User config slideshow mode," and "Freezing current config."

2. When you get to the "User config slideshow mode," stop. This mode plays configurations that you, the user, have saved as presets.

3. Wait until you see a visual effect you like, then hold the Shift key and tap one of the numeric keys (0 through 9) while the desired effect is playing. You can save up to ten different preset effects.

   Note: To get rid of an old preset, just save a new one over it, using the steps above.

   To play your preset, tap the number key that you assigned to your preset configuration. Try tapping different preset keys to the beat of the music for fantastic visual effects.

Visualizer Help

A separate **Help** file of keyboard shortcuts is available in the Visualizer feature of iTunes. While Visuals are turned on, press the **?** key (or the H key) to show "Basic Visualizer Help," a list of keyboard shortcuts that appears on the left side of the visual display.

Press the **?** key again (or the H key) to toggle to another list of keyboard shortcuts, "Visualizer Config Help."

iTunes Equalizer

iTunes provides an **Equalizer** that enables you to make dramatic adjustments to the sound output of your music files. Make adjustments manually or select from over twenty presets. You can even save custom settings as a preset and add it to the preset pop-up menu, as explained below.

An equalizer represents the various frequencies of the sound spectrum, or more specifically, the spectrum of human hearing. The spectrum is expressed as a measurement known as *hertz* (hz).

The iTunes Equalizer represents the frequencies of the spectrum with vertical sliders, also known as **faders.** The faders are used to increase or decrease the volume of each frequency, expressed as decibels (dB).

The lowest frequencies (bass): 32, 64, and 125 hz faders.

The mid-range frequencies: 250 and 500 hz faders.

The highest frequencies (treble): 1K through 16K (kilohertz) faders.

This is the Equalizer button.

To show the Equalizer, click the Equalizer button at the bottom-right corner of the iTunes window. Check the **On** box to activate the Equalizer.

Choose a preset from the pop-up **menu** to automatically adjust the faders.

The **Preamp** slider on the left side of the Equalizer is a secondary volume adjustment. If a music file was originally recorded too quietly or loudly, adjust the volume here. Or if you're looking for maximum room-booming sound, slide the Preamp up to the top.

To save your custom settings as a preset:

1. Adjust the faders to your satisfaction.

2. From the pop-up menu (where it says "Acoustic" in the example above), choose "Make Preset...."

3. In the "Make Preset" dialog box, enter a name for your preset, then click OK.

Your new, custom preset now appears in the pop-up menu.

To apply Equalizer settings to a song, use one of the following two methods.

▼ **Either** Select a song, then click the Equalizer button to open the Equalizer. Select a preset from the pop-up menu, or use the faders to create a custom setting.

▼ **Or** add an Equalizer column to the iTunes Detail window: From the Edit menu, choose "View Options…," check the "Equalizer" checkbox, then click OK. An Equalizer column will appear in the Details window, from which you can choose a preset for each song in the list.

To quickly and easily add an Equalizer column to the detail window, Control-click on a column heading, then choose "Equalizer" from the pop-up Contextual menu.

Experiment with different sound settings by choosing presets in the Equalizer column.

Transfer Songs to an iPod

You can use iTunes to **transfer** one or more Playlists **to an iPod or some other MP3 player.**

1. When you connect a supported MP3 player to your computer using a FireWire or USB connection, the player's name appears in the iTunes "Source" pane.

2. Drag songs from the Library or a Playlist to the MP3 player's name in the "Source" pane.

If you're using an iPod, you can choose to have iTunes automatically transfer all your MP3 songs or selected Playlists to the iPod, or you can manually drag selections to the iPod in the Source pane: with your iPod connected and selected in the iTunes Source pane, click the iPod icon that appears in the bottom-right of the iTunes window; you'll get a dialog box where you can make choices.

Favorite Keyboard Shortcuts

These are the **keyboard commands** that you'll have most fun with:

Command 1	toggles between Show Player and Hide Player
Command T	toggles Visuals on and off
Command F	toggles full-screen mode on and off
DownArrow	turns the volume down
UpArrow	turns the volume up
LeftArrow	first tap selects the beginning of the current song; second tap selects the previous song
RightArrow	selects the next song
Option Command DownArrow	mutes the sound
Spacebar	toggles between Pause and Play
R	instantly changes Visualizer to a new random set of visual effects

Other keyboard shortcuts:

Command N	creates a new Playlist
Shift Command N	creates a new Playlist from the *highlighted* songs (*not* the songs that are checked)
Command A	selects all songs in the current song list
Shift Command A	deselects all songs in the current song list
Command R	shows current song file in the Finder
Command E	ejects a CD
Command M	minimizes Player window to the Dock
Command ?	launches iTunes Help
Command Q	quits iTunes
M	cycles through Visualizer modes
N	toggles between Normal and High Contrast colors
D	resets Visualizer to the default settings
I	displays song information
F	toggles Frame Rate Display on and off
B	displays the Apple logo briefly when Visuals are turned on

iMovie

iMovie

Making movies is incredibly fun and easy with **iMovie 3.** Connect a digital video camera to your computer with a FireWire cable, launch iMovie, and you're ready to create home movies with sound tracks, transitions between scenes, special effects, and customized titles.

If you didn't get a **FireWire cable** with your camera, check the small box that came with your Mac—often there is a FireWire cable in it. If you don't have a cable and need to order one, go to your local electronics store and order one. Or order from one of the many dealers you can find online by searching for "FireWire cables."

This is the icon that designates a FireWire port.

Digital video (DV) requires a lot of disk space: One minute of DV footage uses about 220 MB of hard disk space. A four-minute iMovie that contains sound tracks, transitions, and titles may use 4 to 6 *gigabytes* of disk space.

If you're serious about making iMovies, or if you just can't control yourself after making your first iMovie, buy an extra, very large drive to use when working with video. You'll be surprised how fast you can fill a dedicated 80 GB hard drive when you start making movies.

The Basic Steps

Making an iMovie consists of **five basic steps.** This chapter will walk you through each step.

1. Import video clips to the shelf (page 89).

2. Edit the clips (pages 92–94).

3. Place edited clips into the movie Timeline (pages 95–96).

4. Add transitions, titles, effects, audio, and chapters (pages 99–108).

5. Export the iMovie (pages 110–111).

As you shoot video, keep in mind that every time you start and stop the camera, iMovie will interpret that as a "clip." Each clip will appear in its own little slot on the "shelf." You can then rearrange the order, edit each scene individually, and much more. Clips can be short or long. You can split a clip, cut a segment out of one clip and make it a separate clip, etc. iMovie makes every step of the process easy and fun.

Import Clips to the Shelf

Before you can **import,** of course, you must connect the camera to the Mac.

To connect your camera:

1. With the camera off, plug one end of the FireWire cable into the camera and the other end into the Mac's FireWire port.
2. Put the camera into VTR mode (VTR stands for Video Tape Recorder).
3. Open iMovie.
4. Turn on the camera. In a couple of seconds, the monitor area will display the words "Camera Connected," as shown below.

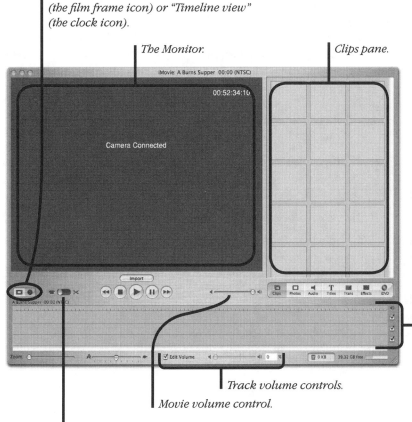

Choose to view the timeline in "clip view" (the film frame icon) or "Timeline view" (the clock icon).

The Monitor.

Clips pane.

There are three tracks in the timeline: the top one is for video (which includes a clip's audio), and the lower two are for other audio tracks. The checkboxes turn audio on or off.

Track volume controls.

Movie volume control.

Toggle between "Camera Mode" to import video (camera icon, on the left) and "Edit Mode" to edit movies (scissors icon, on the right).

To create a new project:

1. From the File menu, choose "New Project...."

2. In the "Save As" dialog box that opens, name your project and choose the location where you want it to be saved.
   Be sure to pick a drive or partition that has plenty of unused disk space. We have several external FireWire drives that we use just for our movie projects.

To preview the raw footage:

1. In the iMovie interface, click the "Camera Mode" button, circled on the next page.

2. Then click the "Play" button to play the video in the iMovie monitor.
   At this point you are just *previewing* the video. iMovie will not digitize and import any video until you click the "Import" button.
   To economize disk space, preview your footage, then rewind and import just the best footage. Use the controls below the "Import" button to rewind, pause, play, stop, and fast-forward.

To import video footage into iMovie:

1. Click the Play button to view the raw footage.

2. When you see footage you want to import, click the "Import" button (see the callout on the opposite page). The Import button is blue when it is selected and importing files.
   You can go backwards while in Play mode (click the Reverse arrows), but not while Importing.

3. To stop importing, click the "Import" button again. Each time you start and stop importing, iMovie will place that segment, called a "clip," into a separate slot in the "Clips pane" at the upper-right corner of the iMovie window.
   If you have plenty of disk space, you can let the camera run. iMovie will import all of the individual segments that were created when you started and stopped the camera (while filming) as separate clips and place those in the Clips pane.

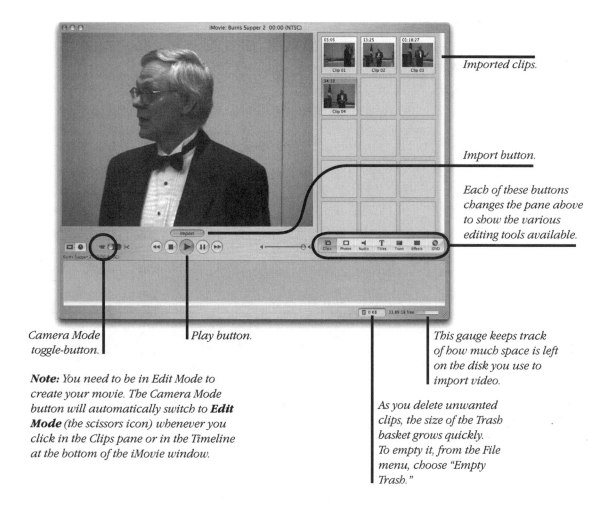

Imported clips.

Import button.

Each of these buttons changes the pane above to show the various editing tools available.

Camera Mode toggle-button.

Play button.

This gauge keeps track of how much space is left on the disk you use to import video.

Note: *You need to be in Edit Mode to create your movie. The Camera Mode button will automatically switch to* **Edit Mode** *(the scissors icon) whenever you click in the Clips pane or in the Timeline at the bottom of the iMovie window.*

As you delete unwanted clips, the size of the Trash basket grows quickly. To empty it, from the File menu, choose "Empty Trash."

Edit Clips

Clips often contain more footage than you want to use in your movie. You can select just the portions of clips that you want to keep.

To display and preview a clip:

1. Click a clip in the Clips pane to select it. The clip is displayed in the monitor. A blue "scrubber bar" appears, as shown below. The scrubber bar represents the time length of the clip.

2. Preview the entire clip by dragging the Playhead (the large white triangle) across the scrubber bar, or click the Play button.

Click on a clip to show it in the Viewer.

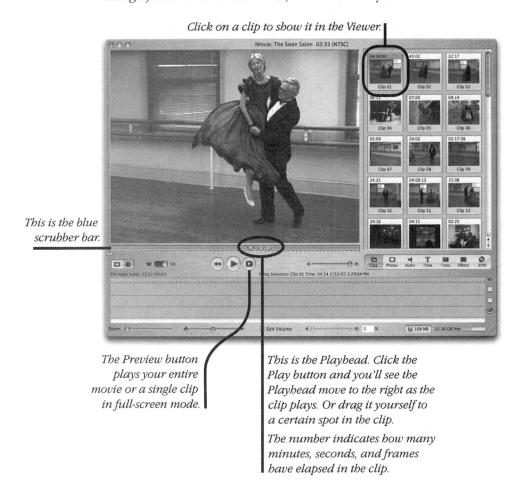

This is the blue scrubber bar.

The Preview button plays your entire movie or a single clip in full-screen mode.

This is the Playhead. Click the Play button and you'll see the Playhead move to the right as the clip plays. Or drag it yourself to a certain spot in the clip.

The number indicates how many minutes, seconds, and frames have elapsed in the clip.

Many **clips** are longer than necessary and should be **trimmed** or **cropped.**

▼ **Trimming** means to select and delete *unwanted* video frames either at the beginning or the end of a clip.

▼ **Cropping** means to delete all frames in a clip *other than* the selected frames.

To trim a clip:

1. Beneath the scrubber bar, locate the "crop markers," two small white triangles. Drag the crop markers (indicated below) to select the segment of a clip that you *want to delete.*

2. From the Edit menu, choose "Clear" to delete all of the selected frames. *Or* press the Delete key.

To crop a clip:

1. Drag the crop markers to select a range of frames in the clip that you *want to keep.*

2. Drag the crop markers individually to select a range of frames. The selected frames are highlighted in yellow.

3. From the Edit menu, choose "Crop" to delete all of the frames that were *not* selected.

Tip: When you crop or trim a clip in the Clips pane, the deleted data goes in the Trash, located just below the pane. Once a clip is in the Trash, you can't take it out.

Because even a moderate amount of editing results in a huge amount of Trash, you can preserve disk space if you keep an eye on the Trash and empty it occasionally: From the File menu choose "Empty Trash...."

The arrows point out the crop markers.

This shows a selection of the clip that is going to be cropped. After choosing "Crop" from the Edit menu, this section is all that will remain of the clip.

After you edit a clip, you're going to drag it to the **Timeline** at the bottom of the iMovie window (as explained on pages 95–96) so you can put your movie together.

Note: When you crop and trim clips as described above, *you eliminate the possibility of ever going back later to use segments of clips that you deleted.*

You might want to keep the original, unedited footage available and accessible. In that case, **copy and paste** a clip segment, as explained on the following page.

To copy and paste a clip:

1. Use the crop markers to select a range of frames that you want to add to your movie.

2. Press Command C to copy the selection.

3. Click in the Timeline at the bottom of the iMovie window.

4. Press Command V to paste the selection into the Timeline.

   If there are already other clips in the movie track, you can place the copied selection wherever you want: click on an existing clip in the movie track. Press Command V (Paste) and your selection will be pasted *to the right* of the clip you clicked on.

If later you decide that you need a longer segment from that original clip (to sync with a music track, for instance), the clip in its entirety is still in the Clips pane instead of forever lost in the Trash.

To trim or crop a clip that's already in the Timeline:

After you've made a "rough cut" of your movie, you often want to fine-tune the duration clips that are in the Timeline to sync with the beat of an imported sound track, or just to change the pacing of the movie.

1. Click on a single clip in the Timeline to show it in the Monitor.

2. Use the crop markers beneath the Monitor's scrubber bar to select a range of frames in the clip.

3. If you want to *crop* the clip (delete everything in the clip *except* the selected frames), go to the Edit menu and choose "Crop." The clip in the Timeline shortens to show the new selection.

4. If you want to *trim* the clip (delete the *selected* frames), use the crop markers beneath the scrubber bar to make a selection of frames, then press Delete.

   If at any time you want to recover parts of the original clip, it is still in the Clips pane, unharmed. This is called non-destructive editing.

To restore clips in which you've deleted frames:

Editing is very much a trial-and-error activity. For that reason, we like to keep the original imported clips in the Clips pane, then cut segments of clips from the Monitor and paste them into the Timeline (instead of dragging the clips straight from the Clips pane to the Timeline). That enables you to go back to the original, unharmed clips in the Clips pane at any time to access any footage you deleted from the Timeline.

Place Clips in a Movie

There are two editing views available for the Timeline: the **Clip Viewer** (click the film frame icon, shown below), and the **Timeline Viewer** (click the clock icon, shown below). If you place a clip in either the Timeline Viewer or the Clip Viewer, it automatically appears in the other area. To switch between the two views, click one of the two icons.

*Click this icon
to display the
Clip Viewer.*

Clip Viewer.

This Timeline display (Clip Viewer) gives a large view of clips, lets you rearrange clips by dragging them, and allows you to drag clips from the Timeline to the Clips pane.

*Click this icon
to display the
Timeline Viewer.*

Timeline Viewer.

This Timeline display (Timeline Viewer) shows the video and audio tracks. In this view you can use the checkboxes on the right side of the Timeline to disable a track's audio.

The Timeline Viewer

Use the **Timeline** to arrange the order of clips, add transitions between clips, add effects, create titles, and add audio to your movie.

To add clips to the Timeline:

- ▼ **Either** drag the clips you imported from the Clips pane to the Timeline.
- ▼ **Or,** as explained on the previous page, copy segments of clips and paste them into the Timeline.

To rearrange clips in the Timeline:

1. Click on a clip in the Timeline to select it.
2. Press Command X to delete it from its current position in the Timeline. —*continued*

3. Next, select a clip (click on it) in the Timeline immediately to the left of where you want the new clip.

4. Press Command V to paste the clip to the right of the selected clip.

Or with the Clips Viewer selected, grab a clip and drag it to a new position in the Timeline.

The **Zoom** slider lets you view the Timeline at different levels of magnification. Move the slider to the right to show the Timeline in greater detail for precise editing. Move the slider to the left to show more clips in the Timeline and reduce the amount of scrolling necessary.

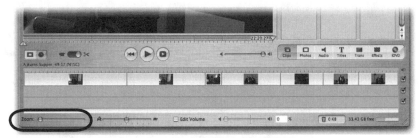

A low zoom level makes more clips visible in the Timeline.

A transition between two clips.

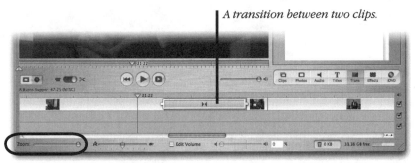

A higher zoom level makes it easier to precisely place the Playhead or to drag a sound track to a certain position. When you use clips of very short duration, you need a higher zoom level to see them clearly.

The Clip Viewer

You can also use the **Clip Viewer,** shown below, to place and rearrange clips, add transitions and effects, and create titles. You cannot work with sound tracks while using the Clip Viewer, but, unlike in the Timeline, you *can* drag clips out of the movie and back to the shelf.

To place clips in a movie using the Clip Viewer, either drag clips from the Clips pane to the Clip Viewer, *or* use the copy-and-paste technique explained on page 94.

To rearrange clips in the Clip Viewer, simply drag a clip to a new location.

This is the Clip Viewer.

You can rename these clips, here in the Clip Viewer, or in the Clips pane. Just click on the clip number to highlight the text, then type the name.

Render clips

When you add a titles or transitions to a movie or add effects to clips, iMovie automatically "renders" them so you can preview them. The progress of the rendering shows as a red render bar moving across a clip or transition.

Clip Viewer: *The render bar shows a clip's render progress.*

The checkerboard icon indicates that an effect is applied to the clip.

Timeline Viewer: *The render bar shows a transition's render progress.*

Tip: To stop a render in progress, press Command Period.

Other effects, such as slow motion and reverse direction clips, also need to be rendered, but that rendering is delayed until you export the movie.

Preview the Assembled Clips

To **preview** your movie, move the Playhead (the white triangle) in the Time-line to the beginning of the movie, or wherever you choose, then click the Play button.

Notice that if you click on a specific *clip* in the Timeline, only that clip shows and plays in the monitor. To load the entire movie into the monitor, click anywhere in the Timeline *except* on a clip (click in the Timeline above the clips or in one of the audio tracks).

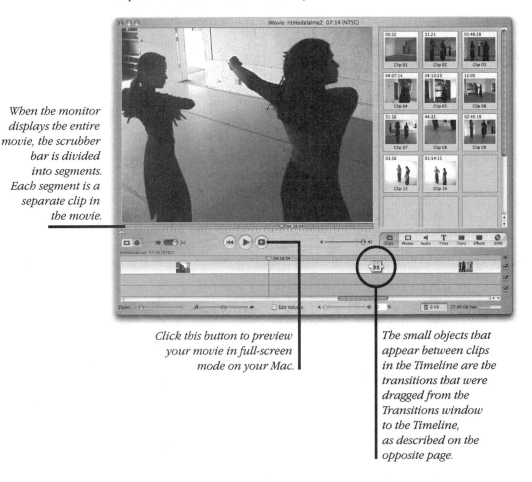

When the monitor displays the entire movie, the scrubber bar is divided into segments. Each segment is a separate clip in the movie.

Click this button to preview your movie in full-screen mode on your Mac.

The small objects that appear between clips in the Timeline are the transitions that were dragged from the Transitions window to the Timeline, as described on the opposite page.

Add Transitions and Titles

If your movie requires precise synchronization between music tracks and video footage, it's best to assemble all your clips in the Timeline before adding transitions because some transitions can alter clip lengths. For some movies, this may not be an issue.

Transitions

A **transition** is a visual effect that creates a bridge from one scene to the next scene. It might be a cross-dissolve, a fade-out, a spinning image, or any of a wide variety of other effects.

To add a transition effect between two clips:

1. Click the "Trans" button to reveal the Transitions pane, as shown below.

2. Click on a transition to see its effect previewed in the small preview window. The "Preview" button plays the effect full-size in the monitor.

3. Use the "Speed" slider to determine the time duration of the transition in seconds and frames (00:00).

4. Drag the selected transition to the Timeline (or Clip Viewer) and drop it between two clips of your choosing.

   To delete a transition at any time: click it in the Timeline and hit the Delete key.

Tip: A limited number of transitions come with iMovie, but you can download others from the Apple web site at **www.apple.com/ imovie,** or buy collections of transitions and effects from third-party vendors that are listed on the Apple web site.

To change a placed transition:
select it in the Timeline, make changes in the Transitions pane, then click "Update."

Cross Dissolve vs. Overlap:
The Cross Dissolve transition smoothly dissolves from one scene to another, retaining full motion of the first scene until it dissolves away.

The Overlap effect freezes on the last frame in a scene as it dissolves into the next scene.

Use the direction control to set the direction of some transitions, such as "Push."

Titles

A **title** is text that you place in its own frame or on top of a clip. A title can show credits, act as a caption, or add comments. There are many styles of titles to choose from and you can use different typefaces, sizes, and colors.

To add titles to your movie:

1. Select a clip in the Timeline (click once on it). The clip you select will show in the thumbnail window when you click on a title style.

2. Click the "Titles" button to reveal the Titles pane, then select a title style.

3. Type your title text into the text fields at the bottom of the window.

4. Use the font pop-up menu to select a font.

5. Use the font slider to enlarge or reduce the type.

6. Click the "Color" box to choose a color from a palette.

7. By default, a title is superimposed over a video clip. If you want to superimpose a title over a black background instead of a clip, check the "Over Black" box in the Titles pane. This option creates new frames for the title sequence and does not affect other clips. It does, however, add to the length of your movie.

8. If you plan to export the movie as a QuickTime file, check the "QT Margins" box to allow the title to expand within the limitations of the QuickTime margin.

    If you plan to burn a DVD and show it on a television, make sure this button is *not* selected or your type may be cut off on the edges, or leave it unchecked all the time to play it safe for any media.

9. Drag your selected title style from the list of styles to the desired position in the Timeline: on top of a clip if you want to superimpose the title over video; adjacent to a clip if you want the title to be against a black background.

To delete a title:

1. If the title is a separate clip "over black," select the title clip, then press Delete.

2. If the title is superimposed over another clip, select the title clip (created when you dragged the title effect to the Timeline), then press Delete.

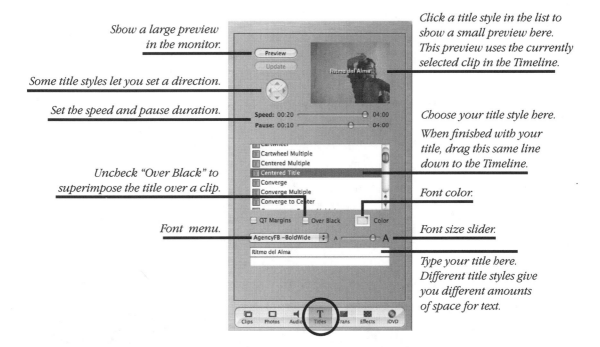

Show a large preview in the monitor.

Some title styles let you set a direction.

Set the speed and pause duration.

Uncheck "Over Black" to superimpose the title over a clip.

Font menu.

Click a title style in the list to show a small preview here. This preview uses the currently selected clip in the Timeline.

Choose your title style here. When finished with your title, drag this same line down to the Timeline.

Font color.

Font size slider.

Type your title here. Different title styles give you different amounts of space for text.

Pan and Zoom Still Photos

The "Photos" button in the button bar shows the "Ken Burns Effect" pane. Ken Burns is a documentary filmmaker who has popularized the technique of slowly panning across still photos and zooming in or out to achieve visually interesting and dramatic effects.

Effect controls.

Preview window.

To apply a "Ken Burns Effect" to a still photo:

1. From the pop-up menu, choose your iPhoto Library or any Album to display in the "iPhoto viewing area."

2. Click a photo in the viewing area to show it in the small Preview window.

3. Click the "Start" button, then set a time length for the effect with the "Duration" slider. In the Preview window, drag the photo to any position you like, then adjust the "Zoom" slider to set the view distance for the start of the effect.

4. Click the "Finish" button, then adjust the "Zoom" slider to set the view distance with which you want to finish the effect. Drag in the Preview window to reposition the image.

5. Click "Preview" to preview the effect, then click "Apply" to apply the effect to the photo and automatically place it in the Timeline at the current playhead position.

iPhoto viewing area.

Add Effects

An **effect** is a visual distortion or alteration that is applied to a clip. The effect may be used for aesthetic reasons or for visual impact. A limited number of effects come with iMovie, but many more are available from third-party vendors.

To add effects to a clip in your movie:

1. Select a clip in the Timeline (click once on it).

2. Click the "Effects" button to reveal the Effects pane.

3. Select an effect from the Effects list.

4. Use the "Effect In" and "Effect Out" sliders to set the amount of time it takes for the effect to fade in and to fade out.

5. If there are other settings sliders below the effects list, set those as well. Some effects have more adjustment options available than others.

6. When you're satisfied with the effect, click the "Apply" button.

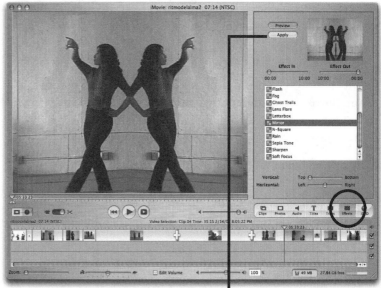

To remove the effect after you click the "Apply" button, select the clip in the Timeline and press the Delete key.

Show a large preview in the monitor.

Click an Effects style in the list to show a small preview here. This preview uses the currently selected clip in the Timeline.

Choose your Effects style here.

When finished with your Effects settings, click the "Apply" button, upper left.

Each effect has its own unique adjustments.

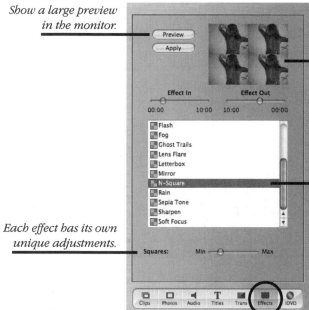

Tip: Some effects, such as Electricity and Fairy Dust, let you grab the effect in the thumbnail preview window and drag it to a new position.

Some effects, such as Electricity and Fairy Dust, let you grab the effect in the thumbnail preview window and drag it to a new position.

The Electricity effect: click anywhere in the thumbnail preview window to set the end-point of the electricity bolt. Click-drag the bolt to position it anywhere in the frame.

Add Audio

Place as many **audio clips** in a sound track as you like. You can drag audio clips to other positions on the Timeline or to another audio track. Audio clips can overlap in the same track or in separate tracks. When two audio clips overlap, both are audible, although you can adjust the volume of individual sound tracks with the clip volume control slider beneath the Timeline.

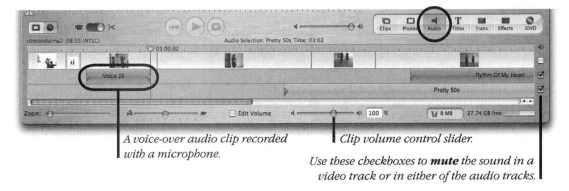

A voice-over audio clip recorded with a microphone.

Clip volume control slider.

Use these checkboxes to **mute** the sound in a video track or in either of the audio tracks.

To add audio files to your movie:

1. Click the "Audio" button to reveal the Audio pane.

2. Position the Playhead (the white triangle) in the Timeline where you want the recording to start.

3. The Audio pane pop-up menu lets you access your iTunes Library, iMovie Sound Effects, or a CD that is inserted in your drive.

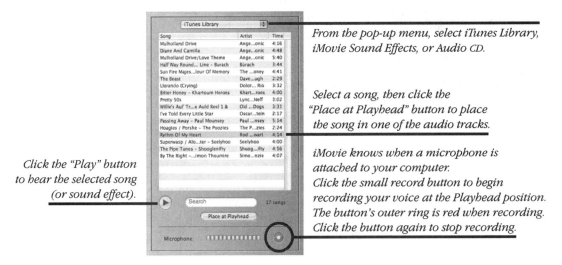

From the pop-up menu, select iTunes Library, iMovie Sound Effects, or Audio CD.

Select a song, then click the "Place at Playhead" button to place the song in one of the audio tracks.

Click the "Play" button to hear the selected song (or sound effect).

iMovie knows when a microphone is attached to your computer.
Click the small record button to begin recording your voice at the Playhead position. The button's outer ring is red when recording. Click the button again to stop recording.

To import an MP3 or AIFF sound file:

You may have audio files stored on your computer that are not in iTunes. You can import an audio file from anywhere on your computer straight into a Timeline audio track.

1. From the File menu, choose "Import File…."

2. In the "Import File" panel, navigate to an MP3 or AIFF file that is stored on your computer, select it, then click "Open." The entire audio file is placed in one of the audio tracks.

   Some of your MP3 file names may be gray, which means you can't use them in the movie because iMovie can only import MP3s that support the QuickTime format.

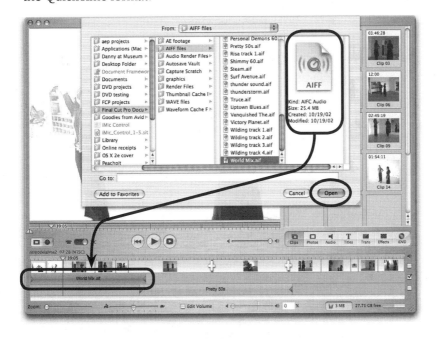

To import a CD sound track:

1. Insert a CD into your CD drive.

2. Select "Audio CD" from the pop-up menu at the top of the Audio Track pane.

3. To review CD tracks without importing them, click on a song, then click the Play button.

4. To import the song, select a CD track from the "Audio CD" list (click on it once).

5. In the Timeline, move the Playhead (the white triangle) to a point where you want to the song to start.

6. Click the "Place at Playhead" button. Click "Stop" when you've recorded as much of the CD track as you want.

To adjust and edit the audio clips:

Adjust the placement of an imported audio file in the Timeline by dragging the clip's color bar left or right (the color of the audio clip is different depending on which audio track it's in).

Edit the start and stop point of audio clips by moving the audio crop markers at either end of the audio clip's bar in the audio track. To fine-tune the placement of an audio crop marker, click it, then use the left and right arrow keys on your keyboard to move it.

You can **drag** an audio clip from one audio track to another. This is very useful when you want to overlap audio files, such as a music track and a sound effect (as shown on the next page).

Shorten the audio clip's duration by dragging one or both of the crop markers towards the middle of the clip.

Advanced audio editing

iMovie 3 adds **advanced audio editing features** that are similar to those used in Final Cut Pro and other professional-level editing software. This feature gives you control over the placement and the duration of audio fade-ins and fade-outs. It enables you to easily create professional effects, such as lowering the volume of a background music track while a voice-over narrates the video, then lowering the video clip volume so the background music is emphasized. Very cool stuff. And easy.

1. Click the "Edit Volume" checkbox.
   A volume level bar (a black line) appears in every audio and video clip.

2. **To set the volume for an entire clip** (audio or video), select the clip, then move the clip volume control slider left or right.

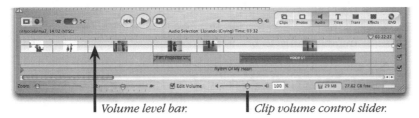

Volume level bar.　　*Clip volume control slider.*

3. **To set various volumes in a single clip,** or to create gradual changes of volume in a clip, click on the volume level bar.

   A yellow marker appears on the volume level bar. Drag the marker up or down to raise or lower the volume. The percentage number next to the clip volume control slider changes as you drag. Create as many markers on the volume level bar as necessary to create the changes in volume you want. When you drag a marker up or down, you see a small red marker at your original click point. Grab that red marker and move it *away* from the yellow marker to increase the duration of the volume change, making it more gradual.

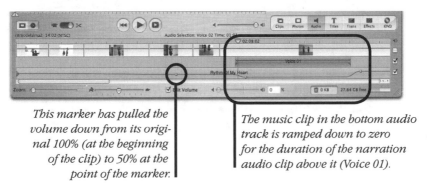

This marker has pulled the volume down from its original 100% (at the beginning of the clip) to 50% at the point of the marker.

The music clip in the bottom audio track is ramped down to zero for the duration of the narration audio clip above it (Voice 01).

Tip: There may be times when you want to use the audio from a video clip—without the video.

To extract audio from a video clip: Select a clip in the Clip Viewer or in the Timeline Viewer. From the "Advanced" menu, choose "Extract Audio." The extracted audio is automatically placed in an audio track in audio track 1 (the top track in the Timeline). The audio remains in the source clip but is muted.

To restore the audio, select the clip, click "Edit Volume," then adjust the slider to the desired volume.

Create Chapter Markers in a Movie

One of the best ways to share movies is to burn them onto a DVD. And one of the biggest advantages offered by iDVD is the ability to jump to predesignated markers in a movie, called "chapters."

Chapter markers you create in iMovie are automatically exported with your movie when you create a DVD project.

To create chapter markers:

1. Open an iMovie project that is completed.

2. Click the iDVD button in the iMovie toolbar to reveal the iDVD Chapter Markers panel.

3. Move the Playhead in the Timeline to the point you want to place a chapter marker.

4. Click the "Add Chapter" button in the Chapter Markers panel. A thumbnail image for the marker appears in the panel.

5. Name the chapter something descriptive.

   Later you can choose to let iDVD use the chapter names when automatically creating menus and submenus for imported movies.

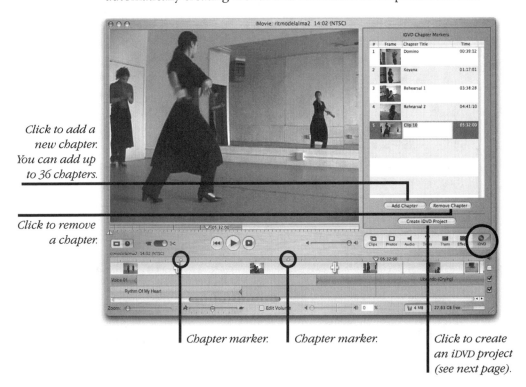

Click to add a new chapter. You can add up to 36 chapters.

Click to remove a chapter.

Chapter marker.   *Chapter marker.*

Click to create an iDVD project (see next page).

Create an iDVD Project

After you create a movie masterpiece, iDVD can immediately transform it into an iDVD project in which menus and submenus are created automatically and an iDVD window opens, ready for you to customize the design and burn your movie onto a disc.

This is a really nifty feature that very quickly creates a DVD project. You can add additional content to the DVD project after it opens, such as other movies, slideshows, and DVD-ROM content. See Chapter 4 for details.

Tip: If you aren't ready to create a DVD project, but you want to **prepare your movie for iDVD,** export the movie "To QuickTime" and format as "Full Quality DV." See page 111.

Later, when you open a DVD project, you can import the DV file into iDVD.

To create an iDVD Project:

1. Open an iMovie project that is finished.

2. Click the "Create iDVD Project" button.

   You may get a message asking if you want to render certain clips. Click "Render and Proceed." After iMovie renders the necessary clips, iDVD launches.

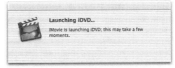

3. In the iDVD window that opens, customize the design if you choose. iDVD automatically creates a main menu with two links: **Play Movie** plays the movie from the start, and recognizes chapter markers; **Scene Selection** links to a submenu in which each chapter has a link. See Chapter 4 for details.

Main menu.   *Submenu.*

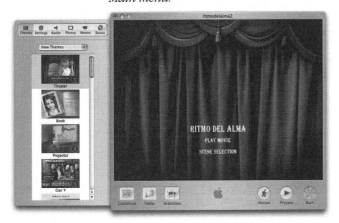

Export a Movie

Once you've finished creating your movie, you can store it on your hard drive, but that uses a lot of disk space, and the only place you can show it is on your computer. Since iMovies are usually large, from several gigabytes on up, you can't pass them around on a Zip disk or even on a CD. So you need to **export the movie.** Fortunately, iMovie is able to export movies in several formats, depending on its final intended use.

To export your movie:

1. From the File menu, choose "Export…."

2. The "iMovie: Export" dialog box appears. From the "Export" menu, choose to export "To Camera," "To QuickTime," or "To iDVD."

▼ **Export To Camera:** Put a writable tape in your camera and put the camera in VTR mode. Make sure it is connected to your computer with a FireWire cable, then click the "Export" button.

Exporting your edited movie back out to your digital camera puts the movie on the digital video tape in your camera. The tape in your camera can usually store from 60 to 90 minutes of movies. You can attach your camera to a TV to show your edited movies, or you can transfer movies from your camera to a VHS tape. If your movie contains scenes that are in slow motion or reversed, iMovie will tell you that it needs to render those scenes before it can export the movie.

▼ **Export To QuickTime:** QuickTime format is a popular standard for multimedia files. QuickTime compresses movies so that their sizes are manageable for transport and delivery, either on the web or other media.

From the "Formats" pop-up menu, select one of the compression options, then click "Export." In the "Expert Settings…" option, you can customize "Image Settings," "Audio Settings," and "Internet Settings."

▼ **Export To iDVD:** This option opens your movie in iDVD, ready for any customization you may want to add. iDVD is amazing software for putting a collection of movies, slideshows, and DVD-ROM content onto a DVD disc that will play on your computer (if you have a supported DVD drive) and will also play on most commercial DVD players. Exporting to iDVD opens iDVD and automatically creates a main menu and submenus based on chapter markers that you placed in the movie. If some scenes in your movie need to be rendered because they use a motion effect such as slow motion, iMovie alerts you that it needs to render those scenes before you can export the movie.

Your movie is now part of an iDVD project open in front of you, but it hasn't been *saved* as a project yet—save it now.

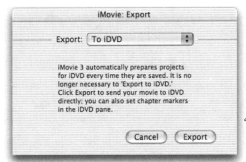

This export option immediately starts a DVD project by opening your movie in iDVD.

If you want to import your movie into a DVD project later, export the movie "To QuickTime" and format as "Full Quality DV," shown above, right.

Preferences

Check the iMovie Preferences to see if there are any options you want to change. From the iMovie application menu, choose "Preferences…" to open the Preferences window.

General

Play sound when export completed: A sound alerts you that your movie has finished the export procedure.

Use short time codes: Abbreviates the time code of 00:00:00:00 (hours:minutes:seconds:frames) to show only the necessary data (for example, 32:12 instead of 00:00:32:12).

Show locked audio only when selected: Choose when to show locked audio clips in the Timeline (see the opposite page).

Import

New clips go to: Choose to place imported clips in the Clips pane or in the Movie Timeline.

Automatically start new clip at scene break: A separate clip is automatically created every time you start and stop the camera while taping. Uncheck this option if you want video from your camera to import as one continuous clip (until you manually stop the import).

Advanced

Extract audio in paste over: Extracts the audio in a new video clip you can use to "paste over" an existing video clip. See the opposite page.

Filter audio from camera: Filters out some noises that may happen during the import process. If you hear beeps or strange noises while importing video, make sure this option is selected.

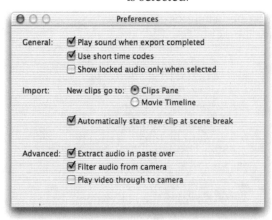

Play video through to camera: Allows you to play a movie simultaneously in iMovie and in your camera. Connect your camera to a TV monitor to see how your movie will look on a TV as compared to your computer screen.

Advanced Tips

Here are a few more tips that you can use to make your movies even more fun and successful.

To lock an audio clip to a video clip:

You may have an audio clip in one of the audio tracks that you want to start playing at a certain point in a video clip. But you want to experiment by moving the video clip around in the Timeline. You can lock the audio clip to the video clip so they move together.

1. Place the Playhead at the point in a movie where you want the audio to start playing.

2. Place an audio clip in the Timeline that lines up with the Playhead.

3. With the audio clip selected, from the "Advanced" menu, choose "Lock Audio Clip at Playhead.

To unlock the clips, from the "Advanced" menu, choose "Unlock Audio Clip."

Pins in the clips indicate the two clips are locked together and can be moved together. The bottom pin in this example is hidden by the audio crop marker (the triangle).

To paste over a video clip:

You may eventually be in an editing situation where you want to replace existing video in the Timeline, but keep the audio of the existing clip. For example, the existing video clip may have narration you want to use, but you want to replace the video with new shots of whatever the narrator is talking about. You can replace the video and retain the audio with a "paste over."

1. Make sure "Extract audio in paste over" is selected in iMovie Preferences.

2. Use the crop markers under the monitor to select the video frames that you want to use to paste over, then press Command C to copy.

3. Position the Playhead where you want the new video pasted.

4. From the "Advanced" menu, choose "Paste Over at Playhead." The audio of the pasted video is muted (set to zero), and the original clip's audio is retained in audio track 1 below the pasted video.

    To replace the original audio with the audio contained in the clip you are pasting, *uncheck* "Extract audio in paste over" in iMovie Preferences.

More Tips

If your edited movie is more than twenty minutes long, the **video and audio may not stay in sync** when you export it as a QuickTime movie or when you open it as an iDVD project. To avoid this problem on long movies, extract the audio from the video clips. The audio tracks will automatically be placed in the Timeline, synchronized with the video.

To extract audio from a clip, select one or more video clips, then go to the "Advanced" menu and choose "Extract Audio." The extracted audio files are placed in the timeline below the corresponding video clip.

Tip: **Create black video clips** by dragging a video clip to the right in the Timeline. Paste video into the black space or use the black space as a transition.

Add a "Fade In" and "Fade Out" transition to either side of the black space to soften the transition.

If you created the black clip by accident, click in the space and press Delete.

Located below the Clips pane, next to the Trash, the **Free Space status bar** alerts you to how much free space is left on the disk or partition being used for your movie. The bar indicator is color-coded to indicate the amount of free disk space.

> **Green:** More than 400 megabytes available
> (about 2 minutes of imported DV footage).
>
> **Yellow:** Less than 400 megabytes available
> (just under 2 minutes of imported DV footage).
>
> **Red:** Less than 200 megabytes available
> (about 1 minute of imported DV footage).

If you have less than 100 megabytes of free disk space available, you cannot import more video until you remove clips from the Clips pane or empty the iMovie Trash.

This is the disk space indicator.

iDVD

iDVD can't help you make movies or photos. But it can assemble finished movies or photos into a beautiful presentation in a medium that's robust, interactive, convenient, and rapidly reaching a ubiquitous status.

iDVD also enables you to create folders of DVD-ROM content. Simply put, the same disc that plays your movies can deliver any kind of data that you want to deliver to your audience: PDF files, applications, archived files, web sites, or almost anything else you want to make accessible on a disc.

Use iMovie to edit your movies and export them for iDVD. Use iPhoto to import, organize, and edit your still images, ready for iDVD slideshows.

Until recently, sharing huge files, such as movies, was difficult or impractical. Even a CD's 650 MB capacity was woefully inadequate for delivering movie files that are usually measured in gigabytes. But now you can put an amazing amount of content on a DVD disc and share it with almost anyone. DVD acceptance in the consumer market is growing much faster than any previous content delivery medium in history.

DVD technology has changed our capabilities and our expectations, both in our creative pursuits and in our approach to business, training, and marketing solutions. Not to mention it's just too much fun, especially when the software is this powerful and easy.

DVDs are going to impact your life, whether you're watching them or creating them, so let's get started.

To take advantage of iDVD's newest feature, the integration of iPhoto and iTunes, open both iTunes and iPhoto while you create a DVD.

What Do I Need to Make DVDs?

If your computer has a SuperDrive, Apple's special drive that reads or writes DVDs, you can use the iDVD software to quickly create professional-looking DVDs that will play on almost any current DVD player, whether it's a DVD-capable computer or a home player.

You also need blank discs to burn your content onto. iDVD uses a type of "general media" disc called DVD-R. You can order them from the Apple store online or buy them from stores that sell Apple products. Although you can find very low prices on the Internet for bundles of generic-branded DVD-R discs, we've had better luck with Apple DVD-R discs and other high-profile brands that do not fall into the dirt-cheap category.

A DVD disc officially claims to hold 4.7 GB (gigabytes), but due to various factors ranging from marketing hype to variances in techniques for translating bits to gigabytes, you really have approximately 4.4 GB of space to work with, or about 60 minutes of video (including video used in motion menus). But that's a lot, especially compared to the 650 MB (megabytes) of storage space you get with a CD-R disc.

Note: iDVD is not meant to **create** content, but to **present** content. Before you open iDVD, you need to have some content you've already created, such as iMovies that have been prepared for iDVD (as explained on page 109) or still photos in iPhoto.

iDVD allows up to a total of 99 movies and slideshows (in any combination) on a single DVD disc. Of course, the length of your movies, the number of images in your slideshows, and how much DVD-ROM content you want to include on the disc will affect exactly how many movies and slideshows will actually fit on your DVD.

Throughout this chapter we refer to the "menu." The world of DVD design and authoring uses the term "menu" to mean the DVD interface that a viewer uses to navigate disc content. We also use "menu" to refer to iDVD's main window in which you create your project's personality and navigation.

Customize drawer.   *Menu.*

Start by Selecting a Theme

DVDs use "menus" to provide navigation to the content on the disc. iDVD provides various **menu themes** for you to choose from. Many of them contain motion and are called "motion menus." If you have a lot of content to squeeze onto a disc, you can economize disc space by using static menus instead of motion menus.

Your iDVD menu can contain a maximum of six buttons which link to movies and slideshows, or to other submenus, which can also contain up to six buttons. One DVD project can contain a maximum of 30 menus.

Double-click the iDVD icon (it's in your Applications folder) to open the iDVD application.

To select a Theme:

1. From the File menu, choose "New Project."
2. In the Save dialog box, name your project and choose the location where you want to save it.
3. Click the "Customize" button in the bottom-left corner of the iDVD window to open the **Themes** panel of the Customize drawer.
4. Click the "Themes" button at the top of the drawer and choose a design from the scrolling list in the drawer.

Tip: If you don't have any content yet, follow the tutorial that came with iDVD and use the content included in the iDVD "Tutorial" folder.

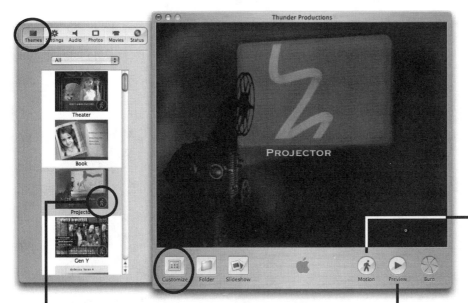

You can turn motion on or off with the Motion button. Turn it off while editing your DVD to make iDVD more efficient, and turn it on when you're ready to Preview or render the final DVD.

To apply a theme, click one of the thumbnails in the Customize drawer. The small "walking man" icon in the lower-right of the thumbnail means that theme contains motion.

To preview your project at any time, click the "Preview" button.

Drop Zones

Tip: **To customize the background of a menu and retain the Drop Zone,** Option-drag a movie or image on top of the background (not into the Drop Zone). A blue highlight will appear around the window to indicate you are replacing the existing *background* image.

Some of the menu themes have **Drop Zones** into which you can drag a movie, a slideshow, or a still image. Drop Zones hold images, movies, or slideshows, but do not link to anything. To remove an image or movie from a Drop Zone, drag the image out of the Drop Zone.

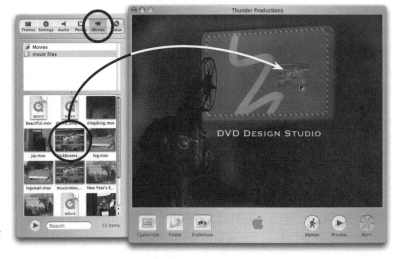

As you drag a movie from the Customize drawer to the Drop Zone, you can see the Drop Zone highlighted with a striped border.

The Settings Panel of the Customize Drawer

You can customize several aspects of your DVD menu. If the drawer shown below is not visible, click the "Customize" button at the bottom of the window. Click the "Settings" button at the top of the Customize drawer.

These wells show the menu's background movie and audio. Drag movies or audio files from the Finder to here to change the menu design.

Click "From Theme" to see a pop-up menu for customizing the appearance of buttons (explained on the following page).

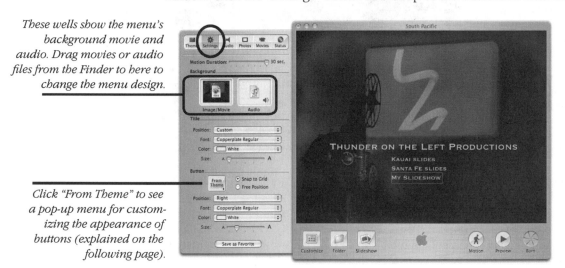

Motion Duration

This slider sets how long a motion menu plays before it loops (repeats). The maximum loop duration allowed is 30 seconds.

Background

Customize the menu background by dragging an image or a movie onto the Image/Movie well. You can also simply drag an image or movie into the background area of the main window.

Customize the menu's background sound by dragging an audio file onto the Audio well.

Title

Each theme includes placeholder text for a title. **To change the title,** click on the text in the main window to select it, then type a new title. If you don't want to use a title, choose "No Title" from the "Position" pop-up menu.

To change the title's position in the menu, select one of the options from the "Position" pop-up menu. To place the title anywhere, choose "Custom."

To change the title's font, color, or size, use the pop-up menus.

Button

To create buttons (links to movies, slideshows, or submenus) and place them in the menu, drag a movie from the Movies browser (click the Movies button at the top of the drawer) to the menu window.

The large **"From Theme"** pop-up button (see the previous page, bottom) lets you customize the appearance of buttons. Press (don't click) on the button to see a pop-up graphical menu of button choices.

- ▼ To use the buttons as they were designed for the selected theme, choose the default, "From Theme."

- ▼ To convert window buttons (buttons containing a movie) to text buttons, choose the "T" option.

  Or choose one of the other custom shapes in the pop-up to change text buttons to window buttons, or to change the appearance of a window button.

- ▼ To customize the placement of buttons, select "Snap to Grid" or "Free Position." When "Snap to Grid" is selected, choose an alignment option from the "Position" pop-up menu.

Save your customized settings as a Favorite

Once you've customized all these settings, you may want to use the same look on another menu or another project. **To save a customized theme** as a "Favorite," click the "Save as Favorite" button at the bottom of the Customize Settings drawer. Now, when you click the "Themes" button at the top of the Customize drawer, you can choose "Favorites" from the pop-up menu and your custom designs appear in the drawer. A single click on one of the Favorites applies it to the current menu.

To delete a Favorite, locate the "Favorites" folder on your computer (look in your Home folder, the Library folder, and then the iDVD folder). Drag the Favorite file from the folder to the Trash wastebasket on your desktop. Or search for it by name. The name will be similar to "yourfilename.favorite."

The ribbon icon indicates a Favorite.

The walking-man icon indicates a motion menu (either the background or the buttons contain movies or slideshows).

Customize a motion button

A **motion button** is a small window that contains either a movie or a slideshow, and links to a movie, slideshow, or another menu. You can set the duration of a motion button movie anywhere up to 30 seconds, and also set the point at which the movie starts playing in the motion button.

1. Click on a motion button in a menu.

    If there's not a motion button in the menu, you can create one by dragging a movie icon from the Movies panel to a menu.

    When you click a motion button, a Movie checkbox and slider appear above the button.

2. Check the Movie checkbox if you want the button to contain motion (play a movie or slideshow). Move the slider left or right to scrub through the movie or slideshow to the point you want the motion to start playing.

3. Uncheck the box if you want the button to contain a static image. If you uncheck the Movie checkbox, the slider position sets a "Poster Frame," a static image that displays in the button to represent the movie or slideshow.

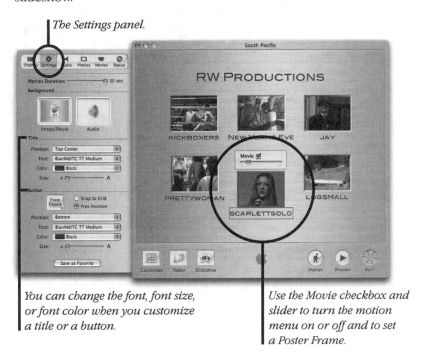

The Settings panel.

You can change the font, font size, or font color when you customize a title or a button.

Use the Movie checkbox and slider to turn the motion menu on or off and to set a Poster Frame.

The Audio Panel of the Customize Drawer

The Audio panel displays the iTunes browser, which includes the iTunes Library and all the playlists you've created. You can select any music file from this browser to use in a menu or slideshow.

▼ **To preview a song,** select it in the list and click the Play button in the bottom-left corner of the drawer.

Click the Play button again to stop.

▼ **To change a menu's background music,** drag a song's icon from the Audio panel into the menu window.

When a blue border highlights the menu window, let go of the icon. The song you dragged becomes the menu's background music.

▼ **To add a song to a slideshow,** open the Slideshow editor: double-click a slideshow button in a DVD menu. Then drag a song's icon from the Audio panel to the Audio well in the Slideshow editor.

The panels that appear when you click the Audio button, the Photos button, or the Movies button are called iMedia browsers because they let you browse through the files associated with iTunes, iPhoto, and iMovie.

You can alter the iMedia browsers to allow more space for browsing their contents: drag the dimpled separator bar up until the top panel becomes a pop-up menu.

The Photos Panel of the Customize Drawer

The Photos panel displays the iPhoto browser, which includes the iPhoto Library and all the iPhoto albums that you've created. You can select any image from this browser to use in a menu, a button, or a slideshow.

▼ **To use a still image** for a menu background, drag the image from the Photos panel into the menu window.

When you see a blue border highlight the edges of the menu window, let go of the image.

▼ **To replace the image** on a menu button (if the menu uses picture buttons), drag an image from the Photos panel and drop it on top of the button.

▼ **To replace an existing image or a movie in the Drop Zone of a menu,** drag an image from the Photos panel and drag it on top of the Drop Zone. When you see a striped border highlight appear around the Drop Zone, let go.

▼ **To add one or more images to a slideshow,** open the Slideshow editor by double-clicking a slideshow button in the menu window (see details on pages 130–134). Then drag the image (or images) from the Photos panel to the Slideshow editor.

This slideshow button was created by dragging multiple photos from the Photos panel to this menu window.

This movie button was created by dragging a movie from the Movies panel to this menu window.

A Drop Zone highlights with a striped border when you drag an image from the Photos panel on top of it.

If the current menu theme uses picture buttons, you can drag an image from the Photos panel on top of the button to change the button appearance.

The Movies Panel of the Customize Drawer

The Movies panel shows the QuickTime movies on your computer that you can drag to menus, buttons, or menu Drop Zones. iDVD always searches the "Movies" folder of your Home folder for QuickTime movie files, but you probably have movies located in other folders or perhaps on other drives. '

To tell iDVD where to find other folders that contain movies so they'll be visible here in the Movies panel, go to the iDVD application menu, choose "Preferences," then click the "Movies" icon at the top of the Preferences window. Click the "Add..." button and choose a folder from the "Open" dialog box that appears.

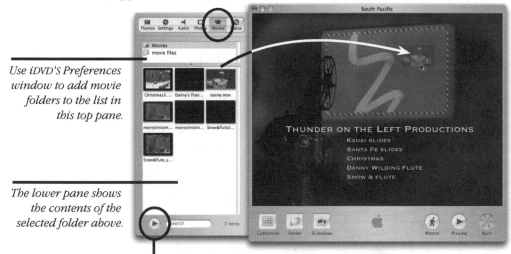

Use iDVD's Preferences window to add movie folders to the list in this top pane.

The lower pane shows the contents of the selected folder above.

To preview a movie in the lower pane, select it, then click the Play button. Or double-click the thumbnail in the drawer.

The flickering projection screen in this menu theme is a Drop Zone.

To add a movie or a slideshow to the Drop Zone, drag and drop it on top of the Drop Zone. iDVD automatically scales the movie to fit the Drop Zone. If part of the movie image area is cut off, use your mouse to drag the movie around inside the Drop Zone.

▼ Drag a movie from the drawer to the menu *background* and the movie will become a button that links to that movie.

▼ Option-drag a movie to the menu *background* and the current theme will be replaced, but the Drop Zone will remain.

▼ Command-Option-drag a movie to the menu *background* and the current theme will be replaced with the movie you drag, and the Drop Zone will disappear.

The Status Panel of the Customize Drawer

In the Status panel you can keep track of your project size and the status of the file encoding.

- ▼ **The disc icon** (circled below, left) and its associated text shows the disc capacity and the current project size. The green color on the disc icon represents the amount of disc space used by video and audio. The blue color represents the disc space used by the DVD-ROM content.

- ▼ **Encoder Status:** This pop-up menu selection shows the status of assets (image files, movies, or music files) that are to be encoded.

This is also where you manage the DVD-ROM content of the disc.

- ▼ **DVD-ROM Contents:** This pop-up menu choice (where it now displays "Encoder Status" in the example below) shows the files and folders that have been added to the DVD-ROM section of the disc.

  Files or folders that are added to the DVD-ROM of a DVD disc can be copied by anyone whose computer has a DVD drive. This section of a DVD acts just like any disc that you use to transport files. See page 135 for details.

The disc icon shows how much of the disc capacity is currently being used.

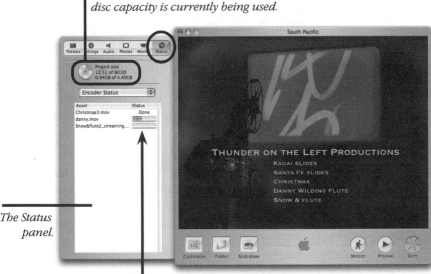

The Status panel.

When "Background encoding" is enabled in the Preferences dialog box (see the following page), iDVD prepares your files for output while you create menus and build your project.

Preferences

iDVD's preferences let you customize some of the settings for making DVDs. From the iDVD application menu, choose "Preferences." Click on one of the three icons at the top of the Preferences window to see the options for that category.

General settings

Project Settings

▼ Check "Show Drop Zones" to show the Drop Zone areas in the Theme menus.

▼ Uncheck "Show Apple logo watermark" if you want to remove the Apple logo from the DVD menu design.

▼ "Enable background encoding" allows iDVD to begin encoding the QuickTime movies you've placed in the DVD menu into the MPEG-2 format required by the official DVD specifications. If background encoding slows down your computer, uncheck this box, and iDVD will postpone the encoding until you're ready to burn the project onto a DVD.

▼ Check "Delete rendered files after closing a project" to preserve hard disk space. If you plan to burn other DVDs of the same project, uncheck this option to avoid having to encode and render the project again.

Video Standard

NTSC and PAL are the two international video standards. The United States, Japan, and some non-European countries use the NTSC format (29.97 frames per second), while most European countries use the PAL format (25 frames per second). Choose "NTSC" if your DVD will be played on a consumer DVD player in the USA.

Slideshow settings

If you check "Always add original slideshow photos to DVD-ROM," a folder of all the original photos are placed on the DVD disc, enabling anyone to drag the photos from the disc to their own hard drive (see page 135). Uncheck this option if you want to conserve space on the DVD or if the viewer doesn't need access to the original images. You can also set this option in the Slideshow editor.

Select "Always scale slides to TV Safe area" to ensure that the entire image displays on a TV. To see the TV Safe area of a DVD menu design, from the Advanced menu in the top menu bar, choose "Show TV Safe Area." What you see inside the gray border is what will be seen on a TV screen.

Movies settings

These settings let you choose whether iDVD will create chapter marker submenus and where iDVD should look for Movie files.

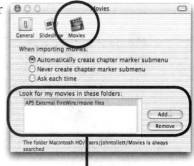

Automatically create chapter marker submenu

Chapter markers allow you to jump to different sections of a DVD movie while it is playing. With this option chosen, when you drag a movie with chapter markers to the menu, iDVD creates two menu buttons: one that plays the movie, and one named "Scene Selection" that links to a new submenu containing buttons that link to the chapter markers in the movie. If there are more than six

chapter markers in the movie, iDVD creates another submenu containing buttons that link to the other chapter markers (iDVD can have a maximum of six buttons per menu).

To create a list of folders for iDVD to search for QuickTime movie files, click the "Add..." button.

Look for my movies in these folders

iDVD automatically looks for movies in the Movies folder that's located in your Home folder. Because movies take up so much disk space, it probably won't take you long to realize you need an additional location (or two) in which to store movies, such as an external FireWire drive. You can add other locations for iDVD to search. Just click the "Add…" button to show the "Open" window, then select any folder on any drive. Your selection will appear in the pane shown above, right.

Create Additional Menus

Considering the fact that a single iDVD menu can't contain more than six buttons, you may need to create submenus that include movies or slideshows.

Create submenus

You can use submenus to work around the iDVD limitation of six buttons per menu. Click the "Folder" button at the bottom of the menu window to create a button named "My Folder." Double-click this button to open its new menu, into which you can drag more movies or create more slideshows. A submenu automatically contains a navigation arrow that enables viewers to return to the previous menu.

If you've already placed the maximum number of buttons on a menu and decide you need a submenu, you can select multiple buttons, then from the Project menu choose "New Menu from Selection." iDVD replaces the selected buttons with a new button called "My Folder," which links to a new submenu containing the buttons that you selected.

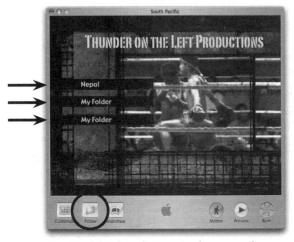

I created the three buttons in the menu above by clicking the "Folder" button at the bottom of the window. The top button's name has been changed from "My Folder" to "Nepal." Each button links to a new submenu, like the one shown to the right.

This submenu contains buttons that link to four different movies. I created the buttons by dragging movies from the "Customize" panel to this submenu background. iDVD takes care of all the design work. Notice the "back" arrow in the lower-left corner that iDVD created.

Create a scene menu

Video-editing software, such as iMovie, enables you to put chapter markers throughout the movie that make it possible to jump straight to those specific sections of the movie on a DVD. iDVD can automatically create "scene menus" that link to the chapter markers in a movie. iDVD can import up to 36 chapter markers for one movie.

1. Drag a movie containing chapter markers into the iDVD window.

   iDVD automatically creates two buttons: a "Play Movie" button that plays the movie, and a "Scene Selection" button that links to a new submenu.

2. Click the "Scene Selection" button (below, left) to go to that submenu. iDVD creates a menu that lists the chapter markers (scenes) as buttons (below, right). If there are more than six scenes in the movie, a right-facing arrow links to the next menu that contains more buttons.

iDVD creates as many submenus as necessary, until all chapter markers in a movie have been accommodated, up to the maximum of 36 chapter markers.

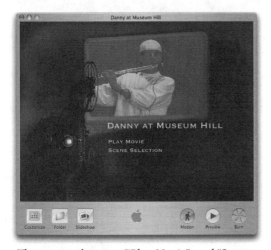 

The two text buttons ("Play Movie" and "Scene Selection") beneath the title were created automatically by dragging a movie that contained chapter markers to the menu window shown here. Double-click the "Scene Selection" button to open the linked submenu that iDVD also created (as shown to the right).

The submenu, its title, and the text buttons that link to the movie's chapter markers were all created automatically. The button names are picked up from the chapter marker names that were set in the video-editing software, iMovie. You can select any button and give it a new name.

Create a Slideshow

DVD slideshows are a quick and easy way to present your photos.

▼ Click the Slideshow button at the bottom of the iDVD window to place a slideshow button in a DVD menu.

▼ To open the Slideshow editor, double-click the button named "My Slideshow" that appears in the menu, as shown below.

Click the "Photos" button to convert the "Customize" panel to the "Photos" panel.

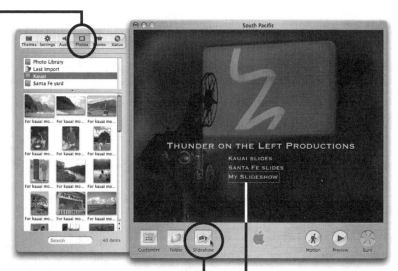

Single-click this Slideshow button to create a new slideshow button in the menu.

Double-click a slideshow menu button to open the Slideshow editor, shown below.

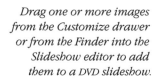

Drag one or more images from the Customize drawer or from the Finder into the Slideshow editor to add them to a DVD slideshow.

Use the Search field to search for images in iPhoto.

Add photos to your slideshow

Use the Finder:

▼ Drag photos from any location on your hard disk to the Slideshow editor window. **Or . . .**

Use iPhoto:

1. Click the "Customize" button at the bottom of iDVD's window to open the Customize drawer.

2. Click the "Photos" button at the top of the drawer.

   The iPhoto Library and any albums you may have created in iPhoto appear in the drawer's top pane. Select any album in the list and its contents appear as thumbnail images in the drawer's lower pane.

3. Select any of the photos, then drag them to the Slideshow editor window.

You can add entire iPhoto albums, or you can make multiple selections from the iPhoto Library and any albums that exist in iPhoto. You can also use a combination of dragging images from the Finder and selecting images from the Photos drawer.

To rearrange the order of photos in the Slideshow editor, just drag a photo up or down the list of images in the editor.

You can choose to display "back" and "next" arrows during a slideshow. If the "Slide Duration" is set to "Manual," the arrows can serve as a reminder to viewers to use the remote control to change images.

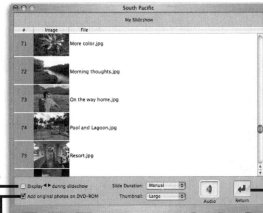

Click the "Return" button to get back to the menu that contains this slideshow.

Check this box to automatically add the original photos to your final DVD disc. iDVD compresses all the images in a slideshow. If you want the viewer to have access to the slideshow's original images, some of which may be a much higher resolution than the compressed slideshow version, check this box.

Select other slideshow options

There are a few more options you'll want to set at the bottom of the Slide-show editor (below).

▼ Check "Display ◄► during slideshow" to add "previous" and "next" arrow buttons to the photos. If "Slide Duration" is set to "Manual," the arrow buttons will remind the viewer they can use the buttons on their remote control to navigate through the photos.

▼ Check "Add original photos on DVD-ROM" to add a folder containing the original images used in the slideshow to the DVD disc. Any viewer will be able to drag the images from the DVD disc to their hard disk. You can also set this option in iDVD Preferences.

▼ The "Slide Duration" pop-up menu lets you set the amount of time a slide displays before advancing to the next slide. Choose from several durations, "Manual," or "Fit to Audio."

Manual requires the viewer to manually change to another slide. You cannot include music when you choose "Manual."

Fit to Audio times each slide's duration so the entire slideshow lasts as long as the selected audio track. The shortest slide duration possible is one second. If the audio track is shorter than the slideshow, the track will repeat until the slideshow finishes.

▼ The "Thumbnail" pop-up menu lets you choose to show large or small thumbnails in the Slideshow editor (not in the final slideshow).

▼ Click the "Return" button to go back to the previous menu.

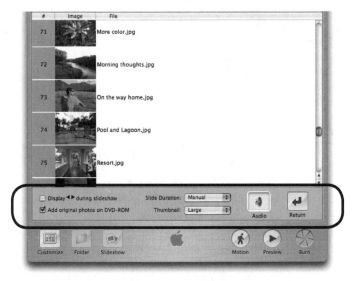

Add music to a slideshow

Use either the Finder or iTunes to add a music soundtrack to a slideshow.

Use the Finder:

▼ Drag an audio file (QuickTime, MPEG, or AIFF) from anywhere on your hard disk to the Audio well at the bottom of the Slideshow editor window. **Or...**

Use iTunes:

1. Click the "Customize" button at the bottom of iDVD's window to show the Customize drawer.

2. Click the "Audio" button at the top of the drawer.

   The iTunes Library appears in the top pane of the drawer, and the playlists appear in the lower pane. Select any song and drag it to the Audio well beneath the Slideshow editor window, as shown below.

Size, Resolution, and Format for Photos

The photos you use in slideshows can be a variety of sizes and formats. iDVD will resize and format them for DVD.

▾ iDVD can use any format that QuickTime recognizes, such as JPEG, PICT, PNG, or Photoshop.

▾ **Image sizes** of 640 x 480 pixels or 720 x 480 pixels work well, but larger sizes can be used and will be resized by iDVD to around 640 x 480.

▾ A resolution of 72 ppi is ideal, although you can use higher resolution images and iDVD will convert them to 72 ppi.

▾ Images smaller than 640 x 480 pixels will be enlarged by iDVD, usually adversely affecting the image quality. If you use a large quantity of high-resolution images in a slideshow, you may notice iDVD acts sluggish, but the final DVD will be okay.

▾ Each slideshow you create can have up to 99 photos.

▾ If, in the Slideshow editor, you set the "Slide Duration" pop-up menu to "Manual," you cannot include music with the slideshow.

Tip: If iDVD determines that it needs to increase the compression to accommodate all your content, it will do so automatically up to 90 minutes. However, it will do this by increasing the amount of compression used on the video files, which may affect the quality of the video. You can monitor the disc capacity in the Status pane of the Customize drawer, shown on page 125.

Create DVD-ROM Content

In addition to menus, movies, and slideshows, DVDs can store any file from your computer, making them accessible to anyone with a DVD drive. This data storage feature is called **DVD-ROM** (Read Only Memory). A small business may want to include PDFs, forms, documents, maps, or other data. When you create a DVD that contains slideshows, you may want to include the original, high-resolution photos on the disc for someone to use in a brochure or family album.

To put DVD-ROM content in your DVD project:

1. Click the "Status" button in the Customize drawer.
2. From the pop-up menu, choose "DVD-ROM Contents."
3. Drag any files and folders from your computer to the drawer.

   ▼ **To delete** an item from the DVD-ROM content, select the item, then press the Delete key on your keyboard.

   ▼ **To reorganize** the DVD-ROM contents, drag the folders up or down in the list, or drag files and folders in or out of other folders.

   ▼ **To create a new folder,** click the "New Folder" button at the bottom of the drawer.

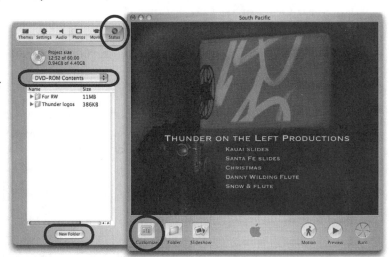

To access the DVD-ROM content that's on a DVD disc:

1. Insert the disc in a DVD drive.
2. Double-click the DVD disc icon on the Desktop.
3. In the window that opens, double-click the folder named "DVD-ROM Contents."

   The folder may also have the same name as your project.

4. Drag any of the folder's content to your computer's hard disk to copy it to your computer.

The iDVD remote control.

Preview your DVD

As you edit your DVD project, you should preview it often. First, click the "Motion" button to turn on motion menus, then click the "Preview" button to see how your final project will look.

While in **Preview mode,** a remote control appears on the screen that lets you test the DVD as if you were using a real remote control on a consumer DVD player. **To return to DVD editing mode,** click "Preview" again. For better efficiency when you return to editing, disable motion menus by clicking the "Motion" button at the bottom of the iDVD window.

Burn Your Project to a DVD

When you're satisfied with all your menus and you've added all the movies, slideshows, and DVD-ROM content that you want, it's time to encode, render, and "multiplex" all those files into the official DVD format and burn them onto a DVD. Happily, all those complex operations happen with a click of the "Burn" button.

Multiplex (also known as "mux") refers to the process of assembling DVD assets into the format that DVD players can use.

1. Place a blank DVD disc in the SuperDrive.

2. Click the "Burn" button in the bottom-right corner of the menu window to open the aperture and reveal the Burn icon.

Depending on the speed of your drive and the amount of content in your project, burning a disc may take anywhere from 10 to 30 minutes.

3. Click once again on the Burn icon which is now pulsating. iDVD starts rendering, encoding, multiplexing, and burning all the files and menus that are part of the DVD project.

Tip: Make sure Energy Saver in System Preferences is not set to "Put the hard disk to sleep when possible." This can interrupt the burning process.

Click the Burn button to start the encoding and burning procedure.

Section two

Mac OS X apps

The applications in this section are productivity applications that were designed specifically to run on Mac's state-of-the-art operating system, Mac OS X, version 10.2 (or later). The following chapters explore the applications that enable the efficient organization, creation, and management of email, contact information, calendars, and to-do lists: **Mail, Address Book,** and **iCal.**

Mac OS X includes communication applications that add convenience, efficiency, and fun to being productive: **iChat** provides instant messaging capability for keeping communication lines open with family, friends, and associates. **Rendezvous** makes file sharing and communication on a local network effortless. **Safari,** Mac's custom-built web browser, offers top browsing speed and cutting-edge features for viewing and organizing web content.

While some applications inspire creativity, these Mac OS X apps enhance the efficiency and productivity of your ever-expanding digital lifestyle.

Mail and Address Book 5

The Mac OS X application for handling email is called **Mail.** As you'd expect, with Mail you can write, send, and receive email messages. Beyond those basic functions, Mail has many useful tools for organizing, formatting, searching, and filtering email.

The **Address Book** is a separate application that works in conjunction with Mail. You can save your favorite email addresses, make a mailing list to send a message to a number of people at once, enter an address in a new message with the click of the mouse, and more.

Mail

The **basic** things you will be doing in **Mail** are checking messages, replying to messages, and composing new messages. On these next few pages are directions for how to do just that, but there is lots more your Mail program can do for you. You can create folders to organize your mail, create "Rules" to filter incoming messages and automatically sort them into special folders, spell-check your compositions, search your mail, and add entries to your Address Book.

But since you probably want to get started right away just using email, jump right in. You must have an Internet connection already set up, and you must have **already set up your email account** with Mac.com (or any other provider, as mentioned below). If you haven't set up your Mac.com account yet, and you want one (you don't have to have one), see page 271.

You cannot get your AOL mail through any other client except AOL or their web site.

If you have an account with any other provider, you can set that up as an account in Mail so you can use Mail as your email "client"; see pages 161–165. In fact, if you have several email accounts, Mail will check them all for you at the same time, and you can send messages from any account.

The Viewer Window

Mail opens up to the **Viewer Window.** If you open Mail and don't see this window, press Command Option N (or go to the File menu and choose "New Viewer Window").

Customizable toolbar, see page 158 (you might see different icons in your toolbar).

Activity Viewer hot spot, see page 179.

Status Bar, see page 179.

Customizable columns, see pages 146–147.

Message List, see pages 146–147.

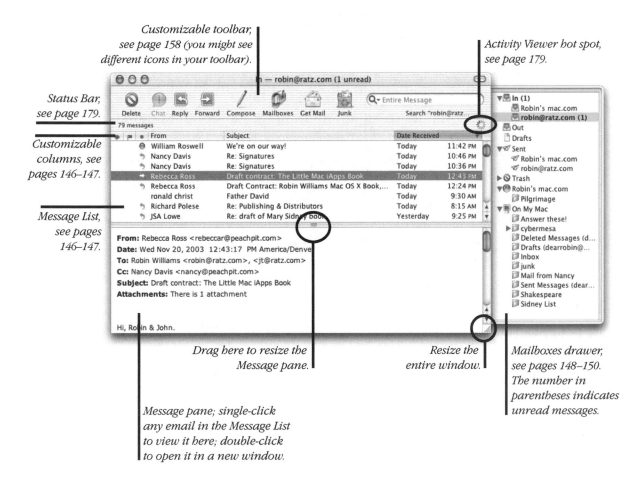

Drag here to resize the Message pane.

Resize the entire window.

Mailboxes drawer, see pages 148–150. The number in parentheses indicates unread messages.

Message pane; single-click any email in the Message List to view it here; double-click to open it in a new window.

Compose

An email address must have an @ symbol, and there must be a "domain name" with a dot, such as "ratz.com," "aol.com," "attbi.net," etc.

Send

Compose and send a new message

1. Click "Compose" in the toolbar to open a "New Message" window.

2. Click in the "To" area (called a field) and type an email address.

3. If you want to send a copy to someone, click in the "CC" field and type an address.

   To send to more than one person in either the "To" or the "CC" fields, separate the email addresses with commas.

4. Click in the "Subject" field and type a message description.

5. Click in the blank message area and type a message.

6. Connect to the Internet if you're not already connected.

7. Click the "Send" icon in the toolbar.

   Your copy of the sent message will be stored in the Mailboxes drawer in the "Sent" folder.

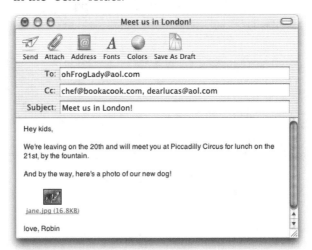

If you can't apply formatting to the selected text, perhaps your mail is set up as "Plain Text." From the Format menu, choose "Make Rich Text."

Save a message as a draft

To finish a message later, click "Save As Draft" in the toolbar, or press Command S. The message will be saved in the Drafts folder within your Mailboxes drawer. **To open the Draft** ("restore" it) later for editing, select the "Drafts" icon in the Mailboxes drawer, then double-click the desired draft in the list. If you don't have a broadband connection, it's handy to write drafts while you're offline, then connect and send them all at once.

Mail automatically creates a draft for you whenever you're writing a lengthy letter just in case something happens and your computer goes down, you won't lose the entire letter. But to make sure, press Command S regularly, as you would in any document.

Address a message to someone in your Address Book

Click the "Address" button in the New Message toolbar to open a limited version of the Address Book. Double-click a name in your list to address your message to that person. **Or** select a number of people and click the "To" button to send the same message to all those people. For all the details about the Address Book, see pages 181–191.

Check for email messages

1. Connect to the Internet if you're not already connected.
2. Click once on the Mail icon in the Dock to open Mail.
3. Click the "Get Mail" icon in the toolbar.

   Mail checks any "Accounts" that you've set up (how to set up accounts is on pages 161–165). Any account in the Mailboxes drawer that receives new email displays a notice next to the Inbox that indicates how many unread messages are in the Inbox.

4. Your messages will appear in the Message List. Single-click a message to display its contents in the Message pane.

Reply to the sender of a message

1. If the message is not already open, select it in the Viewer Window, then click the "Reply" button in the toolbar.
2. A Message window opens which contains the original sender's address in the "To" field, and the original message formatted as a quote. Type your reply above the quote, then click the "Send" button in the toolbar.

Reply to all recipients of a message

Tip: When you select a message and choose "Reply" or "Reply All" from the toolbar, the Reply window that opens also has a "Reply" button in its toolbar. Click the button to toggle it between "Reply" (reply to message sender only) and "Reply to All" (reply to all message recipients).

Mail that you receive may have been sent to multiple recipients, either directly as a Carbon copy (Cc) (or Courtesy copy since it's no longer on carbon paper), or secretly as a Blind carbon copy (Bcc). You can choose to reply to all recipients with one email (the reply will not include anyone in the Bcc list).

1. If the message is not already open, select the message in the Viewer Window, then click the "Reply All" button in the toolbar.
2. Type your reply above the original quoted message, then click the "Send" button in the toolbar.

Send a Bcc (blind courtesy copy)

1. Address and write your message as usual.
2. From the Edit menu, choose "Add Bcc Header." This puts a new field in the address area. Any address(es) you type in this field will *not* be seen by anyone whose address is in the "To" field.

Forward a message

1. Select or open a message in the Viewer Window, then click the "Forward" button in the toolbar.
2. Type any comments above the original quoted message, then click the "Send" button in the toolbar.

Attach a file

Attach: To attach a file to your message, click the "Attach" button in the toolbar, or choose "Attach" from the Message menu. The standard Open dialog box appears so you can find and select the file you wish to attach. Find the file, select it, then click "Open."

Another way to attach a file to a message is to drag the file's icon from its Finder window and drop it in the "New Message" window. This means you need to go to the Desktop and either arrange an open window to the side of your screen, or drag that file out of its folder and let it sit on the Desktop. Then when you are in Mail and writing your message, you can reach the file to drag it into the message window to attach it, as shown below.

To remove an attachment from a message, select the attachment in the "New Message" window (drag across it), then press the Delete key.

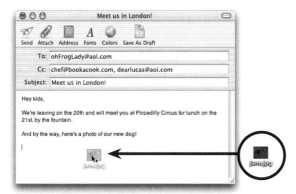

I put the photograph I want to send on the Desktop. Then I opened Mail and wrote my message. Now I can just drag the photo and drop it directly in the message, as shown above.

This is what the attachment looks like once I have dropped it into the message area. The receiver can usually just double-click on the icon to open it. Or drag it to the Desktop first, and then open it.

Depending on the file, you might see the actual image here in the message pane, and the receiver might also see the actual image. She can still just drag it to her Desktop.

Tip: If you want to send photographs as email attachments to a wide variety of computer users on all different sorts of computers, follow these guidelines:

Make sure the file is in the *JPEG format.* If you're not sure, open it in Preview and change the format.

Name the file with a short name with no special characters such as ! ? / or : .

The file must have the extension *.jpg* at the end.

Message List

The **Message List** displays a list of all messages in the currently selected Mailbox. The list is divided into several columns. The Message List provides different views of a list, depending on which column is selected.

The columns of information

Besides the default headings that appear in your Viewer Window, you can choose to show a number of additional **columns.** I explain the ones that aren't so obvious on the opposite page.

Also from the the View menu, you can choose to **hide** any column you don't want to see—just uncheck it from the menu list.

To change the column widths, position the pointer over the gray dividing line in the column headings, then press-and-drag the column left or right.

To rearrange (sort) the list according to the column heading, just click the heading at the top of a column. The column heading that is blue is the one that items are currently arranged by. For instance, I like to keep my email organized by date received, with the newest email at the top of the list, as shown below. But sometimes I want to find an old email from a particular person, so I click the "From" column to alphabetize the names; then I can quickly skim through the collection of email from each person.

These are the column headings. Click a heading to sort the messages by that column.

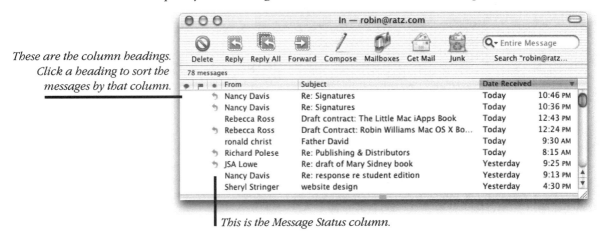

This is the Message Status column.

Icons in the Message Status column

The **Message Status** column (●) uses different icons to indicate if you've read the message, replied to, forwarded, or redirected it. These icons are applied automatically when one of those actions takes place. You can also manually mark an email that you've already read as "unread." Use this as a reminder to go back and read a message again, or make a message stand out: Select one or more messages, then from the Message menu, select "Mark As Unread."

Click the column heading to group similar categories, such as unread or returned messages, together in the list. Click again in the column heading to reverse the order of the list.

Message Status **icons** give visual clues to the status of messages.

- Blue orb: message has not been read.
- Curved arrow: message was replied to.
- Right arrow: message was forwarded.
- Segmented arrow: message was redirected.

Number column: In a series of email exchanges, it may be useful to know in what order messages were received. The Number column keeps track of the order for you. Click the **#** symbol in the column heading to arrange messages by order. Click again in the column heading to reverse the order of the list.

Flags column: Mark a message as flagged when you want it to stand out in the list, or if you want to temporarily tag a group of related messages.
To search for flagged files in a list, click the "Flag" column heading; all flagged messages will move to the top of the list. Click the heading again to reverse the order and put flagged messages at the bottom of the list.

Subject column: The Subject column shows what the sender typed into the Subject header of their email message. Click the column heading to show the subjects in alphabetical order; click again to reverse the order of the list.

Date & Time column: The Date & Time column shows when you received a message. Click the heading of the column to show messages in the time sequence they were received; click again to reverse the order of the list.

Buddy Availability: If you have a Buddy List in iChat (see Chapter 7), this column will display a green orb when a Buddy is online, and a yellow orb when he is online but idle (perhaps his computer has gone to sleep). Supposedly when you see a Buddy is online, you can click the "Chat" icon and start a chat with them. You won't see the Chat icon until you actually start a new message to that person, although you can customize your toolbar (see page 158) and put the Chat button in your Viewer Window toolbar.

Mailboxes Drawer

The **Mailboxes drawer** slides out from the side of the Viewer Window. The drawer might slide out from either side of the Viewer Window, depending on how much screen space is available to the left or right. **To make the drawer appear on one side or the other,** drag a message from the Viewer Window off to the side on which you want the drawer. **To open or close the drawer,** click the Mailbox button in the toolbar, or drag the edge of the drawer.

This is the Mailboxes drawer where all of your email is neatly organized.

For explanations of the individual icons, please see the following pages.

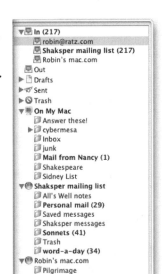

Here you see three email accounts that Mail checks for Robin (in the In box). Each account has its own Out, Draft, Sent, and Trash folders.

Numbers in parentheses indicate unread messages.

All of the folders (Mailboxes) under "On My Mac" are ones Robin created herself and in which she stores messages. Some of these Mailboxes hold messages that are automatically filtered into them; others store messages she has dragged into them.

The crystal balls indicate messages that are on Apple's servers from her two Mac.com accounts. As you can see, she hasn't had a chance to check her Shaksper mailing list for a while.

Icons in the Drawer

Here is an explanation of the various **icons** you might see in your drawer. As you make and delete folders and change your preferences, your arrangement of icons in the drawer will change, so don't worry if you don't see all of these or if you see more than I have listed here.

▼ ▣ **In (4)**
    ▣ **jt@ratz.com (3)**
    ▣ **roadrat@mac.com (1)**

- ▼ The **number in parentheses** is the number of unread messages in that folder. The *first-level* folder (the In box in the example to the left) shows you the **total** number of messages in all accounts, while the *second-level* folders (for the accounts "jt" and "roadrat" in the example), show you specifically how many messages are in that particular account.

- ▼ Single-click the main folder (first level) to show a list in the Viewer window of *all* messages of that sort for *all* accounts. For instance, click the In box to see all mail in all accounts; click the "Sent" icon to see all messages you have sent from any account; etc.

- ▼ Click *one* of the individual folders to see messages for just that selected account.

- ▼ If you have many accounts and want to check for messages from several of them at once, Command-click the accounts.

In box: At the top of the drawer you can tell if you have received any email. Messages contained in these In boxes are stored on your computer.

▣ **In (4)**

If you have **more than one email account,** click the triangle next to the In box icon to show the individual In boxes for each account.

Out box: Stores messages temporarily while waiting to be sent. If you're not connected to the Internet at the moment (you're working "offline" or your connection is down), messages you send are stored in the Out box until an online connection is established.

▣ **Out**

Drafts folder: Stores unfinished messages that you're composing. If you have multiple Mail accounts set up, you'll have separate Draft folders for each account. The messages in the Draft folders are stored on your computer.

▢ **Drafts (1)**

Sent folder: Contains copies of messages that you sent to other people. If you have multiple email accounts, the Sent folder contains other Sent folders named for each account you've set up. The messages in the Sent folders are stored on your computer.

✈ **Sent**

Junk (8)

Junk folder: Stores messages that have been identified by Mail as junk mail. The number in parentheses tells you how many junk messages have not been read. This Junk folder is automatically created when you change the Junk Mail mode from "Training" to "Automatic" in the Mail menu (as explained on pages 153–157).

Trash (2)

Red circle Trash folder: Contains messages that you deleted. If you have multiple accounts, the main Trash folder contains other Trash folders named for each of your accounts. Messages in the "red circle" Trash folders are stored on your computer—they are not *really* thrown away until you choose to empty the trash.

Use the Mail preferences to set up your Trash to **empty automatically** at certain times: In the Accounts pane, double-click an account name, then click the "Special Mailboxes" tab and make your Trash choice.

If you do not set up Mail to empty the Trash at certain times, make sure to **empty all your Trash mailboxes** occasionally. If you have an IMAP account (like Mac.com), you must empty your Trash or your mailbox on the IMAP server may get too full and you won't get any more mail.

To empty all messages in the Trash, select the topmost Trash icon in the Mailboxes drawer, then from the Mailbox menu choose "Erase Deleted Messages" (or press Command K).

roadrat@mac.com
Deleted Messages
Research
Sent Messages
Travel folder

Internet icon: The blue crystal ball indicates this is the Mailbox your Mac.com account (if you have one) and these folders and the files inside of them are stored on Apple's server. You can create new folders in this Mailbox (from the Mailbox menu, make a new Mailbox and choose your Mac.com account), then drag other messages from any account into the folders. You'll have access to everything in this Mailbox from any computer in the world—just open any browser, go to **www.mac.com,** click the Mail icon, and sign in. Everything in this account is stored on Apple's servers for thirty days (then they disappear).

In the Mail preferences, you can set up Rules (see pages 172–175) that tell certain types of email to go into certain folders, including these.

If you delete all of the folders in this mailbox, the entire Mailbox and crystal ball will disappear. If you want it back, make a new Mailbox as described above (or go to www.mac.com, log in to Mail, make a new folder online, and it will appear here in Mail).

On My Mac: Contains custom folders that you create for storing and organizing your messages. If you use Rules (see pages 172–175), you can have certain messages automatically sent to one of these folders. All messages in these folders are stored on your computer.

You might not see the actual little computer icon called On My Mac unless you also create online folders as described above. But even if you don't see the computer icon, all of these folders are stored on your hard disk.

> **Important note:** *If you upgraded from Mac OS X version 10.1 to version 10.2 (Jaguar), you'll find all of your old mail in a folder called "Inbox" located under "On My Mac"!*

▼💻 On My Mac
   🗐 ADC newsletters
  ▶ Book feedback
   🗐 DVD Workshop
   🗐 Online receipts
   🗐 Reply ASAP
   🗐 Shakespeare Readings

Tip: **To create new folders in this section,** Control-click "On My Mac" and choose "New Mailbox."

Drag messages in any account from the Viewer Window to any of your new custom folders.

Mailbox accounts

Some people, like Robin and me, get email at several different addresses, each coming from a different server. **Mail can check all of your email accounts at once.** When you answer mail, you can choose to have it answered from any one of your accounts, no matter to which account the original message was mailed.

If you have more than one account in the Mailboxes drawer, the "New Message" window provides a pop-up **Account menu** that contains the names of any accounts you've created, as shown above. From the pop-up menu, choose the account that you want the message sent from.

To set up your other accounts so Mail can check them all, see pages 161–165.

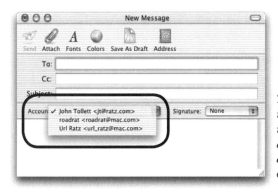

This is my Mail. When I receive an email to my ratz.com account, I can answer it with a return address from any of my other accounts.

Contextual Menus

Mail makes extensive use of **contextual menus:** Control-click on a message, the toolbar, or an item in the Mailboxes drawer to open a pop-up menu that offers various commands, as shown below. If you have a two-button mouse you can right-click on an item to show a contextual menu.

Using contextual menus is just a convenient way to access menu commands—there is nothing in a contextual menu that you can't find in the main menu bar across the top of your screen.

Hold down the Control key (not the Command key) and click on any message in the Viewer window to get the contextual menu.

Junk Mail Filter!

Okay, this is really incredible. You can set Mail so it **automatically deletes junk mail without ever having to see it.** Or if you are a little more cautious, you can have all the junk mail sent to a folder where you can check through it in case something you want accidentally ended up in the junk pile. And this really works—I was getting close to 100 pieces of junk a day in my public email and now I only see two or three a week. The rest are deleted before they even hit my box.

Set up your window

First of all, make sure your viewer window is set up as shown on the following page. This has nothing to do with the junk filter, but it will prevent the following from happening: When you single-click on a junk message to delete it, the message appears in the bottom pane. This does two things—it displays the message, which sometimes can take valuable time, and it often sends back a message to the junk mail sender confirming that this is a valid email address, which means you'll get more email from them and they'll sell your address to other evil junkers! So you don't want to give them the satisfaction of even *opening* a piece of junk mail.

Get rid of the bottom pane, as explained on the following page, and when you want to **read a message,** *double-click* the message name and it will open in its own window.

Tip: To turn off the Junk Mail feature, from the Mail menu choose "Junk Mail," then from the sub-menu select "Off."

—*continued*

To prevent having to open every piece of mail to delete it, follow the one step shown below. When you want to read a message, double-click anywhere in the message line that you see.

When both panes are showing, as in this example, the entire email appears in the bottom pane when you click on a message—even if you want to delete it.

To prevent this, drag this bar all the way to the bottom.

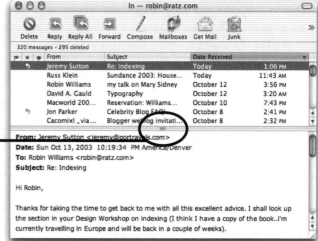

When the bottom pane is gone, you can select one, several, or all email messages and delete them (hit the Delete key) without having to open them first.

To read a message, double-click it and a separate window will open.

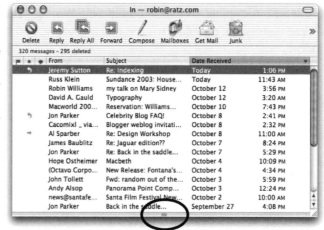

Automatic junk mail detection

Mail automatically analyzes incoming messages and identifies what it thinks is **junk mail** by highlighting the message in brown. If your "Flags" column is showing in the Viewer window, you'll see a junk mail icon (a brown mail bag) in that column.

Mail's default is to turn junk mail brown.

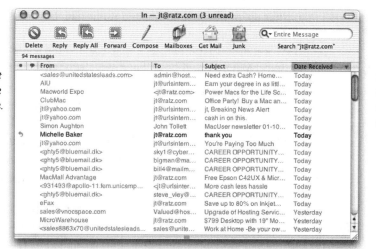

This is my Viewer window. Notice half the junk mail isn't even addressed to me!

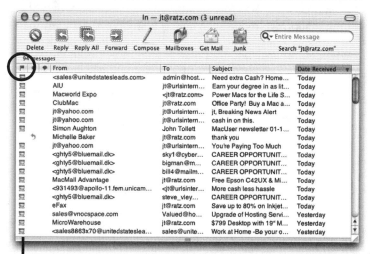

To make the Flags column visible, from the View menu choose "Columns," then from the submenu choose "Flags."

Train Mail to find junk more accurately

You can **train Mail to be more accurate** in determining whether a message is junk:

1. From the Mail menu, choose "Junk Mail," then select "Training."

2. When you receive a new email message, check to see if Mail has correctly identified it.

   ▾ If the new message is unwanted junk mail, but **Mail did not mark it** as such: Single-click the message, then click the "Junk" icon in the toolbar to mark it as junk mail (*or* from the Message menu, choose "Mark as Junk Mail" *or* press Command Shift J).

   ▾ If **Mail Incorrectly identifies** a message as junk mail, you can correct it: Select the message incorrectly marked and notice the "Junk" icon in the toolbar has changed to "Not Junk." Click the "Not Junk" icon to clear the message's junk designation.

3. Continue training Mail in this way for a couple of weeks, or until most incoming messages seem to be correctly identified.

When you're ready to **let Mail automatically handle junk mail,** go to the Mail menu, choose "Junk Mail," and from the submenu choose "Automatic." Mail will create a Junk mailbox (in the Mailboxes drawer) to store all your unwanted mail. You might want to occasionally review the messages in the Junk mailbox to make sure mail is being correctly identified.

When you're satisfied that Mail is accurately finding junk mail, you may want to change your setting so **Junk mail is instantly deleted.** Be careful with this! If you choose this option, you will never see the mail, nor can you undo the action or find it in any "Trash" mailbox—it's gone. And good riddance.

Instantly delete junk mail

You can have Mail delete junk before you ever see it—spam will instantly be deleted and you won't even be able to find it.

To delete junk mail before it ever appears in your box:

1. From the Mail menu, choose "Junk Mail," then from the submenu choose "Custom…." This opens the "Rules" pane of Mail preferences, with the "Junk" Rules edit sheet available for editing, as shown below.

   For more details about making Rules, see pages 172–175.

2. Below you see how I have set up my Mail preferences so Junk is deleted before it ever lands in my box. Remember, you have to be very confident that you're not getting any real mail mixed up in your junk mail (personally, if something gets accidentally labeled as junk and disappears, that's too bad—it's not worth it to me to sort through hundreds of pieces of junk mail to see if there's one good message).

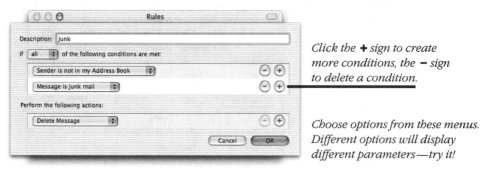

Click the + sign to create more conditions, the − sign to delete a condition.

Choose options from these menus. Different options will display different parameters—try it!

Tip: If you buy airline tickets online, the email confirmation might be considered spam and thus deleted. I set up a special Rule (see pages 172–175) that allows mail from places like Southwest or Delta to be delivered.

The Favorites Toolbar

The buttons in the **favorites toolbar** are duplicates of some of the commands that are also available in the menu bar at the top of the screen. You can customize this toolbar just like you customize the one in the Finder window.

To add additional tool buttons to the favorites toolbar, go to the View menu and choose "Customize Toolbar...." A pane of buttons appears that represent various functions, as shown below. Drag any of these buttons to the favorites toolbar for easy access.

To remove a button from the toolbar, Command-drag it off the bar.

To rearrange a button, Command-drag it to another position.

Command-click this button at any time to switch the toolbar between icons, icons with text, or just text.

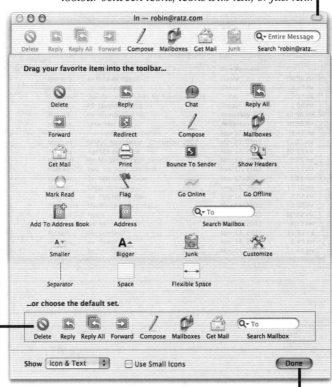

To restore the toolbar to the way it was when you first opened Mail, click anywhere in this bar.

Click Done when you're finished to put this pane away.

Other buttons that don't have obvious functions are "Bounce To Sender" and "Redirect."

The **Bounce To Sender** button is meant to discourage unwanted email: Select an unwanted message in the Message List pane, then from the Message menu, choose "Bounce To Sender" (or click the button in your toolbar, if it's there). The sender will receive a reply that says your email address is invalid and that the message was not delivered. The unwanted message is moved to your "Deleted Messages" folder. The recipient cannot tell if the message has been read. Unfortunately, this does not work for most spam (junk email) because spam return addresses are usually invalid (to prevent spammers from being spammed).

Bounce To Sender

Redirect is similar to "Forward," except that redirected mail shows the original sender's name in the "From" column instead of yours, and shows the time the message was originally composed in the "Date & Time" column of Mail's Viewer Window. When you redirect mail, your name remains in the "To" header at the top of the message so the new recipient will know that you received the message and that you redirected it.

Redirect

Mail Search

You can search a specific account or folder, or all mailboxes at once.

To search a specific account or folder, single-click an account or folder in the Mailboxes drawer, then click the triangle next to the magnifying glass in the Search field. From the pop-up menu, under the heading that identifies the account or folder you selected, choose whether to search entire messages or just one of the header fields (From, To, or Subject).

To search multiple mailboxes and folders, Command-click items in the Mailboxes drawer to search, then set the search criteria as explained above.

To search all mailboxes, from the Search pop-up menu, choose a search criteria under the heading "In All Mailboxes."

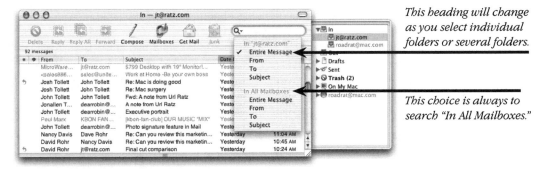

This heading will change as you select individual folders or several folders.

This choice is always to search "In All Mailboxes."

IMAP vs. POP

Apple's Mail program can handle two types of incoming mail "protocol": **IMAP** and **POP** (or POP3, to be specific). A protocol is a particular set of standards or Rules having to do with communications between computers.

Email from a POP account is stored "locally," which means on your hard disk.

POP3 (Post Office Protocol 3) is a protocol in which the server automatically downloads the mail to your computer when you check mail, then *deletes* the mail from the server. With POP you cannot read mail until it has been downloaded to your computer. POP works best for users who always use one computer on which the email files are stored and managed. Although Mac OS X uses IMAP to handle Mac.com email accounts, you can also setup POP accounts in Mail just as easily (pages 161–165).

You can choose to leave your mail on the POP server after it has been downloaded to your Mac (see page 163–165), but check with your service provider before you do that—it might make them mad to have all of your email clogging up space on their server.

Email from an IMAP account is stored on a remote server (although you can keep copies on your hard disk).

IMAP (Internet Message Access Protocol) is a protocol that receives and *holds* email on a server for you a certain amount of time, typically thirty days. IMAP allows you to view email before deciding whether or not to download it to your computer.

One advantage of IMAP is that you can manage your email from multiple computers because the email files are kept on the IMAP server for storage and manipulation; this means if you check your mail on one computer while you're away from home, say in Glasgow, then when you come home and check your mail, you can get the same messages at home that you read in Glasgow.

Another advantage is that you can choose *not* to download emails that have large attachments or email from people you don't want to hear from. You can wait until it's convenient, until you know who an attachment is from, or you can just delete unwanted or unsolicited email and attachments before they ever get to your computer.

America Online uses an IMAP server. That's why you can choose whether or not to download a file, and your email disappears automatically after thirty days whether you like it or not.

When you sign up for a Mac.com email service through .Mac, you're assigned a fifteen-megabyte mailbox on Apple's IMAP mail server. All unread messages within an account, *even deleted messages,* are stored on Apple's server for one month by default, unless you designate a different length of time (see the account preferences on the following pages). If you get more than fifteen megabytes of mail and attachments, people will not be able to send you any more email at that account until you clear it out. (See page 271 about a .Mac account, also called a Mac.com account.)

Set Up a New Account or Edit an Existing Account

Use **Mail Preferences** to create new mail accounts, edit existing accounts, and to customize Mail's behavior.

To open Preferences and get the Accounts pane:

1. From the Mail menu, choose "Preferences...," then click **Accounts.**

2. The **Description** list shows all the email accounts you've created.

    To **create** a new account, click "Add Account" and then see the following page.

    To **edit** the preferences of an existing account, select the account in the list, then click "Edit." See the following pages for detailed descriptions of the options.

To remove an account from the list, select it, then click "Remove." *Or* leave it there, but make it **inactive:** double-click the account name, click the "Advanced" tab, and uncheck the first two checkboxes.

Check for new mail: Set how often you want to check for new mail. This only works if Mail is open (if the triangle is under its icon in the Dock). If you don't have a full-time, always-on connection to the Internet (such as DSL or cable modem), you'll probably want to select the "Manually" option to avoid having your modem dialing and trying to connect when you least expect it.

New mail sound: Choose various sound alerts, or "None," when new mail appears in your In box. If you have various Rules set that filter your mail, you can have different sounds for each of the Rules so you know exactly when junk mail has been deleted, a letter from your lover has arrived, or mail for your family has gone into the Family mailbox; see pages 172–175.

*Mail cannot get your AOL email. Nothing can get AOL email except AOL (although you can use any browser anywhere in the world and go to **www.aol.com** to get your mail).*

Add or Edit an Account: You may have more than one email account in your life. For instance, you might have one that is strictly for business, one for friends and family, one for your lover, and one for your research. Mail can manage them all for you.

1. From the Mail menu, choose "Preferences...."

2. Click "Accounts" in the toolbar, then click "Add Account" to create a new one, or double-click the name of an existing account.

3. You should see the "Account Information" pane; if not, click the tab.

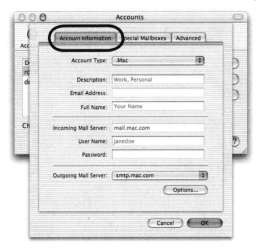

4. Choose an **Account Type** from the pop-up menu.

   Choose ".Mac" if you're setting up an email account that you created using the Mac.com web site.

   If you're setting up an account that comes from some other service provider, they can tell you if they use POP or IMAP (most likely POP).

5. In the **Description** field, type a name that will identify the account in the Mailboxes drawer. You can name it anything, such as "Lover Boy," "Research Mailing List," "earthlink," etc.

6. If you're setting up a Mac.com address, the **Email Address** field will automatically be filled in with your Mac.com email address.

7. **Incoming Mail Server:** If your account type is "Mac.com Account," the host name will automatically be filled in with "mail.mac.com."

   If you're setting up another account type, the mail service provider can tell you what name to use. Tell them you need the "incoming" mail server name, also known as the "POP address." (It's probably something like "mail.domainname.com," where "domainname" is the name in your email address, such as mail.ratz.com).

8. If you're setting up a Mac.com account, **User Name** and **Password** are the same ones you chose when you signed up for a Mac.com account. You should have received an email from Apple verifying this information.

   If you're setting up a POP account, your user ID and password may have been assigned by your provider, or they may have been chosen by you. *These are not necessarily the same user ID and password that you use to access your email.* If necessary, ask your provider for the User ID and password information.

9. **Outgoing Mail Server:** No matter where your email account *comes* from, the outgoing mail server (the SMTP Host) for every account is always the one you're paying money to for your Internet service—it's your Internet Service Provider's name, such as "mail.providername.com" because that's how your email is going *out*. Mac.com is *not* the SMTP host for your Mac.com account.

   If "smtp.provider.com" or "mail.provider.com" don't work, you might have to call your provider and ask them what their SMTP Host is named.

My friend Joannie made up a great pnemonic for SMTP: Send Money To Person.

Next, click the **Special Mailboxes** tab of the window. The items in this tab change depending on whether you're creating an IMAP account (such as a Mac.com account) or a POP account (most others).

These are the IMAP options. The advantage to storing items on the server is that you can access them from anywhere in the world; they're not stored on your computer. If you have a Mac.com acount, you can go to www.mac.com and log into your account on any computer that has a browser and an Internet connection.

These are the POP options. These refer to the items that are in the Mail program and stored on your Mac, not on a remote server.

—continued

See the opposite page for the POP options.

If you're creating an IMAP account, the following options are shown in the Advanced pane:

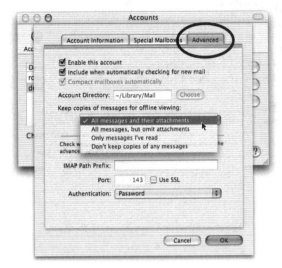

Enable this account: Check to make the account active. Uncheck it to make the account inactive, which does not delete the account—it just tells Mail to ignore it.

Include when automatically checking for new mail: UNcheck this box to prevent Mail from checking email at this address. This is useful if you have several email addresses and you choose not to check some accounts as often as others.

Compact mailboxes automatically: On an IMAP server, when you select and delete messages, they don't really get deleted—they get placed in a "Deleted" folder on the server. The server stores these deleted files for a user-specified length of time before they are erased. Apple doesn't give you a choice about this with your Mac.com email account—the files you delete will be erased immediately when you close the Mail application; this frees up your email space on their server.

Keep copies of messages for offline viewing: This menu offers options for copying email messages from an IMAP server onto your own Mac.

"All messages and their attachments" will copy all of your email, plus any attachments you were sent, to your hard disk.

"All messages, but omit attachments" will copy the body of the email messages, but not attachments.

"Only messages I've read" will only copy and store messages if you've read them. You can mark a letter as "Unread" or "Read" whether you really have or not—use the Message menu.

"Don't keep copies of any messages" will not copy any of your mail to your hard disk. This option provides you with extra security and privacy if other people have access to your computer.
If you choose this option, be aware that your IMAP server will eventually erase messages whether you've read them or not that have been stored for a user-specified length of time (thirty days at the most, generally).

If you're creating a POP account, the following options are shown in the Advanced tab.

See the previous page for the IMAP options.

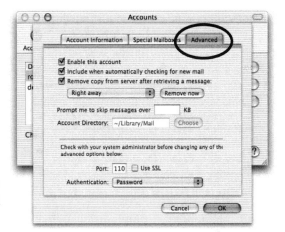

Enable this account: Check to make the account active. Uncheck it to make the account inactive, which does not delete the account—it just tells Mail to ignore it.

Include when automatically checking for new mail: UNcheck this box to prevent Mail from checking email at this address. This is useful if you have several accounts and you choose not to check some email as often as others.

Remove copy from server after retrieving a message: POP servers prefer that you check this so your mail is deleted from the server as soon as it is down-loaded to your Mac. Uncheck it only when you need to temporarily keep a copy of your mail on the server. In the pop-up menu you have some options for length of time to store messages.

Prompt me to skip messages over __ KB: When checking for mail, you can choose to skip over messages that are larger than you want to receive. This can eliminate unsolicited attachments. Enter the maximum file size that you'll permit Mail to download. A typical email message with no attachments is about 1 to 10 KB (kilobytes).

All done?

When all the "Accounts" preferences are set, click OK. Your new account will appear in the Mailboxes drawer, under the "In" icon.

See When iChat Buddies are Online

Mail detects when an **iChat Buddy is online** (see Chapter 7 regarding iChat and Buddies) and notifies you: a green dot next to a Buddy's message means she's available and you can send an Instant Message to her computer.

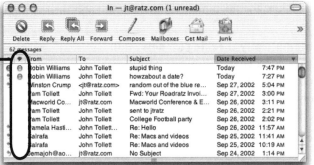

This is the "Buddy Availablity" column. When someone in your iChat Buddy List is online, a green dot will appear. A yellow dot indicates your Buddy is online, but idle; her computer is probably asleep.

If you don't see the "Buddy Availability" column in your Viewer Window, go to the View menu, select "Columns," then choose "Buddy Availability."

Chat with a Buddy

If you see that a Buddy is online, you can open a chat with her directly.

To open a chat with a Buddy:

1. Single-click an online Buddy's email message in the Viewer Window.
2. Press Command Option I, *or* from the Message menu, choose "Reply with iChat," which will open an iChat window, as shown below, right.

Or

1. Double-click a Buddy's email message in the Viewer Window.
2. Click the Reply button as if you were going to write a letter.
3. Click the Chat icon (the blue speech balloon) in the toolbar to open an iChat message window.

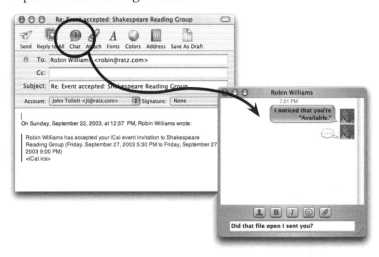

Fonts & Colors

You can select **fonts, font sizes,** and **text colors** for various parts of your email messages.

Fonts & Colors

To open Preferences and get the Fonts & Colors pane:

1. From the Mail menu, choose "Preferences…."
2. The "Mail Preferences" toolbar shows six buttons representing different categories of preferences. Click **Fonts & Colors.**

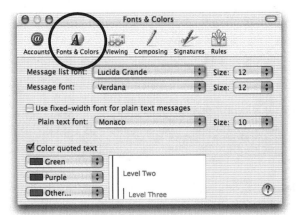

Message list font is the font used in the list of messages.

Message font is the font in which you will type your email messages. If you choose a font that your recipient does not have installed on their computer, it will turn into their default font.

Email replies often contain quotes from previous emails. Color coding and indenting the quotes makes messages easier to read and helps to visually organize the quotes in a hierarchy of responses. To apply color to quotes, check the **Color quoted text** box. Choose colors for up to three levels of quotes from the three color pop-up menus.

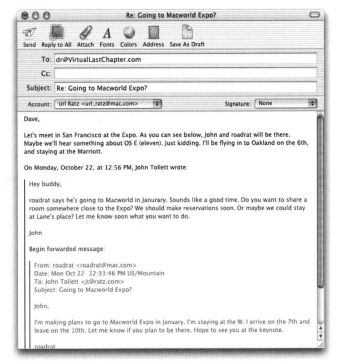

Viewing

Viewing

The **Viewing** preferences affect the information you see in the main window.

To open Preferences and get the Viewing pane:

1. From the Mail menu, choose "Preferences...."

2. The "Mail Preferences" toolbar shows six buttons representing different categories of preferences. Click **Viewing.**

Show header detail: This menu lets you choose how much, if any, header information (all that to/from/date stuff) shows at the top of emails. Choose "Custom..." to customize what information shows in headers. "Default" means the stuff you usually see.

Show online buddy status: Click this to display the Buddy Availability column in your Viewer Window. When someone in your Buddy List is online, a green dot appears in this column; a yellow dot if they are online but idle.

Highlight thread of selected message in color: If you check this and then click on any message in your Viewer Window, all other messages with the exact same subject will be highlighted in the color you chose.

Display images and embedded objects in HTML messges: If it makes you crazy when you get big, complex web pages through your email messages, uncheck this box so only the text will appear, not all the fancy graphics.

Composing

The **Composing** pane applies to email messages as you write them.

To open Preferences and get the Composing pane:

1. From the Mail menu, choose "Preferences…."
2. The "Mail Preferences" toolbar shows six buttons representing different categories of preferences. Click **Composing**.

Format: "Rich Text" allows you to stylize messages with fonts and formatting, but not everyone will be able to see these features. "Plain Text" can be seen by everyone, but does not show any color and style formatting. Choose the format you'll use most often as the "Default message format," then change to the other format when necessary (choose it from the Format menu in the main menu bar).

Check spelling as I type: Check this to catch spelling errors immediately. When Mail doesn't recognize a word, it underlines the word with a dotted red line. If you need help with the correct spelling, from the Edit menu choose "Spelling," then choose "Spelling…" from the submenu.

Always Cc myself to send a copy of outgoing messages to yourself.

Automatically complete addresses: As you type a few letters in the "To" field, Mail will add the rest of the address for you. If there are more than one match, you'll get a list to choose from. If the correct one is in the field, just hit Return. If you get a list, use the DownArrow to move down the list, selecting each one; hit Return or Enter when the proper address is chosen.

Tip: If you select some text in an email message and hit the Reply button, only the selected text will appear in the reply as a quoted message.

When sending to a group, show all member addresses: When you send a message to a group (mailing list, as explained on pages 187–190), Mail will display everyone's address. Unless you have a specific reason to do this, UNcheck this box so the actual addresses are hidden.

The other options are self-explanatory.

Signatures

A **signature** is a blurb of pre-prepared information about you or your company that can be added to the end of a message, either manually or automatically, as shown on the opposite page. You can create different signatures that include different types of information for various types of messages. For instance, in addition to a signature for personal mail that may include your address and phone number, you may want to create a different business signature that doesn't include personal information.

To open Preferences and get the Signatures pane:

1. From the Mail menu, choose "Preferences…."

2. The "Mail Preferences" toolbar shows six buttons representing different categories of preferences. Click **Signatures.**

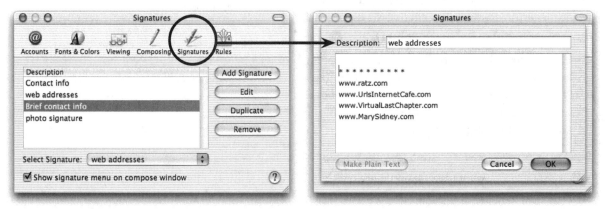

Create a signature: To create a signature, click the "Add Signature" button. In the "Description" field, enter a name for the signature that is descriptive to you. In the big box, enter any information you want to include in the signature. If you want to add a photograph, drag it into the text field. The image format should be JPEG (.jpg) to optimize file size and to minimize translation problems across computing platforms. If your message is going to another Mac, other formats will work, such as TIFF, PICT, or PNG, but JPEG is still the recommended format.

To create a new signature that's similar to an existing signature, select the signature you want to use as a model, then click the "Duplicate" button. This duplicate now shows up in the list of signatures; select it, then click the "Edit" button. Make necessary changes to the signature, change its name in the "Description" field, and click OK.

To edit the information in a signature, choose a signature in the Description list, then click the "Edit" button. Make changes in the signature file, then click OK.

To remove a signature from the list, select it, then click the "Remove" button.

To choose a default signature, select its name in the "Select Signature" pop-up menu. This signature will be used in all messages unless you override it by choosing another signature or "None" from the pop-up menu (discussed below) when you're writing a new email.

Show signature menu on compose window: Check this to install a pop-up menu in the "New Message" window that contains all of your signatures. Then in any email message, just choose the one you want to include at the end of that message.

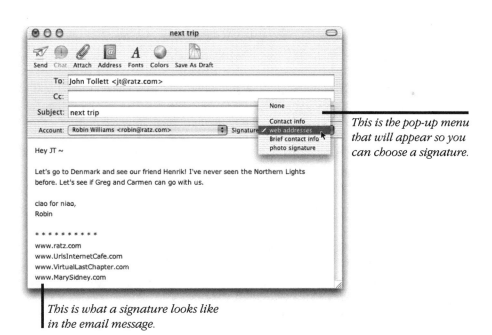

This is the pop-up menu that will appear so you can choose a signature.

This is what a signature looks like in the email message.

Rules

Rules

Use **Rules** to manage and organize your messages automatically. Rules act as filters that sift through your messages and put them in their proper mailboxes, delete them, forward them, or follow other actions, according to your directions. You might belong to a mailing list about pack rats, so you can have every email that comes in from that mailing list automatically delivered to the Pack Rat Mailbox. Or you might want to delete every email with a subject that contains the words "mortgage," "enlargement," "babes," "hot," "free," or other obvious junk-mail words.

To open Preferences and get the Rules pane:

1. From the Mail menu, choose "Preferences...."

2. The "Mail Preferences" toolbar shows six buttons representing different categories of preferences. Click **Rules.**

Before you create a new Rule: If you want your mail to be automatically organized into different mailboxes, you can create those mailboxes *before* you make the Rules.

To make a new mailbox:

1. If the Mailboxes drawer is not open, open it (click the Mailbox icon in the toolbar).

2. From the Mailbox menu, choose "New Mailbox...."

3. Choose whether you want this mailbox to be on your hard disk (On My Mac) or on Apple's server, if you have a .Mac account (choose your account name from the pop-up menu).

4. Name the mailbox and click OK.

To create a new Rule:

1. Click the "Add Rule" button. You'll get the dialog box shown below.

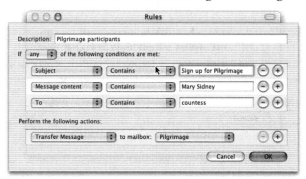

2. The **Description** field contains a default name, such as "Rule #5."
   Change this name to something that describes your intended Rule.
   In the example below, I want all the mail from my son Ryan to go into a
   special mailbox, so I named it "Mail from Ryan."

3. In the **following conditions** section, specify which elements of an email
   message are to be searched and what the subject of the search will be.

   The first pop-up menu contains types of message **headers** that usually
   are included with an incoming message, such as To, From, Subject,
   etc., or you can choose to find text in the body of the message. Choose
   which area to search.

   Then choose a "modifier" from the second pop-up menu, such as
   "Contains," "Does not contain," or others.

   Type an appropriate word or words into the text field. The Rule above
   will search for messages whose "From" field "Contains" the word "Ryan." *—continued*

4. **Perform the following actions:** Determines what actions will be applied to messages that match the criteria you specified. You can check as many or as few of these actions as you like.

> **Transfer Message:** Select an existing mailbox (that you previously made according to the directions on page 172) to transfer the messages into. (If you didn't make a mailbox already, you can do that now: just go to the Mailbox menu and choose "New Mailbox.")

> **Set Color of Message:** Choose a color for highlighting messages that match the criteria. Then you can quickly identify various categories of filtered email that may appear in a message list.

> **Play Sound:** Choose a sound that will alert you when you receive a message that matches the criteria.

> **Reply to Message:** This opens a text box in which you can type a message that will automatically be included before the original message being forwarded or replied to.

> **Forward Message:** To forward targeted incoming mail to another email address, check and enter an email address in the text field that you want the forwarded mail sent to. After you choose this you will get a little button, "Message…"; click it to enter a message that will appear at the beginning of the forwarded email.

> **Redirect Message:** *Forwarded* mail shows *your* name in the "From" column of the email, plus the date and time you forwarded it. *Redirected* mail shows the *original* sender's name in the "From" column, and shows the time the message was originally composed in the "Date & Time" column of Mail's message list. When you redirect mail, your name will remain in the "To:" header at the top of the message so the new recipient will know that you received the message and redirected it.

> **Delete Message:** Trash any message that meets the criteria. You can use the header information of mail you don't want and create a Rule that automatically deletes messages like that one.

> **Mark as Read:** Removes the blue dot from the Message Status column (if it's showing) even if you didn't really open and read it.

> **Mark as Flagged:** Puts a little flag marker in the Flags column (if it's showing) to call your attention to this message.

> **Stop evaluating Rules:** Just like it says.

5. **OK:** Click OK and the Rule is made. All incoming mail will now be searched and sorted using the criteria you just created.

Rules are listed in an order and will be applied in that order. **Change the priority order** by dragging a Rule to another position in the list.

Make a Rule active or inactive with the checkbox in the **Active** column.

To **edit a Rule,** select it in the list, then click the "Edit" button, *or* double-click the Rule name in the list.

Duplicate a Rule if you want to create a new Rule that is similar to an existing one. Select an existing Rule in the list, click "Duplicate," then select and edit that new Rule.

To remove a Rule, select it in the Rule list, then click the "Remove" button or press the "Delete" key on your keyboard.

Rules affect new messages that are received *after* a Rule was created. **To apply Rules to older messages,** select the desired messages from the Message List. From the "Message" menu, choose "Apply Rules to Selections."

News from Apple: The Rule is set so these messages from Apple are highlighted in blue. You can change this, delete the Rule, etc.

> **Tips:** If you won't be able to respond to your mail for a while, set up an **autoresponder** that will automatically return a message saying you are away and will respond later:
>
> > Choose "If sender is in my Address Book," and "Reply to message," then click the button to enter your message. You might say something like, "Thank you for your email. When I return from the Amazon on October 27, I will answer your lovely message."
>
> Or **forward** all of your own email to yourself at another address.

Menu Commands

Following are some of the items in the **menus** that aren't explained elsewhere.

File menu

New Viewer Window: If you've closed the main Viewer Window and realize that you need it back, use this command, or press Command Option N.

Import Mailboxes: Mail can import the mailboxes of many popular email applications. If you have custom mailboxes already set up in another email application, from the File menu, choose "Import Mailboxes…." Select one of the email clients in the list, then click the right arrow button for instructions. Mail will open a directory window so you can navigate to the appropriate mailbox file and import it.

You can't import AOL mailboxes (not because of Mail's limitations, but because of AOL's prohibitions).

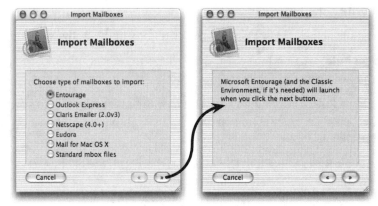

To print an email message: Double-click a message to open it. Click the "Print" icon in the open message's toolbar to open the Print dialog box.

Or select a message in the Message List pane, choose File and "Print…."

Make the appropriate selections in the Print dialog box and click "Print."

To print multiple email messages: From the Message List pane, select multiple messages. From the File menu, choose "Print…." All selected messages, including header information, will print out in continuous fashion—it will not print a separate page for each message.

Mailbox menu

Go Offline: If you have a dial-up account that ties up your phone line while you're connected to the Intenret, you can "Go Offline." This disconnects you from the Internet, but leaves Mail open. Before you go offline, transfer any messages you want to read to another mailbox (just drag them over and drop them in). Then go offline, read your mail, compose messages, print them, etc. Messages you compose while offline are stored in the Outbox in the Mailboxes drawer, where you can open and edit them. When you're ready to send mail, from the Mailbox menu, choose "Go Online."

Get New Mail in Account: If you have more than one account in Mail, go to this menu to selectively check the mail in just a single account.

Edit menu

These are some of the items in the **Edit menu** that aren't explained else-where in this chapter or that are not self-explanatory.

Paste As Quotation: Use this command when you want to paste text from another document into an email message as a quotation. In Mail, a quota-tion is styled with indentation, a vertical bar, and a user-specified color, as explained on page 167.

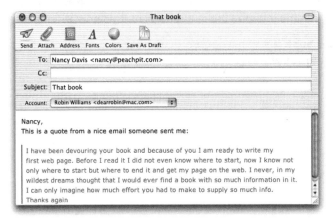

Append Selected Messages: This will add entire email messages you have received onto the end of a message you compose. Compose your message; in the Viewer Window, select the email message you want to append, then choose this command from the Edit menu.

View menu

Focus on Selected Messages: Select messages (Command-click to select more than one), then choose this option so *only* those messages will be visible in the Message List. To show all of the messages again, go back to the View menu and choose "Show All Messages."

Hide Status Bar or **Show Status Bar:** The Status Bar is located just below the toolbar. The left side of the Status Bar provides information about your Internet connection when checking for mail, and it displays the number of messages in the current Mailbox.

Activity Viewer: The right side of the Status Bar displays a revolving wheel when connecting to a remote server to send or receive mail. Click that revolving wheel (or click where it would be) to open the **Activity Viewer,** as shown below, and see what's going on as it connects.

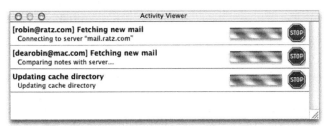

Click the revolving wheel again to close the Activity Viewer (or click the red Close button in the upper-left corner of this window).

Format menu

In the Format menu, under "Font," there is a command to make the selected text **Bigger.** The menu says the keyboard shortcut is Command +, but that doesn't work—use Shift Command +. Sometimes even that doesn't work.

Make Plain Text changes messages from "Rich Text" format to "Plain Text" format, which will strip out all of the formatting, different fonts, colors, etc. If the message is already in Plain Text, this command appears as "Make Rich Text." This will *not* restore any formatting that was removed.

Text Encodings: If you receive email that does not display correctly because it was originally written in a foreign language on a foreign keyboard, it may help to choose "Text Encodings," then select one of the text encoding options from the list.

Increase Quote Level: To format text as a Mail-style quote or to increase the existing quote level, click within a line of text, then choose "Increase Quote Level." Choose the command again to further increase the quote level, as shown below.

The operation is much easier and faster if you learn the keyboard shortcuts: Click within the appropriate text, then type Command ' (that's the typewriter apostrophe, just to the left of the Return key) to "Increase Quote Level," or type Option Command ' to "Decrease Quote Level."

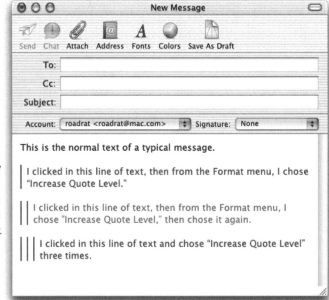

Each of these quoted sections has been increased one more level than the one above it.

The **Address Book** works both independently and with Mail to create Address Cards that store contact information for individuals or groups. When *Mail* is open, you can automatically create an Address Book entry for anyone who sent mail to you. When *Address Book* is open you can automatically address email to an individual or group. You can search the Address Book by name, email address, or by a user-defined Category.

*Single-click here to open the dialog box where you can choose an image to apply (TIFF, GIF, or JPG; not EPS format). **Or** drag an image from your Desktop and drop it in this space.*

Once you add an image, it will appear in a chat session with this person.

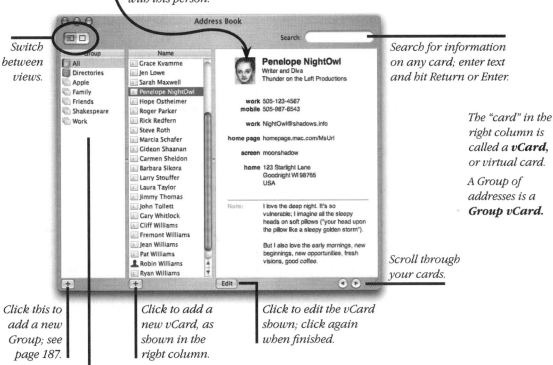

Switch between views.

Search for information on any card; enter text and hit Return or Enter.

*The "card" in the right column is called a **vCard,** or virtual card.*

*A Group of addresses is a **Group vCard.***

Scroll through your cards.

Click this to add a new Group; see page 187.

Click to add a new vCard, as shown in the right column.

Click to edit the vCard shown; click again when finished.

Organize *your cards into Groups; see pages 187–188.*

Add *any Name into any number of different Groups; every Name will always appear in the "All" list.*

*If you **add** a Name directly into a **Group,** it is automatically added to the All list.*

*When you **delete** a name from a Group, it is not deleted from the All list.*

*If you address an **email** message to the name of a **Group,** the message goes to everyone in that Group. See page 188.*

Add New Names and Addresses

There are several ways to **add a new vCard of information** or just a name and email address to the Address Book, depending on whether you are using Address Book or Mail at the moment.

To add a new address card while using Address Book:

1. Single-click the **+** sign at the bottom of the "Name" column (or at the bottom of the visible card).

2. This makes a new vCard automatically appear and the name of the person is already selected for you, waiting for you to type, as shown below.

   Type the person's first name, then hit the Tab key. Type the last name, then hit Tab, etc. Continue to fill in all the information you know.

3. If a label is changeable, you'll see two tiny arrows. For instance, maybe you want to change the label "mobile" to "cell." Single-click the tiny arrows and you'll get a little pop-up menu, as shown below. Either choose one of the pre-named labels, or choose "Custom..." and type in the name of the label you want.

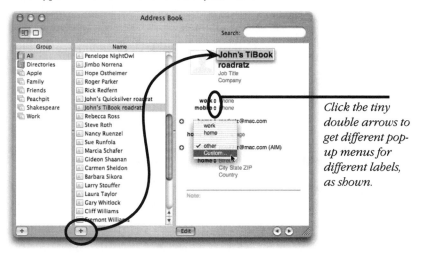

Click the tiny double arrows to get different pop-up menus for different labels, as shown.

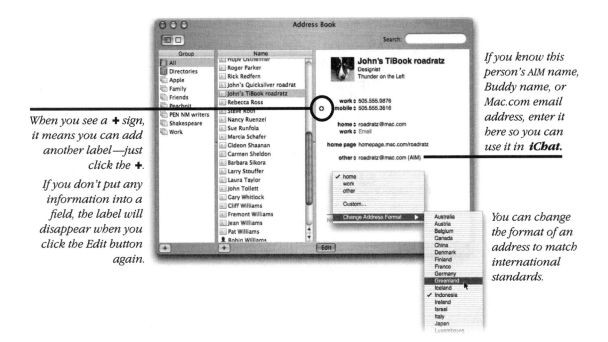

When you see a ✚ *sign, it means you can add another label—just click the* ✚.

If you don't put any information into a field, the label will disappear when you click the Edit button again.

If you know this person's AIM name, Buddy name, or Mac.com email address, enter it here so you can use it in **iChat**.

You can change the format of an address to match international standards.

An Aside: Use the Sticky Note Service

You can use Services to make a Sticky note out of the text in any field of your Address Book, as shown below.

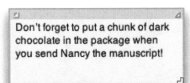

Don't forget to put a chunk of dark chocolate in the package when you send Nancy the manuscript!

This is a Sticky note made from the Notes field in the Address Card.

Just select the text in a field (press Command A to select all of the text, even if you can't see all of it). From the Address Book menu, choose "Services," then choose "Make New Sticky Note." *Or* press Command Shift Y instead of going to the menu at all.

To add a sender's email address to your Address Book instantly:

1. In the **Mail** program, either single-click on an email in your list, or open an email message.

2. From the Message menu in the menu bar across the top of your screen, choose "Add Sender To Address Book," *or* press Command Y. The Address Book will not open, but the sender's address will be added.

   Check on that address later, though, because if a person's first and last name are not included in their own email address, you'll find the new address in your Address Book at the very top of the "Names" column as <No Name>. Edit that vCard to add the person's name so he is sorted in the list properly.

Click on a sender's email in your list, then press Command Y.

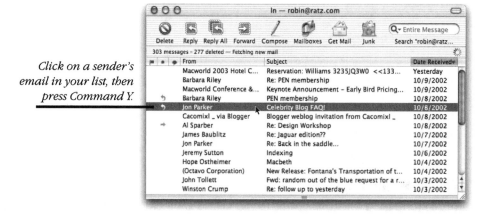

To add someone's address from your History list:

1. In the **Mail** program, go to the Window menu and choose "Address History." This brings up a window, shown below, that has kept track of everyone you have sent email to (not everyone who has sent *you* email because then you'd have thousands of junk mail addresses).

    If an address has a vCard icon to its left, that name and address is already in your Address Book.

2. Single-click the name of someone you want to add to your Address Book, then click the button "Add to Address Book." Ta da! You won't see anything happen, but that address has been added.

Note: *At the bottom of this list are all the people you have emailed but whose actual names are not shown.*

If you add one of those to your Address Book, it will show up in the Name column in your Address Book at the top of the list, called <No Name>.

Select <No Name> to display its vCard, then click the Edit button so you can add the person's name to the vCard.

Label Options

The various entries in a vCard each have different **options,** as shown below. Single-click on each entry *label* (the bold word on the left, not the entry data) and see what the options are.

Experiment with the options to become familiar with them. If you see pop-up menus that say things like "work" and "home," that means you're still in Edit mode—click the Edit button again to get out of Edit mode.

See a fax number from across the room

You can choose to see phone and fax numbers in type large enough to fill your screen so you can see it across the room when you fax someone. Try it. (Or type a love note instead of a phone number and flash it to your sweetheart on the other side of the room.)

Send an email (and other options)

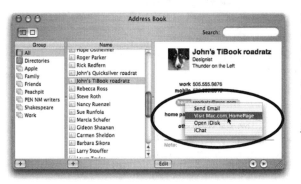

You will see more or fewer options here depending on whether the person is a .Mac member or not.

Regardless, you can always click on their email address to open an email message pre-addressed to this person.

Go to a web page or open a chat

Go directly to a person's web page, if you included the address in the vCard.

Click on his Instant Message name to open a chat with him (as explained in Chapter 7).

Create and Use a Group Mailing List

You can make a **Group** in the Address Book, which not only helps organize your
address list, but a Group acts as a **mailing list;** that is, you can send an email
message to the Group name and the one message will go to everyone in that
list. You can put the same name in more than one list.

To make a Group/mailing list:

1. In the Address Book, make sure you see all three columns, as shown
   below, left. (If you only see one panel, the "Card" panel, click the "View
   Card and Column" button shown below, right.)

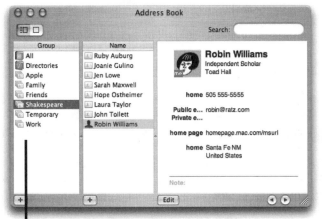 

*In the left column you see the Groups I have made, and
the "Shakespeare" Group is currently selected. In the
center column are all the people in that selected Group.*

*If you only see one vCard,
click this button.*

2. Under the Group column, click the **+** sign. A "Group Name" will
   appear in the Group column, selected and ready for you to type a new
   name, as shown below. Just type to replace the selected name. When
   done, hit the Enter key.

*I'm going to name
this new group
"PEN NM writers."*

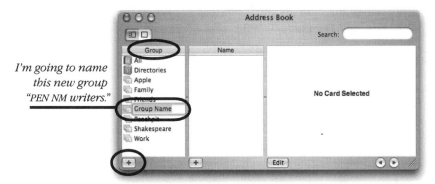

—continued

3. Now you can do one of two things: **Either** in the "Name" column, click the **+** sign and add a new address; this new address will be added to your "All" group *and* to the new Group that you just made (which is still selected, right?).

Or click the "All" Group so you see all of the addresses in your book, then drag an existing address and drop it on the Group name, as shown below.

"All" contains the name of every person in every Group, as well as those who are in no Group at all. Each Group actually contains "aliases" to the one address card.

Now Denise is in the "All" list, as well as in the "PEN NM writers" Group. You can put the same person in any number of Groups.

Shortcut to make a Group

Here's an **even faster way** to make a Group:

1. Hold down the Command key and click on all the names in the list that you want to put into a new Group.

2. Let go of the Command key.

3. Go to the File menu, and choose "New Group From Selection."

4. Change the name of the Group, as shown on the previous page.

Send email to an entire Group

Once you've made a Group mailing list, you can send a message to everyone in the group simply by sending the email to the Group name.

To send an email message simultaneously to every person in a Group:

1. You don't have to have the Address Book open. In **Mail,** start a new email message.

2. In the "To" box, type the name of the Group. That's all—write your letter and send it and it will go to everyone in the Group.

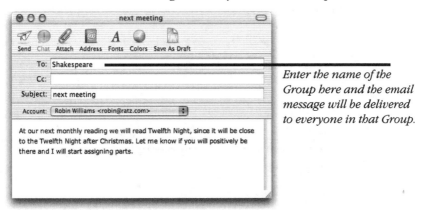

Enter the name of the Group here and the email message will be delivered to everyone in that Group.

Tip: It's polite to suppress the address list when mailing to a group so you don't broadcast personal email addresses. See the following page for directions on how to suppress the list.

Suppress the address list when sending mail to a Group

It's polite to **suppress the address list** when sending to a Group. For one thing, it's *really* annoying to have to scroll through a long list of addresses to get to the message. For another, *some* people don't want their private email address broadcast to everyone else on the list.

To suppress the Group list of addresses:

1. In the Mail program (not the Address Book), open the Mail preferences (go to the Mail menu and choose "Preferences…").

2. Click the "Composing" icon in the Toolbar, as shown below.

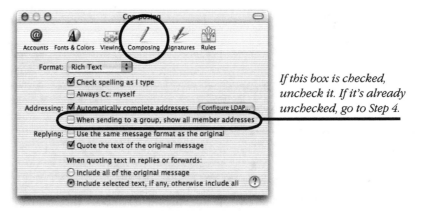

If this box is checked, uncheck it. If it's already unchecked, go to Step 4.

3. UNcheck the box (if it's checked) "When sending to a group, show all member addresses."

4. Put the Preferences away (click the red Close button).

Export an Address or a Group of Addresses

You can **export** a single address, a collection of selected addresses, or a Group. Once exported, any other Address Book users can import the addresses into their application. There are two simple ways to export:

▼ Drag a Group, a Name, or a collection of Names from the Address Book and drop them on the Desktop or inside any Finder window. It will make an icon like the ones shown below.

▼ Select the Group, a Name, or a collection of Names in the Address Book. From the File menu, choose "Export vCard(s)..." or "Export Group vCard...." You will be asked where you want to save the exported vCard. An icon like the ones shown below will appear where you chose to save it.

Drag a selection of vCards to the Desktop and the Mac will create this icon.

Drag a Group to the Desktop and the Mac will create an icon for you with the name of the Group.

Important tip: What you **don't** want to do now is double-click this icon! I know, it's almost irresistible. But if you double-click it, it will look like nothing happened. So you'll probably double-click again. And maybe a third time just to make sure you didn't miss something. Every time you double-click, the addresses in the file are added to your Address Book! So if you double-click three times, you'll have each person's address in your Book four times! So let's say you open your Address Book and delete three of those extra names — if any of those names were in a Group, you could be deleting them from their Group because only one of those four duplicates are actually in the Group — but which one? Sigh. How do you think I know this?

You can **send this file** to anyone with the current version of Address Book—they double-click the file **(once)** and those addresses are now in their Book.

Import Addresses

Caveat: This is supposed to work and it did work in previous versions of OS X and it should work again. But if you try it and it doesn't work, it's not *you* who is doing something wrong —we have to wait until Apple fixes it. Check their web site.

If you want to **import addresses** from an application *other* than Address Book, first open the other email client and export the address information as a "tab-delimited" file. Then open Address Book, and from the File menu, choose "Import." Use the "Open" window to select the tab-delimited file on your computer, then click "Open."

Keep in mind that if you had information in the other address list that was in a different order from your list in Address Book, data might appear in odd places. It's a good idea to **save a copy** of your original Address Book file in case you need to replace the new one; see below.

You can *export* selected addresses from your Address Book so someone can *add* them to their Mac OS X Address Book; see page 191.

Save your Address Book

If you plan to reformat your hard disk, **save a copy of your Address Book** file so you can place it in the same location after you reinstall Mac OS X. To find the Address Book file, open your Home folder, then open the "Library" folder, then the "Application Support" folder. The address book folder is located here, named **AddressBook**.

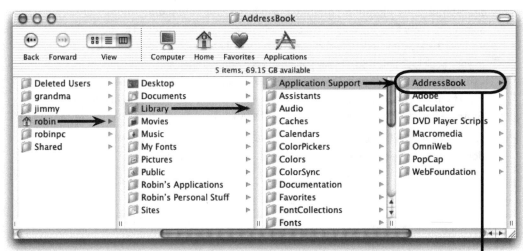

This is the AddressBook folder that contains your list of email address and contact information. Before you do anything that might change it, drag a copy of this original file into another folder, like your Documents folder: Hold down the Option key and drag it to another folder.

Email Etiquette

Many people use email everyday without being aware of **email etiquette** and without realizing that they're **1)** annoying co-workers, friends, and relatives; **2)** making themselves look naive and amateurish in the email world; and **3)** turning themselves into junk mailers, albeit well-intentioned.

If no one has complained about your email etiquette, you're probably in good shape. Or it could be that family members and friends do not want to risk embarrassing you. To be safe, consider the following suggestions and see if your email manners are up to date.

1. **Get permission before you add someone to a mailing list.**
   You may be well-intentioned, but most people get so much spam and junk mail that they'd rather not receive the inspirational messages that someone sent you—especially since they probably received five other copies already. Not everyone is a curmudgeon about getting email like this, but it's polite, professional, and considerate to ask for permission before putting someone on your mailing list. And please, don't take it personally if they decline. Privacy on the Internet is hard to come by, and many people try to keep their email address off as many mailing lists as possible. When you add someone's address to your mailing list without their permission, you're publishing private information.

2. **Clean up the email headers.**
   Even if someone *wants* to be on your mailing list, it's extremely annoying to get email that has dozens (or hundreds) of lines of header information before the message. This happens when you receive an email message that was sent to a list, then someone sent it to their list, then someone else sent it to their list. This kind of email makes the senders look like the clueless amateurs they are. Before you send a forwarded message, **delete** all that header stuff so the recipient can see the message at a glance without having to scroll through pages of junk. (To delete the header information, click the Forward button to forward the message, select all that useless stuff, and hit the Delete button.)

3. **Hide the mailing list addresses.**
   When you send a message to your mailing list (called a "group" in Mail), you are essentially providing every reader of the message with the email addresses of all your friends and relations. Then if those people forward your message, all of their recipients have the email addresses of all your friends and relations. Not many people appreciate that. Use the tip on page 190 to hide the list of addresses when you send a message. Not only is it neater, it is more polite to everyone involved. *—continued*

4. Take the time to personalize your email.

If you send well-intentioned junk email to an aquaintance, friend, or relative, it will be appreciated if you take the time to add a personal note to the forwarded message, such as "Hi Jay, I thought you might enjoy this." When I receive an unsolicited, unsigned, almost-anonymous, forwarded email, it makes me wonder when I can expect to start receiving the rest of the sender's postal service junk mail and Sunday supplements.

5. Identify your email attachments.

Tip: If you want to send photographs as email attachments to a wide variety of computer users on all different sorts of computers, follow these guidelines:

Make sure the file is in the *JPEG format.* If you're not sure, open it in Preview and change the format.

Name the file with a short name with no special characters such as ! ? / or : .

The file must have the *extension .jpg* at the end.

When you attach a file to an email message, don't make the recipient guess what kind of file it is or what program might open it. Include a description of the attachment and the file type, or what program is needed to open it. Say something like, "Barbara, the attached file is a photograph that I saved as a .tif in Photoshop 7 on a Mac running OS X." Dealing with attachments can be confusing, and any helpful information is usually appreciated.

6. Don't fall for the urban legends and hoaxes that travel around the Internet.

When you get a panic-stricken email from a friend warning you of an apocalyptic virus and to "Please forward this email to everyone you know," do not forward it to anyone you know. This email message usually contains the words "THIS IS NOT A HOAX!" That means that this is a hoax. These messages float around the Internet constantly and some of them are many years old. If there's a deadly virus about to destroy the world as we know it, you're more likely to hear about it from the national news services and online news sites than from your cousin who's been using email for three months.

Also, do not forward the email messages that tell you Microsoft will pay you one dollar every time you use HotMail or visit the Microsoft web site. And don't forward the warning that the postal service is going to start charging us for every email, or that the phone company is going to tax every message, and please stop sending the Neiman Marcus cookie recipe around, and that little boy in the hospital who is waiting for your postcard went home years ago.

And make darn sure your email recipient has *begged* you to send all those messages that say "Send this to at least ten other people. Do not break this chain!"

iCal

iCal

iCal is a personal calendar, an organizer, and a scheduler built around the idea that you need more than one calendar to manage the different aspects of your life. You can create as many specialized calendars as you want: one for work, one for family, another for school, etc. You can choose to display just one calendar at a time, or any selection of calendars.

Use iCal's **To Do list** to prioritize and manage your busy day, week, or month. Add an **event,** such as a party, to iCal and let iCal email invitations to selected people in your Address Book. iCal can **notify** you of upcoming events and appointments with an alarm sound, email alert, or display message on your screen. And iCal's **search** feature enables you to easily find any event or To Do item that you've added to your calendar.

iCal requires Mac OS X 10.2 or later.

You can even **publish** your own calendar online so you (or friends, co-workers, or family) can check it from any computer, anywhere in the world. The number of calendars you create is limited only by the amount of free disk space on your computer. All sorts of iCal calendars are available online that you can subscribe to—many organizations, bands, and entertainment companies are posting iCalendars on their web sites.

Here iCal is displaying the events from six different calendars.

The iCal Window

iCal's customizable window provides access to all calendars, views, events, and lists. The color-coding makes it easy to view multiple calendars in one window and instantly know whether there are any overlapping events—for instance, you can easily tell if Mom's meetings might make her miss a soccer game, or a family vacation might coincide with a comet sighting.

Calendar list

The upper-left pane of the iCal window shows the **list of calendars** that you have created or to which you have subscribed. You can select any calendar in the list to show just that calendar's information (check its box) in the View pane, or you can select multiple calendars so they show simultaneously in iCal (check any or all of the boxes).

Checkboxes are color-coded to match that calendar's items in the View pane.

*To **hide** a calendar's events, uncheck the box.*

*This area is the main **Calendar View pane**.*

*This is the **To Do pane**.*

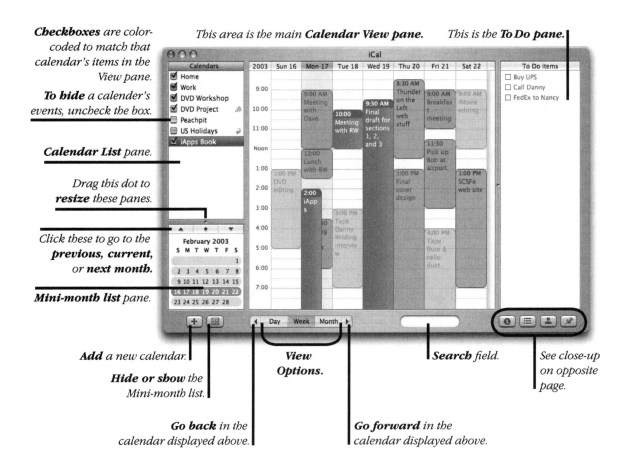

Calendar List pane.

*Drag this dot to **resize** these panes.*

*Click these to go to the **previous, current,** or **next month.***

Mini-month list pane.

Add a new calendar.

Hide or show the Mini-month list.

View Options.

Search field.

See close-up on opposite page.

Go back in the calendar displayed above.

Go forward in the calendar displayed above.

This is an enlargement of the important **Hide-and-Show buttons** in the bottom-right corner.

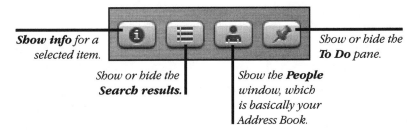

Show info for a selected item.

Show or hide the Search results.

*Show the **People** window, which is basically your Address Book.*

*Show or hide the **To Do** pane.*

Calendar View pane

The appearance of the iCal Viewing pane changes according to which View Option you choose: Day, Week, or Month.

To choose a view preference, click one of the View Options at the bottom of the iCal window.

Mini-month list

The Mini-month list allows you to go to any day, week, or month of any year.

- ▾ **To display a particular month** in iCal's main Viewing pane, click the month you want to see in the Mini-month list.

- ▾ **To scroll forward or backward in time through the monthly calendars,** click the up or down triangle located at the top of the Mini-month list.

- ▾ **To choose a calendar view,** click one of the View Option buttons located at the bottom of the iCal window—select "Day," "Week," or "Month."

- ▾ **To go to the "previous" or "next" day, week, or month in any view,** click the triangles on either side of the View Option buttons.

There are several easy ways **to get back to the current date** after working with future dates in iCal. Do one of the following:

- ▾ **Either:** In the Mini-month list, click the diamond-shaped icon at the top of the list (between the up and down triangles).

- ▾ **Or** from the Calendar menu at the top of your screen, choose "Go To Today."

- ▾ **Or** press Command T.

Create a New Calendar

Keep track of the schedules of selected family, friends, and colleagues. If you share the same user account on your Mac with other family members, you can view their individual calendars in your iCal application.

To create a new calendar, click the "plus" button on the bottom-left of iCal, then enter a name for the calendar and choose a color.

To change the color of a calendar, select the Calendar (click once on its name), click the "Show Info" button, and choose a color from the pop-up menu.

To change a calendar name, double-click a name in the Calendars list, then type a new name.

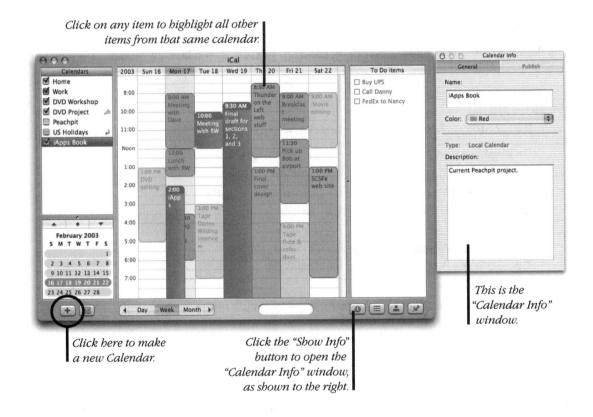

Click on any item to highlight all other items from that same calendar.

Click here to make a new Calendar.

Click the "Show Info" button to open the "Calendar Info" window, as shown to the right.

This is the "Calendar Info" window.

Create a New Event in a Calendar

Items that you enter into an iCal calendar are called **events.** An event can be an appointment, a party, a reminder, an all-day class, or a week-long seminar. Or anything else that's in your schedule.

To create an event:

1. Click on a calendar in the Calendars list to select it. If none of the calendars in the list seem appropriate for the new event you want to add, create a new calendar as explained on the opposite page.

2. In the Calendar View pane, click and drag vertically in the time-slot in which you want to place an event. Once you've created the event, you can drag it to any other position in the calendar.

3. When you create a new event, the text "New event" is already selected (highlighted), so all you have to do is start typing a description of your event.

   Type as much information as you want for an event description, even if the description is too long to fit in the colored event box.

To see the entire description of an event, select it, then click the "Show Info" button in the bottom-right corner of the iCal window. The Event Info window shows your description in the "Subject" pane.

This is the Show Info button.

If you need to include extensive notes, click the "Notes" button (upper-right, circled) to display a scrollable notepad.

Create an All-Day event or a Multiple-Day event

All-Day and **Multiple-Day events** are represented by colored shapes in a row at the top of the calendar. Instead of stretching an event shape from 9 A.M. to 5 P.M., the All-Day designation leaves room in the calendar for other items without overlapping too many events in the same column.

This is an All-day designation.

This is a Multiple-Day event, as shown in Week view.

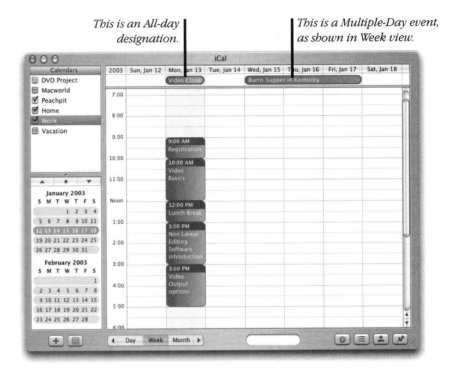

To create an All-Day event:

1. To create an event in the Calendar View pane, drag your mouse across the time period, then enter a name for that event.

   Or select an existing event that you want to change to an All-Day event.

2. Click on an item in the calendar to select it, then click the "Show Info" button in the bottom-right corner of the iCal window.

3. In the "Event Info" window, click the "All-day event" checkbox.

4. Press "Return" on your keyboard to apply your settings.

These buttons determine what information shows in the "Event Info" window.

To create a Multiple-Day event:

1. Create a new event as explained above, or select an existing event.

2. Click the "Show Info" button.

3. Check the "All-day event" checkbox.

4. Set the "from" and "to" buttons to show the dates of the event.

5. Hit Return on the keyboard to apply your settings.

To create recurring events:

1. Click an event box to select it.

2. Click the "Show Info" button.

3. Click the "Recurrence" icon in the "Events Info" toolbar, as circled to the right.

4. Choose a frequency option from the pop-up menu directly below the toolbar.

5. Choose the other options that your frequency choice offers.

6. Hit Return on your keyboard to apply your settings.

iCal provides a visual indication of **schedule conflicts.** The example below shows three calendar items with overlapping times. If the items belong to different calendars (upper-left pane of Calendar window), the color coding will indicate to which calendar an item belongs.

All-Day event.

Multiple-Day event.

Conflicting events.

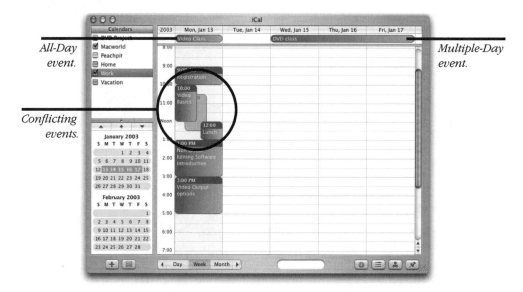

*iCal's **Month view** shows an All-Day event as an event bar that stretches across one or more days within the main calendar grid.*

All-Day event.

Multiple-Day event.

Delete an event

To manually delete an event, select it, then press the Delete key on your keyboard.

iCal can **automatically delete events** that have passed.

1. From the iCal menu, choose "Preferences…"

2. Click the first checkbox ("Automatically delete events and To Do items") in the "Events and To Do Items" section, then enter the number of days after which events are to be deleted.

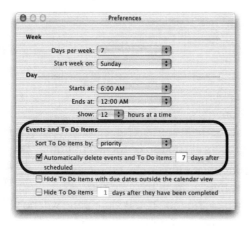

Invite people to an event

Tip: If you have more than one email account, you can specify which account is the default: Open the Mail preferences and click the Account icon. The account name at the top of the list is the default. To change it, drag another account name to the top of the list.

iCal uses Mail and your Address Book to invite people to an event (Mail will send the message from your default email account, if you have more than one account).

To invite people:

1. Make sure the event to which you want to invite people is visible in the View pane.

2. Click the "People" button at the bottom-right corner of iCal. This will display the People window (shown to the right), which contains your Address Book contacts.

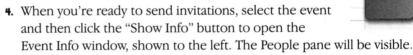

3. Drag people from the People window and drop them on top of the calendar event.
A small "people" icon appears at the top of the event item.

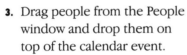

4. When you're ready to send invitations, select the event and then click the "Show Info" button to open the Event Info window, shown to the left. The People pane will be visible.

5. Click the button at the bottom, "Send Invitations." Mail opens and sends email messages to all of the people in the Event Info list.

6. The recipient gets a message like the one shown below.

Not everyone will be able to open the link, but they will at least get the email message about the event.

7. When she clicks on the link, it opens an invitation with a response. Because the button to "Mail your answer" is checked, when she clicks either "Decline" or "Accept," you'll receive an answer, and iCal will automatically update the status in the Event Info window.

If she has iCal on her Mac—and she accepts—the event will automatically appear in her application in the calendar she chose.

Move an event

To move an event to another day or time, drag the event to a new location in the calendar window. If the date is not visible in your current view, change to a broader view. For instance, in Month view you can drag an event anywhere in the month.

To move an event to another month or year:

1. Single-click the event to select it.
2. Click the "Show Info" button.
3. Change the date and time information to the new event date.

To move an event to another calendar:

iCal lets you reorganize your calendars with ease.

- ▾ **Either:** Control-click the event, then choose a calendar from the pop-up menu that appears, as shown below. The event will change to the color associated with the other calendar category.

- ▾ **Or** select an event, click the "Show Info" button, then choose a calendar from the "Calendar" pop-up menu.

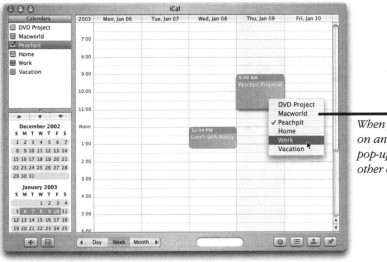

When you Control-click on an event, you'll get a pop-up menu listing your other calendars.

Let iCal notify you of an upcoming event

Don't worry about possibly forgetting some important event in your calendar. iCal can notify you of upcoming events with three different alarm types, even if the iCal application is not active.

To set an Event Alarm:

1. Click on an iCal event to select it, then click the "Show Info" button to open the Event Info window.

   Or in Day and Week view, double-click the "time" bar at the top of an event to open the Event Info window.

   In Month view, double-click the color circle to the left of an event.

2. At the top of the Event Info window, click the "Event Alarm" icon to show the alarm options.

3. Choose one or more of the alarm options: "Display message," "Send email to me," or "Play sound."

4. Enter the number of minutes, hours, or days before an event to notify you.

This is an example of a message alarm that will appear on your screen.

This icon indicates an alarm has been set.

Click the "Event Alarm" icon to display the alarm options.

iCal Search

Use iCal's **search** feature to locate any event you've added to a calendar.

To search for an event:

1. In the text entry field at the bottom of the calendar, type a key word or phrase—all possible matches to what you type will appear in the Search Result panel. The list of possible matches gets shorter as you continue to type.

2. When you finish typing, click the item you want. iCal selects and shows that item in the Calendar View pane.

To show or hide the Search Result panel, click this button.

To open the "Show Info" window for a found item, double-click the item in the Search Result panel (*or* double-click the title bar of the event in the Calendar View pane).

To change the information for an event, double-click the text on the colored event box, then type your changes.

Or click an event to select it, then click the "Show Info" button (the "i" icon) to open the "Event Info" window. Make changes, then press Return.

Create a To Do list

Use iCal to keep a reminder list of things you need to do.

To create a To Do list:

1. Select a calendar in the Calendars list.

    Note: When you create a To Do item, it is automatically color-coded to match the *selected* calendar. If you need to switch the To Do item to a different calendar, Control-click on the item and choose another calendar from the pop-up menu that appears.

2. Click the "To Do" button in the bottom-right corner of the iCal window (the push-pin icon) to show the "To Do items" panel.

    To resize the panel, drag the tiny dot on the left-edge of the panel.

3. To open the "To Do Info" window, select a To Do item, then click the "Show Info" button (the "i" at the bottom of the window).

4. Type a description of your To Do item, and make the other possible choices in this window. Close the window when you're done.

After a To Do task is completed, click in the little checkbox to mark it off. Woo hoo. *Or* click the "Completed" checkbox in the "To Do Info" window.

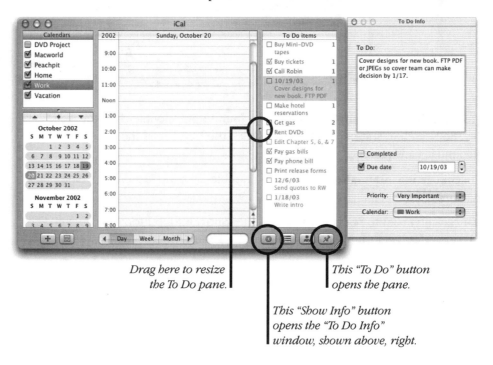

Drag here to resize the To Do pane.

This "To Do" button opens the pane.

This "Show Info" button opens the "To Do Info" window, shown above, right.

Rate the importance of a To Do item

To Do items are placed in alphabetical order in the list. You can **assign priorities,** ranked from 1 to 3, to items to move them up in the list.

An item with a "Very Important" priority is marked with a "1" in the To Do panel. "Important" is marked with "2," and "Not Important" with "3." Multiple items with the same priority are listed alphabetically within that group. All items that do not have an assigned priority are listed alphabetically below the prioritized items.

1. Click on a To Do item to select it.
2. Click the "Show Info" button to open the "To Do Info" window.
3. From the "Priority" pop-up menu choose a priority. Close the window.

The "To Do Info" window

The "To Do Info" window also has several other uses.

▼ Make editing changes to a task's description.

▼ Sometimes a task's description is too long to show in the To Do panel. In that case, open its "To Do Info" window, where the entire description appears.

▼ Check off a task as "Completed." You can also do this in the To Do panel by clicking the checkbox next to a task.

▼ Set a "Due date" that will appear above the task in the To Do panel.

▼ Assign a selected task to a different calendar: from the "Calendar" pop-up menu, choose a different calendar.

Print a To Do list

When you print a calendar, you can choose to include that calendar's To Do list (see the illustration on page 211).

Hide or Show various To Do lists

To Do items from different calendars all share the same To Do list. They are color-coded to match the calendar to which they belong. When you hide a calendar (uncheck its box in the Calendars list), all the To Do items associated with that calendar are also hidden. If you have a lot of items in your To Do list, hiding some of them can make finding things easier.

iCal Preferences

To customize the appearance of iCal calendars and some of its settings, use the iCal Preferences.

1. From the iCal application menu, choose "Preferences...."

2. In the "Week" section of the Preferences window, choose how many days a calender shows and on what day of a week to start a calendar.

3. In the "Day" section, choose the hours that a calendar shows.

4. In the "Events and To Do Items" section, make choices for the settings listed.

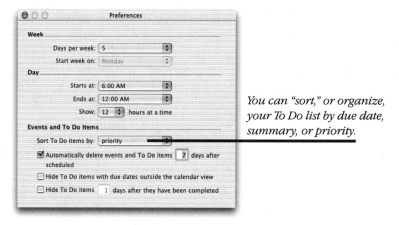

You can "sort," or organize, your To Do list by due date, summary, or priority.

If you want iCal **to store your past schedules and appointments, uncheck** the first checkbox, "Automatically delete events and To Do items."

Print Your iCal Calendar

No matter how convenient the digital lifestyle may be, sometimes you need an old-fashioned paper **printout.** It's easier to stick a paper calendar on the fridge than a PDA. But that'll probably change soon.

1. Select the calendar you want to print in the Calendars list.

2. From the File menu, choose "Print...."

3. From the pop-up menu, shown below, choose "iCal" to show iCal's printing options.

4. Click the checkboxes of items you want to print, then select a date and time range to print.

5. Click "Print."

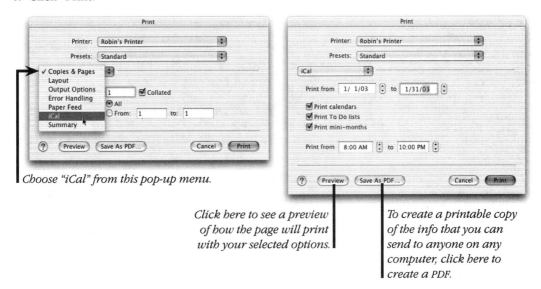

Choose "iCal" from this pop-up menu.

Click here to see a preview of how the page will print with your selected options.

To create a printable copy of the info that you can send to anyone on any computer, click here to create a PDF.

Publish Your iCal Calendar

If you have a .Mac account and you want to **make your calendar available to others,** you can "publish" it. Published calendars can be viewed from any computer in the world using a web browser.

To publish your calendar (you must be connected to the Internet)**:**

1. In iCal, select a calendar in your Calendars list.

2. From the Calendar menu at the top of your screen, choose "Publish...."

   You'll get the "Publish Calendar" window, as shown to the left.

3. Choose which options you want to apply.

   ▾ Choose "Publish on .Mac" to publish to the Apple server provided with your .Mac account.

   ▾ Choose "Publish on a web server" if you plan to publish to a WebDAV server other than your .Mac account. (See the sidebar on the opposite page for more information about WebDAV.)

4. Click the "Publish" button.

5. When your calendar has uploaded to the server, the "Calendar Published" window shows the address where others can go to subscribe to that particular calendar.

   To see your calendar online, click "Visit Page."
   To notify people that you've published a calendar, click "Send Mail."

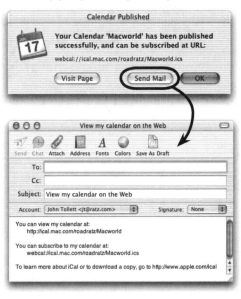

When you click "Send Mail," your default email application automatically opens and creates an email that lists the web addresses for viewing or subscribing to your calendar.

Tip: Send a copy of this email to yourself so you have a record of the addresses to access your calendar.

Add password protection to a published calendar

If you want to add a password to protect a published calendar, select "Publish on a web server" in the Publish Calendar window. This option displays text fields for entering a WebDAV server address and for setting a login name and password.

For an alternative to publishing calendars on the .Mac site, check iCal Exchange at www.icalx.com. iCal Exchange offers free iCalendar publishing to its own WebDAV server.

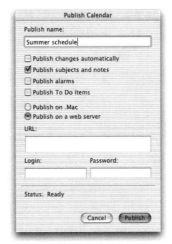

WebDAV (Web Distributed Authoring and Versioning) is a standard for collaborative authoring. Generally speaking, WebDAV servers enable web-based enterprise collaboration, such as a large corporation developing a business plan or a team of programmers creating software.

Most of us are content just to know that WebDAV allows us to share calendars that have been created using the industry-standard iCalendar specification (.ics).

Make changes to a published calendar

When you make changes to a calendar that has already been published, you can update the published calendar in several ways.

- ▼ **Either:** Select a calendar from the Calendars list, then from the Calendar menu at the top of your screen, choose "Update."

- ▼ **Or** select a calendar from the Calendars list, then from the Calendar menu at the top of your screen, choose "Publish." Give the calendar the exact published name as the existing one. This new, updated calendar will replace the old one.

- ▼ **Or** when you first publish a calendar, set iCal to automatically update changes. From the Calendar menu at the top of your screen, choose "Publish," then select "Publish changes automatically." If you have a full-time Internet connection, iCal will **automatically** upload the changed calendar to your iDisk. (If you don't have a full-time connection, *don't* choose to publish the changes automatically; instead, dial-up and publish changes when necessary.)

Unpublish an iCal calendar

If you decide to **unpublish** a published calendar, it's easy to do.

Make sure you're connected to the Internet. Select the name of a calendar in the Calendars list, then from the Calendar menu choose "Unpublish." You'll still have the original copy of the calendar on your computer, but it will no longer be available for viewing by others.

Subscribe to iCal Calendars

You can **subscribe to calendars** that have been published by family, friends, colleagues, or total strangers. You do not have to have a .Mac account to subscribe to a calendar that's hosted on .Mac.

To subscribe to any iCal calendar:

1. From the Calendar menu at the top of your screen, choose "Subscribe...."

2. In the "Subscribe to Calendar" window that appears, enter the URL (web address) that was given to you or that you may have received in an email from the publisher of the calendar.

   OR if you know the web address of a site that offers iCalendars for subscription (such as **http://apple.com/ical/library**), use your browser to visit the site and click one of the available calendar links. The window titled "Subscribe to Calendar" will open with that particular iCalendar address entered in the "Calendar URL" field.

3. Use the checkboxes to set your preferences for the options listed. The "Refresh" option assumes you have a full-time Internet connection such as cable, DSL, T1, etc.—don't bother to check it if you have a dial-up modem.

4. If subscription to the calendar requires a password, click the "Advanced options" triangle to show the "Login" and "Password" fields. Click the "Needs authentication" checkbox and enter the Login and Password that was given to you by the calendar publisher.

5. Click "Subscribe."

6. The subscribed calendar appears in the Calendars list in your iCal application. Select it to show the calendar in the main viewing area.

Other calendars available for subscription

In addition to subscribing to the calendars of friends, family, and colleagues, there are many special-interest calendars available online to which you can subscribe. It's quite amazing—there are public calendars that list graphic design and typographic events, hundreds of athletic games, school calendars, religious events, sci-fi events, movies, television, and so many more. Visit these sites to see some of the possibilities:

> www.apple.com/ical/library

> www.iCalshare.com

Refresh Calendars

To make sure that you **see the most current version** of a subscribed calendar, you can refresh it. Refresh downloads the current calendar from the server, ensuring that you have the latest published information. If you don't have a full-time connection, make sure you dial up to connect to the Internet before you choose to refresh.

1. Select a subscribed calendar in the Calendars list.
2. From the Calendar menu at the top of your screen, choose "Refresh."

If you have a full-time Internet connection, you can set up an automatic schedule that determines how often your subscribed calendar is updated:

1. From the Calendar menu, choose "Subscribe…."
2. Click the "Refresh" checkbox, then from that pop-up menu, choose a time interval to set how often your computer downloads a new version of the subscribed calendar.

Import Calendars

An iCal file is actually a text file (.ics) that can be sent as an email attachment. iCal can import iCal files and vCal files (iCal and vCal are similar calendar/scheduling formats).

Although the iCal Import window offers an option to "Import Entourage data," the two are not compatible at the time of this writing and Apple says they are investigating the issue.

Click "Import" to open the "iCal:Import" window, then navigate to the .ics file that you want to import.

Import a calendar into iCal from Palm Desktop

If you use the application Palm Desktop (version 4.0 or later) to keep calendar and scheduling information, you can import that data into iCal.

Tip: An even easier way to import a vCal file into iCal is to drag the vCal file onto one of the calendars in the Calendars list. The events in the vCal file are added to that calendar. Large calendars can take several minutes to import, so be patient.

To import a calendar from Palm Desktop into iCal:

1. Open the Palm Desktop application.
2. From the File menu, choose "Export."
3. In the "Save As" field type a name.
4. From the Module pop-up menu, choose "Date Book."
5. From the Items pop-up menu, choose "All Date Book Items."
6. From the Format pop-up menu, choose "vCal."
7. Click the "Export" button. Close Palm Desktop.
8. Open iCal.
9. Select a calendar in the Calendars list into which you want to import the Palm Desktop events.
10. From the File menu, choose "Import."
11. Choose "Import a vCal file."
12. Click the "Import" button.
13. Locate the vCal file you exported from Palm Desktop, and select it.
14. Click the "Import" button.

Export Calendars

You can export a calendar as an ".ics" file, a standard calendar format. The exported .ics file can then be imported to a calendar on another computer, attached to an email for someone else to import into their iCal, or imported into another device such as a Palm or iPod.

To export a calendar:

1. Select a calendar in the Calendars list.
2. From the File menu, choose "Export." The iCal Export window opens.
3. Choose a location in which to save the exported ".ics" file.
4. Type a name for your exported calendar in the "Save as" field. The ".ics" extension will be automatically added to the file name.

Tip: If you have an iPod (Apple's MP3 player), you can transfer your calendar information to your iPod and carry it with you wherever you go—see Chapter 14 to learn about iSync.

You can also drag a calendar from the Calendars list in iCal to the Desktop to export it.

iCal Help and Keyboard Shortcuts

You can find **additional information** in the Help menu while iCal is open: choose "iCal Help."

To see a list of keyboard shortcuts, choose "Keyboard Shortcuts" from the Help menu.

Back up Your Calendars

If iCal is storing a lot of valuable information, don't forget to back up your calendars. Copy your calendars to an external drive or to some removable media, such as a CD or Zip disk.

To find your calendars, which are saved as .ics files in the Calendars folder:

1. Go to your Home folder, open the Library folder, then locate the Calendars folder.

2. To make a backup copy, drag the Calendars folder to another drive, or drag it to an icon that represents any removable media that may be connected to your computer (Zip, CD, or DVD).

For detailed information about Backup, see Chapter 13.

Another way to backup calendars is to use **Backup,** an application provided with .Mac memberships. You can make backup copies of files locally or to your .Mac iDisk (storage space on Apple's computers that's provided with .Mac membership). Backup makes the process simple and easy.

1. Download Backup from the .Mac web site if you don't already have it on your computer.

2. Open Backup.

3. From the pop-up menu, choose where to put your backup copies. You can choose your iDisk or a local drive (Zip, CD, or DVD).

4. Click the checkbox next to "iCal calendars."

5. Click the "Backup Now" button. The Backup application knows where to find your calendars.

The checkmarks indicate which items are selected for backup.

iChat and Rendezvous

7

iChat

If you've ever used a chat program or "instant messaging" program such as AOL Instant Messenger or ICQ, you'll figure out how to use **iChat** in about four seconds. If you've never used a chat program, it will take you about one whole minute.

With Apple's iChat you can have private written conversations over the Internet with people who already have a .Mac account or an AIM or AOL account; it is not compatible with MSN Messenger, Yahoo Messenger, IRC, Jabber, or ICQ (although it will soon be compatible with ICQ).

iChat

If the iChat icon isn't in the Dock, you'll find it in the Applications window.

Set Up iChat

The first time you click the **iChat** icon in the Dock, the Welcome window asks you to enter the information for your iChat account. The "Account Type" pop-up menu lets you choose between using your Mac.com account (if you have one) or an existing AOL Instant Messenger account (called AIM, if you have one; go to **www.aim.com** to get your *free* account; you don't need to have AOL to get an AIM account).

If you don't have a Mac.com account and you want one (see page 271), you can click that button to sign up for it right now. Otherwise, enter your information, and click OK.

Your iChat "Buddy name" (Account Name) is the same as your Mac.com membership name. Your online Buddies will use that name to find you and send Instant Messages or files. You can even have both an AOL Instant Messenger Buddy name and your Mac.com Buddy name and switch between them (only one can be *active* at a time).

Note: You must be connected to the Internet to use iChat!

If you are connected to other computers in your office, you can use Rendezvous to chat, even when you're not online. See page 248.

This is your "Buddy" name. In the case of a Mac.com account, your Buddy name is your entire email address (including "@mac.com").

If you use AOL, this would be your name at AOL (without the "@aol.com" part).

If you have an Internet AIM account, this would be the Buddy name you've been using.

What Is It Like?

What is it like to "talk" with someone through iChat? Below is a typical iChat window and how it basically works; I'm chatting with my mother, who uses AOL. You type a message to someone; they type back to you.

*Each person in the window has her own bubble of talk and an icon that represents her. You can **customize the icon** for yourself or for others; see page 227.*

Type your message into this edit box and then hit either Return or Enter to send it.

*Click the **paperclip** button to find a file to send (or drag a file into the edit box and hit Return).*

*Use the **B** and **I** buttons to make text bold, italic, or both:*

Either: *Select the text after you type it, as you would in a word processor, then click one or both buttons.*

Or: *Click a button or press Command B or Command I **before** you type —the next words you type will be in bold or italic (or both, if you pressed Command B I). You will continue to type in that style until you either click the buttons again or use the keyboard shortcuts again.*

*Click the **Smiley** button to get a list of Smilies to insert into your message — just click the one you want.*

If you type a standard Smiley, iChat will substitute a real Smiley. For instance, if you type ;-) as a wink, it will automatically turn into a round Smiley icon in the message. Try it.

You can customize the color of your bubble, the typeface, and the color of the typeface for both yourself and your participants. See page 242.

When either you or another participant starts to type, a thought bubble appears to let the other person know.

Click the person-head icon to open this "drawer" on the side that shows you a list of participants.

Instant Message, Direct Message, Chat, or Rendezvous?

With iChat, you can communicate with others in **four different ways:** Instant Messages, Direct Messages, Chats, and Rendezvous. I'll explain here how each one is different from the others and on the following pages tell you how to do each one.

An **Instant Message** opens a small window in which you can "talk" back and forth with *one other person,* and your talk is **totally private** (unless someone is looking over your shoulder). You must be connected to the Internet.

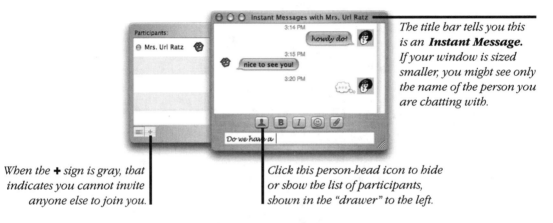

The title bar tells you this is an **Instant Message.** If your window is sized smaller, you might see only the name of the person you are chatting with.

When the ✛ sign is gray, that indicates you cannot invite anyone else to join you.

Click this person-head icon to hide or show the list of participants, shown in the "drawer" to the left.

A **Direct Message** looks just like an Instant Message and is even more private. Instant Messages go through a central messaging server on the Internet, while a Direct Message goes directly to *one other person's* computer, bypassing the central server. Some network or firewall security settings will not allow Direct Messages to be sent or delivered. You must be connected to the Internet.

The title bar in a **Direct Message** also says it's an Instant Message, but inside the box you can see you have actually started a Direct Message session.

A Direct Message is between two people —you cannot invite anyone else to join you.

A **Chat window,** or Chat Room, is a public "room" where you can invite *any number of people.* These people might be spread all over the world, but you can all gab together. People can come and go as they please and the room stays open until the last person leaves. You must be connected to the Internet.

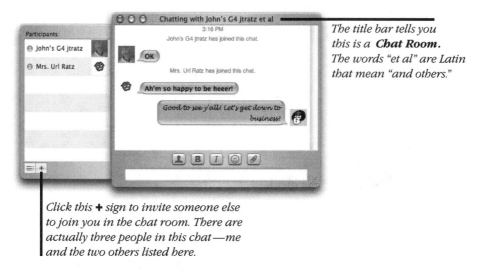

*The title bar tells you this is a **Chat Room.** The words "et al" are Latin that mean "and others."*

Click this ✛ sign to invite someone else to join you in the chat room. There are actually three people in this chat—me and the two others listed here.

A **Rendezvous message** does not go through the Internet—it goes through your local network in your small office or school directly to another computer on the same network. You do not have to be connected to the Internet to send Rendezvous messages. See pages 245–248 for details about Rendezvous.

*This is actually a **Rendezvous** Instant Message, although you can't tell by looking at it—you only know because you sent it to that person on your network.*

You cannot have a Chat session with multiple users through Rendezvous.

Create Your Buddy List

If you plan to **chat often** with certain people, **add them to your Buddy List** so you can easily see when they're online, and with the click of a button you can start a chat or send a file.

This is a typical Buddy List. The people whose names are in bold are online and you can start a chat with them; the others are offline and unavailable at the moment.

To open your Buddy List and add people to it:

1. Click the iChat icon in the Dock, if iChat is not already open. If you don't see your Buddy List, press Command 1 (that's the number one), *or* go to the Window menu and choose "Buddy List."

2. In the Buddy List window that opens, click the **+** button (circled, above). A "sheet" will drop down from the top of the window, as shown below.

3. The sheet that drops down in front of the Buddy List window contains all of your Address Book contacts (as above).

If the person you want to add is in your Address Book, select that contact, then click the "Select Buddy" button. The new Buddy can now be seen in the Buddy list.

If you have not put that person's AIM name (Buddy name or Mac.com email address) in your Address Book yet, you'll get another sheet like the one shown below.

If the Buddy you want to add is NOT in your Address Book, click the "New Person" button in the Address Book panel, which will bring down a different sheet, as shown below.

4. From the "Account Type" pop-up menu, select "Mac.com" *if* the new person uses their Mac.com account for instant messaging.

Or choose "AIM" if the new person uses an AOL or AIM screen name.

5. Enter the "Address Book Information" if you want this person to be added to your Address Book as well.

6. To make a photo or custom icon appear next to a *new* Buddy's name, drag an image on top of the Buddy Icon window in the New Person panel (the photo or image must be a JPEG, GIF, or TIFF file). This picture will appear in your Address Book, in the Buddy List, and in Chat windows.

To add or change the photo of an existing Buddy, see page 227.

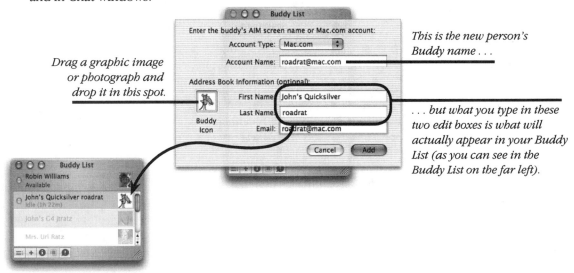

Drag a graphic image or photograph and drop it in this spot.

This is the new person's Buddy name . . .

. . . but what you type in these two edit boxes is what will actually appear in your Buddy List (as you can see in the Buddy List on the far left).

7. Click the "Add" button and that person is added to your Buddy List (and to your Address Book if you entered that information).

Tip: If you're colorblind between red and green, go to the Preferences (see page 242) and choose to have the availability buttons displayed as squares and circles. They'll still be red and green, but at least you'll be able to tell which is which.

Status and messages in your Buddy List

Your name appears in the top-left corner of the **Buddy List.** The **colored status buttons** indicate the online status of you and your Buddies: green means "Available," red means "Unavailable," and yellow means "Idle," which usually means that person's computer has gone to sleep due to inactivity.

A message indicates your **availability:** "Available," "Away," or any custom message that you can create. *It's not just a message—it actually changes whether people can see you or not.* When you choose any message with a red dot, no one can send you messages.

To change the status message, click the existing message ("Available" or "Away"), then from the pop-down menu (shown below) choose another.

To create a custom status message, click the existing message ("Available" or "Away"), then from the pop-down menu choose "Custom…" and type your message.

Once you have created other messages, choose one from this list whenever you want to display it.

Photos in your Buddy List

If you have put a **photo or image** for someone (or yourself) in your Address Book, it will appear in your Buddy List and iChat windows. If your AOL Buddy has added a photo or image in AOL or their own iChat application, their photo or image will appear instead of the one you placed.

But perhaps you don't like the image your friend uses. **To override his image,** select his name in your Buddy List, then click the "**i**" button at the bottom of the list, which will give you the box shown below, left. Either add a different photo or leave the "Picture" box blank, then check the box to "Only use this picture." You may have to quit iChat to make the new image appear.

Choose to show the "Address Card" if this is not what you see.

*Drag a photo or image (GIF, JPEG, or TIFF) to the "Picture" box. **If it's the wrong size,** you'll get a separate window where you can resize the image and choose which section you want to display, as shown above, right.*

***To remove a picture,** click on the "Picture" box and hit the Delete key.*

*To add or change **your** picture, use the Address Book (see page 181).*

When you drag a picture from your hard disk and drop it into the Picture well, most of the time you'll get this great little window.

Drag the blue dot along the slider to enlarge or reduce the entire image.

Press on the image and drag it around until the portion of the image you want is visible in the little square.

Click "Done."

Create actions for a selected Buddy

Every Buddy has "actions" associated with it. You can have iChat announce that your Buddy has arrived or left (logged on or logged off), if you got a new message from her, or if she finally sent you a reply, etc.

To create actions for a selected Buddy, select his name in your Buddy List, then click the "**i**" button at the bottom of the list, which will give you the Info box *for that Buddy.* From the Show menu, choose "Actions," then set your preferences. You can see here that when my sister logs in, my Mac says out loud to me, "Your sister's here."

The voice used is the one you last chose in the Speech preferences: Click the "System Preferences" icon in the Dock, then click the "Speech" icon on the bottom row. Click the "Default Voice" tab and choose a voice.

My sister's iChat tells her, when our mother logs on, "Talk to your Mother."

Store information about a selected Buddy

In the same information box described above, choose the name of your Buddy's account in the "Show" menu. If that person has written a profile in America Online or AIM, it will appear here. You can also store notes about this person in the lower area, as shown.

The iChat File Menu

The **iChat File menu** is a little misleading, as explained here:

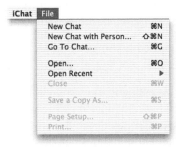

"New Chat" and *"New Chat with Person…"* might open a Chat Room in which you can invite a number of people, **or** it might open an Instant Message or Direct Message in which you can communicate with only one other person. It depends on which "Chat Option" is set for that particular window, as explained below.

"Go To Chat…" really **does** always open a Chat Room in which you can invite a large number of people.

Chat options

You don't really have to worry about this until you bump into a problem, like not being able to invite anyone into your Chat Room. What makes the difference between whether the first two commands in the File menu open an Instant Message window, a Direct Message window, or a Chat Room window is which of the **Chat options** have been chosen. *Most of the time* these two File commands seem to open an Instant Message window, but you can change the open window to a Direct Message or a Chat Room window *before* you start to talk to someone.

To choose between an Instant Message, Direct Message, or Chat Room window:

1. From the File menu, choose "New Chat" or "New Chat with Person…." (as explained above).

2. Before you send a message to anyone, go to the View menu and choose "Chat Options…."

3. Press on the little pop-up menu called "Mode," as shown below. Change the window to a different mode if necessary. Click OK.

You can only change the mode if you haven't yet sent a message. Once you start a dialog, the window is set in the selected mode and can't be changed.

Three Ways to Send an Instant Message

There are three ways to send an Instant Message to someone else. If someone is in your Buddy List and you notice they're online, the third method is the quickest and easiest.

You need to know a person's **AIM name.** It might be someone's Mac.com email address (including the part "@mac.com"), an AOL screen name (without the "@aol.com" part), or an AIM name that a person signed up for at www.aim.com.

To end an Instant Messaging session, just close the window. When either participant closes his or her window, the session ends.

1) Send an Instant Message to anyone whose AIM name you know:

1. From the File menu choose "New Chat." As explained on the previous page, this command *usually* opens an Instant Message (IM) to one other person; you cannot ask anyone else to join the two of you.

2. Click the little person-head icon at the bottom of the IM window; this will pop out a drawer to the side.

3. At the bottom of the drawer, click the + symbol to get the menu, as shown below. Anyone in your Buddy List who is online will appear in this menu; click that person's name to invite him.

   Or choose "Other…" and enter the AIM name of any person to whom you wish to send an IM.

4. Type a message at the bottom of the IM window, then hit Return or Enter. A message is sent to the other person, inviting him to chat.

5. When he writes back to you, you're on.

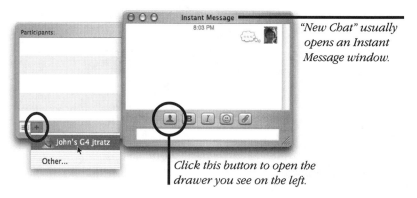

"New Chat" usually opens an Instant Message window.

Click this button to open the drawer you see on the left.

2) Send an Instant Message to anyone whose AIM name you know:

1. From the File menu choose "New Chat with Person…." As explained previously, this command *usually* opens an Instant Message (IM) to one other person; you cannot ask anyone else to join the two of you.

2. In the text field of the panel that drops down, type the AIM name of someone you know. Although it says to type the "address," it really wants the *screen name* of an AOL or AIM member.

   If you are trying to contact a Mac.com member, type their email address, including "@mac.com." Click OK.

3. Type a message at the bottom of the IM window, then hit Return. A message is sent to the other person, inviting him to respond.

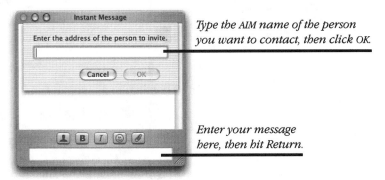

Type the AIM *name of the person you want to contact, then click* OK.

Enter your message here, then hit Return.

3) Send an Instant Message to someone on your Buddy List:

1. If your Buddy List is not open, press Command 1.

2. Select any Buddy whose name is dark, which means she is online (to select someone, click once on her name).

3. At the bottom of the Buddy List, click the Instant Message (IM) symbol: ![symbol]. *Or* press Command Option M.

4. An Instant Message window will open with your Buddy's name in the title bar.

5. Type a message in the edit box, then hit Return to invite him in.

Select a Buddy who is online, then click the IM symbol.

Or Control-click on a Buddy name and choose "Send Instant Message…."

Type something in the edit box, then hit Return or Enter.

Send an Email to Someone on Your Buddy List

Send **email** to anyone on your Buddy List, whether or not that person is online.

1. Select a Buddy in your list (if your Buddy List isn't showing, press Command 1).

2. Click the "Compose email" icon at the bottom of the Buddy List window. It looks like a postage stamp: ![stamp].

3. Mail will open. Compose your email message in the message window that appears, and send as usual.

Send a Direct Message

Instant Messages go through a central messaging server on the Internet. If you have a message to send that requires more privacy, you can use a **Direct Message** that goes directly to another person's computer, bypassing the central server. (Some recipients may have network or firewall security settings that do not allow Direct Messages to be delivered.)

To send a Direct Message to someone in your Buddy List:

1. Select a Buddy in your Buddy List window who is online (if your Buddy List isn't showing, press Command 1).

2. From the Buddies menu at the top of the screen, choose "Send Direct Message...."

   Or Control-click on a Buddy name, then choose "Send Direct Message..." from the contextual menu.

3. Type a message, hit Return or Enter, and wait for a reply.

To end a Direct Instant Message session, either you or the recipient close your window (click the red button).

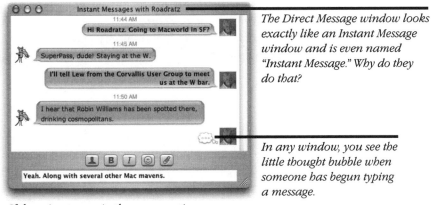

The Direct Message window looks exactly like an Instant Message window and is even named "Instant Message." Why do they do that?

In any window, you see the little thought bubble when someone has begun typing a message.

If there is a pause in the conversation, the time will appear in the window.

To send a Direct Message to someone who is NOT in your Buddy List:

1. From the File menu, choose "New Chat with Person...."

2. Enter the person's AIM name.

3. From the View menu, choose "Chat Options...."

4. Click on the Mode pop-up menu and choose "Direct IM." Click OK.

5. Enter your message in the edit box at the bottom of the window and hit Return or Enter to send it. Although the title bar in your window claims this is an "Instant Message," it is really a Direct Message.

Chat with Several Buddies at Once

A **Chat Room** is different from an Instant or Direct Message in that you can have a number of people around the world in the same "room" (which looks amazingly like an Instant Message window) all chatting at once. Here are your options:

- ▾ You can **create a new Chat Room** with a unique name and invite a large number of people to join you. Mac.com members, AOL members, and AIM users can all be invited into the Chat Room. (The limit in America Online is 23 people in a room, but I am not sure what the limit is in iChat.) Caps and lowercase don't matter when typing the name of a new Chat Room.

- ▾ You can **join an existing Chat Room** that another Mac.com member has created if you know the exact name of the room. (You cannot join any Chat Room that an AOL member has created within AOL.)

Note: If you enter the name of a Chat Room that other Mac.com users in the world have already set up, you will land in their room! So you want to be sure to type the correct name of the room you want to join. Caps and lowercase don't matter when typing the name of an existing room.

Create a new Chat Room

This opens a room where you can chat with a large number of people.

To create a new Chat Room and invite others to join you:

1. From the File menu, choose "New Chat."

2. A new message window appears. *Before you type anything or choose anyone to invite,* go to the View menu and choose "Chat Options...."

3. From the pop-up "Mode" menu, choose "Chat," as shown below.

4. iChat supplies a unique Chat Room name for you, but you can change it. If you change it, be sure to enter a name that no one else in the world would be using at this moment or you might end up in someone else's Chat Room. (How do you think I know this?) Click OK.

If you don't see this Participants drawer, click the person-head icon at the bottom of the message window, or go to the View menu and choose "Show Chat Participants."

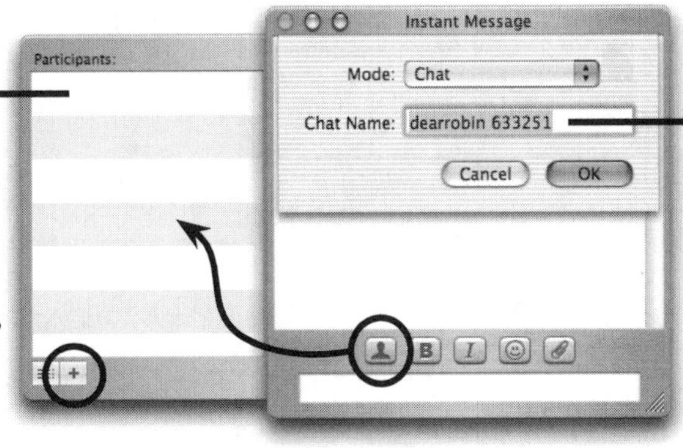

iChat automatically supplies a Chat Room name that no one is currently using. You can change the name.

5. **To invite one or more of your Buddies** to the new Chat Room, click the **+** button at the bottom of the Participants drawer, then choose people from your list who are online at the moment. You can also drag names from your Buddy List to the Participants drawer.

   To invite someone who is not on your Buddy List, click the **+** button at the bottom of the drawer, choose "Other ...", then type their screen name and click OK. Any invited person must be online already.

—continued

6. Once you have added the participants to the list, type a message into the text field at the bottom of the window, hit Return, and that message will go out to everyone on your list.

You can always add more people at any time, and anyone in the world can enter your Chat Room name and drop in to your window. For instance, if someone is not yet online when you send out an invitation, you can send them an email telling them to join you in that particular room as soon as they are online.

7. All of your participants will get a message on their screens inviting them. As soon as they respond, they will appear in your window.

This is your new Chat Room with three participants, which includes you.

This is the same chat in AOL. Sad but true — it's ugly. And too many commercials.

Yet another method . . .

You can also **start a new Chat Room** this way: *Command*-click on each person in your Buddy List whom you want to invite. Then *Control*-click on any selected Buddy in the list, and choose "Invite to Chat…" from the contextual menu that pops up. A Chat Room will open and every selected Buddy will receive an invitation.

Join an existing Chat Room

You can **join an existing Chat Room** that another Mac.com member started if you know its name. You cannot join a chat that an AOL user started in AOL.

1. From the File menu, choose "Go To Chat…."

2. Type in the exact name of the Chat Room you wish to join, then click "Go."

   If a Chat Room by this name exists somewhere in the world, you will appear in it and it will appear on your screen.

   If there is no such existing room, an "Empty Chat Room" will appear on your screen. People can join you there if they know the name, and you can send invitations to other users (as explained on the previous page).

Caps and lowercase don't matter in a Chat Name, nor do spaces; that is, "tea room" is the same as "TeaRoom."

Send or Receive Files through iChat

You may want to **send a picture or some other file** to a Buddy in your list. This technique only works if your Buddy is also an iChat user. If he is an AOL user, you'll have to send the file as an email attachment.

To send a file to another iChat Buddy on your list:

1. Drag a file icon and drag it on top of a Buddy's name in the Buddy List.

2. A panel appears on your computer screen to show you the status of the file transfer.

On the recipient's computer (assuming she is an iChat user, not an AOL user), an alert appears warning of an incoming file, as shown below.

1. Click in the alert window (shown below, left) to open the "Incoming File Request" window (shown below, right) which identifies the file and its sender.

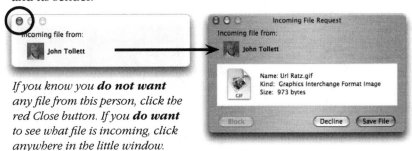

*If you know you **do not want** any file from this person, click the red Close button. If you **do want** to see what file is incoming, click anywhere in the little window.*

2. Either "Decline" the file or click the "Save File" button and download it. If you save the file, it will appear on your Desktop.

Save Transcripts of Chats

You can save a transcript of any chat—Instant Messages, Direct Messages, and Chat Rooms—to document a conversation, read later, or store in your box of love letters.

To save an individual chat:

1. Make sure the chat you want to save is the "active" window on the screen—click once on it to make sure.

2. From the File menu, choose "Save a Copy As…."

3. Name the document and choose a folder in which to store it. Click "Save."

To automatically save all chat transcripts:

1. From the iChat menu, choose "Preferences…."

2. Click the "Messages" icon in the Preferences toolbar.

3. Check the box to "Automatically save chat transcripts." This creates a new folder inside your Documents folder, called "iChats." Every conversation you have in iChat will automatically be recorded and stored in this folder—you don't ever have to choose to "Save."

To read any saved chat, just double-click on its icon; the file will open in a Chat window. If your chats are saved in the iChats folder, you'll find that folder inside your Documents folder.

Customize the Chat Background

You can **customize the background** of any chat window by adding a picture or graphic. This comes in handy when you've got several chats going on and don't want to get confused about who is in which window.

This image will appear only on *your* computer—the person you are chatting with will not see it. As soon as you close this chat window, that background disappears and will not automatically re-appear anywhere.

To customize a chat window:

1. Click anywhere in the chat window that you want to customize (this is just to select that window).

2. From the View menu, choose "Set Background...."

3. In the dialog box that appears, select an image file that's on your computer, then click "Open."

   Or simply drag any image file from your Desktop and drop it directly into an empty space in the chat window.

Small images will "tile" (repeat over and over) to fill the window space. Large images will display full-sized, cropping off the image where necessary.

As shown by the examples below, a simple or subdued background image increases the readability of the window.

To remove a background, click once in that chat window, then go to the View menu and choose "Clear Background."

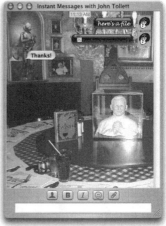

This is actually a large photograph. If I open the chat window larger, I see my Aunt Lois sitting at the table with the Pope.

Set up Additional iChat Accounts

In addition to your Mac.com account, you can also set up an existing AOL Instant Messenger Account (AIM), another Mac.com account, or use your AOL screen name as a different account. No matter how many different accounts you have, though, only *one* can be *active* at any time. Every account can create a different Buddy List; if you use an existing account, it will pick up your Buddy List from that account.

To set up another iChat account:

1. From the iChat menu, choose "Preferences…."

2. Click the "Accounts" icon in the toolbar.

3. Click the "Log Out" button so you can make changes.

4. Type in a new "Screen Name."

   Either: This would be another Mac.com account name you own, which would be your email address including the "@mac.com" part (or click the little arrows to get a menu where you can choose to go to Mac.com and buy a new account).

   Or: Use an existing AIM account name that you got at **www.aim.com**.

   Or: Use your AOL name. Do *not* include the part "@aol.com."

5. Enter the login password you chose when you set up that particular account.

6. Hit Return to add the new account to the "Screen Name" pop-up menu.

7. Close the Preferences window.

8. From the iChat menu, choose "Log Into AIM" to go online with the currently selected screen name.

To switch accounts,
see the following page.

Switch to a different account

Also see the note about Accounts preferences, below!

Once you have set up different accounts, as explained on the previous page, you can switch from one to the other.

To switch to a different iChat account:

1. From the iChat menu, choose "Preferences…."
2. Click the "Accounts" icon in the toolbar.
3. Click the "Log Out" button so you can make changes.
4. From the "Screen Name" pop-up menu, choose a different account that you previously set up (see above). Close the Preferences window.
5. From the iChat menu, choose "Log Into AIM" to go online with the currently selected screen name.

Preferences

Most of the options in **Preferences** are self-explanatory, but here are a few tips:

Accounts: If you have several accounts set up, as described on the previous page, you may want to select a particular account *before* you actually go online. You can save a couple of steps if you do this:

1. Open the iChat Preferences, then click the "Accounts" icon.
2. **Uncheck** the box, "When iChat opens, automatically log in." Close the window.
3. Next time you open iChat, you will not be logged in, so open Preferences and choose an account from the "Screen Name" pop-up menu. Close Preferences.
4. Go to the File menu, and choose "Log Into AIM."

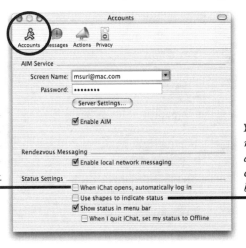

This technique lets you open iChat without being actually logged in, which means no one will know you are online under the previous account.

*You can choose to see the red and green status lights as circles and squares, in case you are **colorblind** between red and green.*

Messages: Use the Messages pane to customize many features of your Chat windows, such as the color of your balloon and the balloons of other people, the font you use and they use, and the colors of the fonts. As you make choices, your choices will be shown in the little window space, as you can see below.

See page 238 regarding this option.

Actions: In the Actions pane, you can have certain actions happen as the result of certain events. For instance, you can make sure your computer tells you how wonderful you look everytime you log in, just in case no one else in your office tells you so.

—continued

Choose an event from the menu, then choose the actions you want to happen upon that event.

The text you enter will "speak" in the voice chosen in the Speech system preferences. If you change voices while iChat is open, you'll have to quit iChat and reopen it before the new voice will take effect.

This is continued from the previous page.

Privacy: If you want to be **invisible** to certain people, or you want to be **visible only** to certain people, click the "Privacy" icon in the Preferences toolbar, then from the Privacy Level pop-up menu, choose a setting.

> **To allow or block specific people,** choose "Allow people listed below" or "Block people listed below," then click the plus sign at the bottom of the pane to add a screen name.

> **To remove people from a list,** select the screen name, then click the minus button.

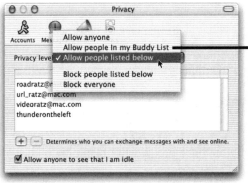

If you choose to "Allow people in my Buddy List," it automatically limits who can see you online to the people you know well enough to have in your List.

Share Files with Rendezvous

iChat

Rendezvous is part of the **iChat** software that comes with Jaguar. You can also send email, Instant Messages, or files to anyone on Rendezvous.

To use Rendezvous, you don't need to have a Mac.com account, nor an AIM account, as you must to use iChat. But both machines do need to have iChat installed (which automatically includes Rendezvous) and must be connected through some sort of network.

To set up Rendezvous:

1. Open iChat: either single-click on its icon in the Dock, or double-click its icon in the Applications window.

2. The first time you open iChat, you get the dialog box shown below. Setting up iChat also sets up the information for Rendezvous.

   First and Last Names: This is how the other people on your network will identify you.

   Account Type: You don't need to choose an account type if you plan to use only Rendezvous. But if you are setting this up for iChat as well, choose "Mac.com" if you have a Mac.com account. Choose "AIM" if you have an AOL or an AIM screen name.

   Account Name and Password: Enter your screen name and password, if you have one of the accounts mentioned above. Otherwise, you can leave it blank if all you plan to do is Rendezvous.

   Click OK. Another message window will appear.

3. In the Rendezvous window, shown below, right, click "Yes."

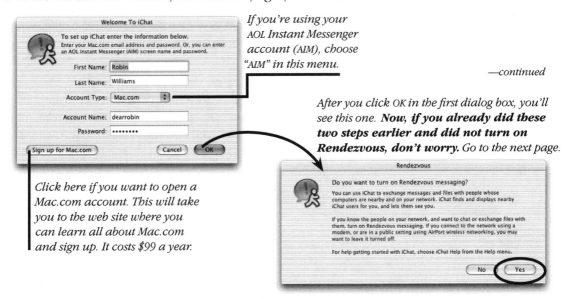

If you're using your AOL Instant Messenger account (AIM), choose "AIM" in this menu.

—continued

After you click OK in the first dialog box, you'll see this one. **Now, if you already did these two steps earlier and did not turn on Rendezvous, don't worry.** *Go to the next page.*

Click here if you want to open a Mac.com account. This will take you to the web site where you can learn all about Mac.com and sign up. It costs $99 a year.

It's not too late to set up Rendezvous

If you previously opened iChat and set it up but did not turn on Rendezvous, **or** if you want to change any of the settings (**or** turn off Rendezvous), use the iChat preferences:

1. While iChat is open, go to the iChat menu and choose "Preferences...."

2. In the "Accounts" pane, as shown below, check the box to "Enable local network messaging." Adjust any of the other settings per your liking.

If you uncheck "Enable AIM," Rendezvous will still work, but iChat will not.

If you're colorblind between red and green, check this button so the red and green status dots will be circles and squares instead of both circles.

Check this box to turn on Rendezvous; uncheck it to turn it off.

Read the iChat information also! Just about everything that applies to **iChat** (preferences, images, opening and closing, changing your availability message, what all the icons indicate, etc.) also applies to **Rendezvous.** So if you haven't already, read the other pages in this chapter about iChat to fill in any gaps you might have regarding Rendezvous.

Send a file to another computer user

You can send a file to any other user on your network with just a drag-and-drop. It's the best.

To send a file to another computer on your local network:

1. Open iChat, which will activate Rendezvous.

2. If the Rendezvous window (shown below, left) doesn't appear, press Command 2, *or* go to the Window menu and choose "Rendezvous." Other users who also have Rendezvous set up and running will appear in the little window.

3. To send *one* file or a *folder* containing several files, drag it to the Rendezvous window and drop it on a name. You will be asked to confirm the transfer.

4. The other computer will get a message, shown below. When that user clicks "Save File," the file will be sent from one machine to another. Now that was pretty easy.

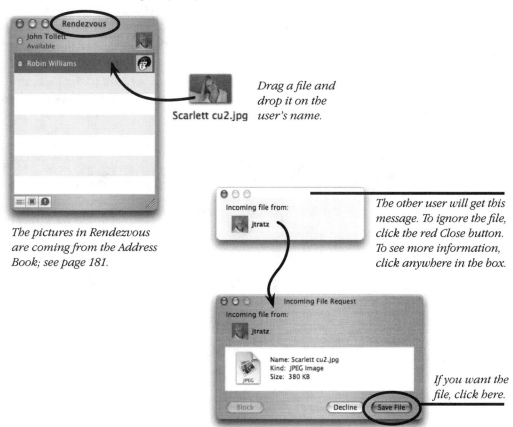

Drag a file and drop it on the user's name.

Scarlett cu2.jpg

The pictures in Rendezvous are coming from the Address Book; see page 181.

The other user will get this message. To ignore the file, click the red Close button. To see more information, click anywhere in the box.

If you want the file, click here.

Send a file through an Instant Message

This is **another way to send a file through Rendezvous:**

1. Open iChat, which will activate Rendezvous.

2. If the Rendezvous window (shown below) doesn't appear, press Command 2, *or* go to the Window menu and choose "Rendezvous." Other users on your network who also have Rendezvous installed and running will appear in the little window.

3. Select the name of the user to whom you want to send a file, then click the "Instant Message" icon at the bottom, the one with the little bubble. This opens an Instant Message (IM) window, shown below-right, on both your computer and the other user's computer.

4. Start a dialog with the other person—send at least one message.

5. Now you can do one of two things:

   Either: Drag the file into the message box and send it (hit Return or Enter).

   Or: Click the paperclip icon to open the standard Open dialog box where you can find and select the file you want to send, then send it (hit Return or Enter).

6. The receiving user will see the file in the sender's message bubble. Click once on the file name and it will download to the Desktop (unless you changed your downloads default in the Internet system preferences' Web pane).

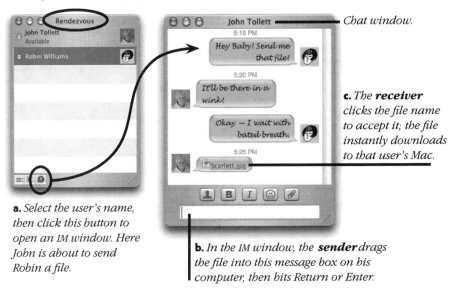

— *Chat window.*

a. Select the user's name, then click this button to open an IM window. Here John is about to send Robin a file.

*c. The **receiver** clicks the file name to accept it; the file instantly downloads to that user's Mac.*

*b. In the IM window, the **sender** drags the file into this message box on his computer, then hits Return or Enter.*

Safari

The World Wide Web is looking better than ever, thanks to **Safari,** Apple's new web browser which was built just for Mac OS X. You'll love the simple elegance of its appearance and the speed with which it gets you from page to page. Because Safari complies with W3C (World Wide Web Consortium) standards, web pages display as they were meant to, including pages that use advanced technologies such as XML, XHTML, CSS, Java, and JavaScript.

Safari makes text on web pages look its best with high-quality anti-aliasing (a technique to reduce the "jaggy" look text can have on a computer screen). Safari and Jaguar work together to take advantage of Unicode, which makes it possible to display text on web pages in languages such as Japanese, Chinese, Arabic, or Korean.

Safari is based on *open source* software, creating the opportunity for software engineers around the world to tinker with the source code to develop amazing browser enhancements that we haven't even thought of yet. Meanwhile, Apple's engineers have had some brilliant ideas of their own: an integrated Google search field, a space-saving progress bar in the search field, SnapBack technology, improvements in bookmark management, and a filter for those incredibly irritating pop-up advertisement windows.

If you find web pages that don't work perfectly, it's because Safari is a very young new kid on the browser block and while it's really good, it's going to get even better. Besides, it's not as if those other browsers are flawless, even at version 5 and above.

Note: As I write this, Safari is still in beta, which means it's not really finished yet. So things will undoubtedly change as the days go by. If you see things in your version of Safari that are not addressed in this chapter, I apologize. We'll catch up in the next edition!

Download Safari

*Safari runs best on
Mac OS X version
10.2.3 or later.
You must be using at
least version 10.2.*

If Safari is not already on your Mac, you can download it free from Apple's
web site: **www.apple.com/safari.**

Once you download Safari, your Software Update will automatically find and
download the updates as they appear.

To download Safari, of course, you need to open another browser. You
should have Internet Explorer on your Mac—just go to the web site and
click the link to download, then follow the directions on-screen.

*A nice feature of Safari is that it will not leave all the mess around
after a download—it automatically deletes all the files you don't need
(as long as you're running at least Mac OS X version 10.2.3).*

Quick Tips

Here are just a few quick tips in Safari.

Bigger or smaller text on the web page

Depending on how the web designer designed the page, it is often possible for you to make the reading text larger or small. This will not affect any text in graphics, however.

Make text bigger: Command +

Make text smaller: Command –

Or if you have the "Text Size" button displayed in your Safari toolbar, as shown on page 255, click the large or small A icon.

Death to pop-up windows

Do you hate those annoying little advertisement windows that pop up without your permission? Press **Command K** to prevent their appearance. If you decide you want them, press Command K again to allow their presence. You'll find this command in the Safari menu.

Web address tips

If a web address ends in **.com,** all you need to type is the main name, such as **apple, toyota,** or **NFL,** then hit Return. That is, you never have to type **http://** or **.com.** To go to a web site that ends in anything besides **.com,** you will need to type that part (such as **.org, .edu,** or any country code).

You'll notice **as you type a web address** that previous and similar addresses appear below the Address field. When you see the correct address appear, stop typing, then use the DownArrow key to select the address you want to go to. When it's highlighted, hit the Return key and off you'll go.

*This is one of my favorite features: just double-click in the domain name between **www** and **com,** and **only that one word,** the one you need to change, is selected. No more trying to press-and-drag across that tiny word in the tiny Address field to select it!*

Email a link

It's easy to send an email link to someone. Just open the email message, then drag the tiny icon to the left of a web address in the Address bar, and drop it in the email message.

Drag this icon to an email message and drop it in the message at the point where you want it to appear.

Links tips

Sometimes you want to open several links at once without losing the page you're on.

To open a link in a new window, Command-click on it (that is, hold down the Command key and click on the link). The page will open in a separate window.

To open a link in a new window that is *behind* the current window, Shift-Command–click on it. This is one of my favorite features—I can go to a search results page and open a dozen windows in five seconds, then go see what they are about.

To get a contextual menu of options, as shown below, Control-click on a link. The options that appear in the menu depend on what kind of item you Control-click on.

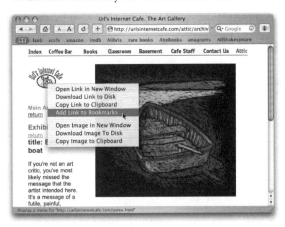

View a link's location in the status bar

If the **Status Bar** in Safari is showing, you can position your mouse over a link (don't click), and the address of where the link will take you is visible in the Status Bar.

To show the Status Bar, go to the View menu and choose "Status Bar," *or* press Command \. (The backslash is right above the Return key.)

*The **progress bar** slides right across the web address as the new page loads. Watch for it. When the bar stops progressing, the page is fully loaded.*

Status bar.

Notice the mouse is positioned over the link to the "Art Gallery." In the status bar, you can see the address where that link will take you if you click it.

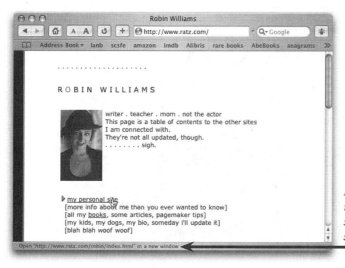

If the link will open the new page in a new, separate window, Safari's status bar will tell you so.

Make a Web Location of any link

A **Web Location** is a tiny file that will open your browser (if it isn't already) and go to that web page. The advantage of a Web Location over a bookmark is that you don't have to have the browser already open before you can use a Web Location—double-click a Web Location icon (.webloc) and it will automatically open Safari and go straight to that page.

Louvre.webloc

This is what a Web Location file looks like.

To make a Web Location, just drag a link off of a web page and drop it on the Desktop.

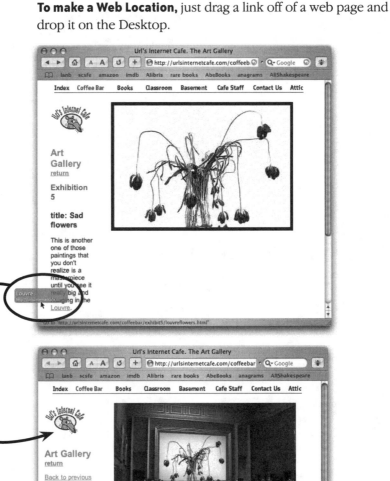

Louvre.webloc

Open a Web Location icon

Once you've made a Web Location icon, as described on the opposite page, there are several things you can do with it.

Louvre.webloc

Put the location in the Dock: Drag it to the right side of the dividing line (on the side where the Trash basket is). When you click on this icon in the Dock, that web page will open in a new, separate browser window (meaning it won't replace any existing browser windows that are already open).

Open that web page in a new and separate window: Double-click this icon.

Open the page in a window that's already open on your screen: Drag this icon and drop it in the middle of the window (*not* in the Address field). The new page will *replace* the existing one.

Customize the Toolbar

You can choose what you want to see in the toolbar. Go to the View menu and look under the gray "Show" heading (shown to the right). The items you see in the menu shown to the right are in the same order the items will appear, left to right, in the toolbar shown below.

Back and Forward; see page 256.

Home button; see Preferences on page 270.

Add Bookmark; see page 260.

Report bugs (problems) to Apple.

Address Bar.

Bookmarks Bar; see page 261–265.

Text size; click to make larger or smaller.

Status Bar.

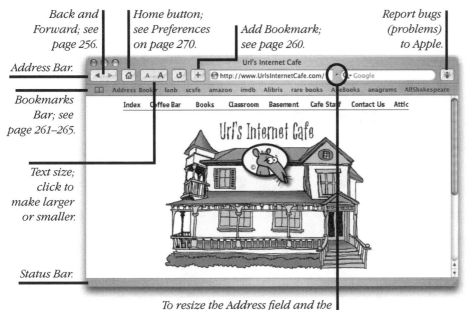

To resize the Address field and the Google field, drag this dot left or right.

To remove items from the toolbar, *you must uncheck them from the View menu; you can't drag or Command-drag them off (in this beta version, anyway). Nor can you rearrange. (But try in a newer version.)*

Back and Forward Menus

As you may already know, you can *press* on the Back or Forward button and you'll get a menu showing the pages you can go back to, or pages you have come from that you can go forward to, as shown below.

*Press on the Back or Forward button to get a menu of the pages you've been to. The menu displays the **page names** (what the designers named the pages.)*

But did you know that if you hold the Option key down while you press on either the Back or Forward button, you will **see the actual web addresses** of the pages you have been to?

*Option-press on the Back or Forward button to see the **actual web addresses** displayed in the menu.*

Address Book

If you have entered web addresses for people in your **Address Book** (see Chapter 5), you can access those web sites directly from the Bookmarks Bar in Safari, as shown below.

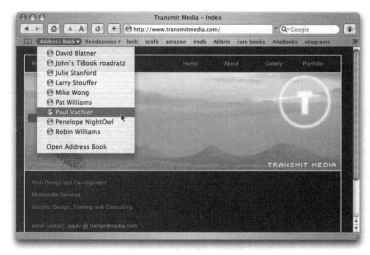

These are the people in my Address Book whose contact page includes a web address.

To put the Address Book item in your Bookmarks Bar:

1. Open the Safari Preferences (go to the Safari menu and choose "Preferences…").

2. Click the "Bookmarks" icon in the toolbar. You'll get the little window shown below.

3. Check the box to "Include Address Book." Close the Preferences.

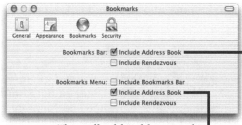

This will put an Address Book menu in your Bookmarks Bar, as shown above.

This will add "Address Book" to your Bookmarks Menu, the one at the top of your screen.

Tip: If you don't want to take up the space in your Bookmarks Bar with the Address Book, don't forget that you can always access the Address Book in the Bookmarks Window; see page 261. And you can add it to your main Bookmarks Menu, the one at the top of your screen.

Google Search

If you've ever used **Google** as your search engine, you know how amazing it is. If you haven't yet, once you do you might never use anything else. Because it's so great (it even figures out if you've misspelled something you're looking for), Apple has included it in your Safari toolbar. Use it just as you would if you went directly to the Google.com site. Here are a few extra tips for searching (these tips apply to any search tool, actually).

If you don't see the Google search field in your toolbar, go to the View menu and choose "Google search."

Type your search term in this little field.

To delete whatever is in there, click the X.

Put quotation marks around words that should be found together, as explained below.

With quotation marks *around a phrase, Google will find only those pages where those two words are next to each other.*

Notice with quotation marks, Google found 33 pages.

Without quotation marks, *Google displays 88 pages because it finds every page that has the word "brenda" on it and the word "euland," whether they are next to each other or not.*

Limit your search even more

Use ***Boolean operators*** to limit your search. That is, put a **+** sign in front of any word or phrase (in quotation marks) that you want to make sure Google finds; put a **−** sign in front of any word that you do not want to appear on a page. Do not put a space after the + or −.

For all the details about this very useful SnapBack button that you see in the Google field, see pages 268–269.

▼ A search for just the word **safari** gave me 2,370,000 results.

▼ A search for **safari +apple −africa** gave me only 94,300 results, and pages about Apple's Safari were right at the top.

▼ A search for **safari +browser +apple −africa** gave me only 47,900 results, again with Apple's Safari at the very top.

Extra tips

Here are a couple of handy menus for Google.

▼ Click on the tiny magnifying tool and triangle in the Google field and you'll get a menu listing the **last ten searches** you did in Google, as shown to the right.

Safari maintains this list no matter how many windows you open or even if you quit Safari.

▼ Select a word or phrase on any web page, then Control-click on that word. A **contextual menu** will appear with the option to do a "Google Search," as shown to the right. Choose it and the new results will appear instantly.

Click this icon to show the Bookmarks Window or to hide it.

Bookmarks

Make a **bookmark** of a page that you want to return to anytime in the future; this bookmark will then be available in the Bookmarks Menu at the top of your screen. Just choose that page from the menu to go directly to it. Bookmarks of course, are the handiest features of any browser.

The biggest problem with bookmarks is they are *so* handy you end up making hundreds of them, and then it can be difficult to find the one you want (which defeats the purpose of a bookmark in the first place). All browsers allow you to create folders and to store collections of bookmarks in those folders, but Safari has made it more convenient.

To bookmark a web page:

1. Go to the web page that you want to bookmark.

2. **Either:** Click the **+** button in the toolbar, if it's there
(if the **+** is not in your toolbar and you want it, see page 255).

   Or: Press Command D.

   Or: Go to the Bookmarks Menu and choose "Add Bookmark...."

Tip: To add a page to the Bookmarks Menu **without** displaying the drop-down sheet asking you to rename and file it, press **Command Shift D.**

3. A small "sheet" drops down from the title bar of the window, as shown below. This sheet offers the opportunity to **change the name of the bookmark**—just edit as you would anything else.

   From the menu in the sheet, you can also choose to **store this bookmark in an existing folder** that you previously made, (see the following page), *or* in the main Bookmarks Menu, *or* in the Bookmarks Bar (the thin bar beneath the toolbar, shown below).

This is the Bookmarks Bar.

Edit the name of the bookmark here.

Choose an existing folder here, or choose the Bookmarks Menu or Bookmarks Bar.

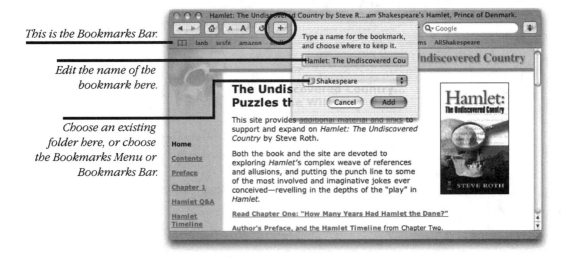

The Bookmarks Window

Below you see the **Bookmarks Window.** On the left side is the **Collections pane,** which holds your entire assortment of bookmarks. You can have "collections" (folders) of bookmarks that *do not* show up in the Bookmarks Menu; this gives you the option to keep your menu short, sweet, and useful instead of two-yards long and difficult to wade through.

Hide or show the Bookmarks Window.

This is what my Bookmarks Menu looks like, both in the menu itself (above) and in the Bookmarks Window (left).

The "Bookmarks Menu" is selected, and to its right is a display of all the bookmarks I have created and that I store in the Bookmarks Menu. As you can see, most of my bookmarks are organized into folders.

Bookmarks Bar: Anything you put in the Bookmarks Bar will appear in the bar itself, as explained more fully on the following page. This gives you instant access to your most-visited web pages.

Bookmarks Menu: Anything in here will appear in the list that drops down from the Bookmarks Menu at the top of your screen, as shown above, right.

Address Book: Any web sites you have added to any contacts in your Address Book (see Chapter 5) will appear here. Also see page 257.

Rendezvous: Web sites for printers, routers, webcams, or administrative sites on your network will automatically appear here.

History: Every web page you have visited for the past week is here; see page 265 for details.

Folders: *Folders in the Collections pane do not appear in the Bookmarks Menu.* This is a good place to keep bookmarks you don't need often, like those for a specific client or project. See the following pages.

Organize your bookmarks

You can create as many folders as you like and store as many bookmarks in those folders as you like. You can choose to have folders appear in the Bookmarks Menu or not, or you can put an entire folder of bookmarks into the Bookmarks Bar.

To make a new folder in the Collections pane:

1. Click the **+** sign at the bottom of the Collections pane.

2. The new folder appears and is ready for you to name it, as shown below—just type.

*This is a new Collections folder. It will appear in the drop-down sheet menu when you make a new bookmark, but as long as it is sitting in this Collections pane, **it will not appear** in the Bookmarks Menu.*

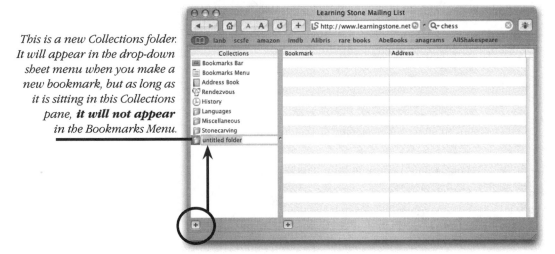

To put a NEW bookmark into the new folder in the Collections pane:

1. Make a new bookmark as usual (as described on page 260).

2. In the sheet that drops down (as shown on page 260), press on the little menu and you will see the new folder you just made. Choose it and the new bookmark will be stored inside that folder.

To move an EXISTING bookmark into a new folder in the Collections pane:

1. Click on any other collection in the Collections pane, such as History, Bookmarks Menu, or any other folder. The existing bookmarks that are stored in that collection will appear on the right.

2. Drag a bookmark from the *right* side of the window and drop it into the new folder in the Collections pane, as shown at the top of the opposite page.

To move a COPY of an existing bookmark, Option-drag it.

I made a new collections folder and named it "Chess."

Then I clicked on the "Bookmarks Menu" collection to display the bookmarks I made earlier.

*I found the chess bookmark I had made, and here you can see me dragging it from the right side over to the folder on the left. When I drop it, that bookmark will **move** into the new folder.*

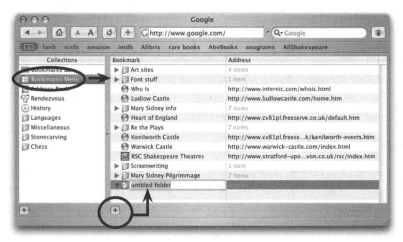

All of the folders and single bookmarks shown on the right side of this window are the ones that are stored in the Bookmarks Menu; you can see that "Bookmarks Menu" is the selected collection.

To make a new folder inside an existing collection (such as the Bookmarks Menu collection):

1. Select a collection in the Collections pane, such as "Bookmarks Menu." (To select it, click once on its name.) *Any bookmarks and folders stored in the Bookmarks Menu collection will appear in the Bookmarks Menu at the top of the screen.*

2. On the *right* side of the window, click the **+** sign at the bottom. This will make a new, untitled folder on the *right* side, which means it is stored inside the selected collection.

3. Make new bookmarks and choose this folder to store them within, or drag existing bookmarks from the same collection into other folders. For instance, in the example above, I should make a new folder and drag the English castle bookmarks into it.

The Bookmarks Bar

The **Bookmarks Bar** is where you can store your most-often visited web sites. You can put folders in the Bookmarks Bar as well as individual links.

To add a bookmark to the Bookmarks Bar:

If the Bookmarks Bar is not showing in your browser window, press Command B.

▼ **Either:** When you are at the page you want to bookmark, **drag the tiny icon** in the Address field and drop it on the Bookmarks Bar.

▼ **Or:** Press Command D to get the drop-down sheet. Edit the bookmark so its name is short, then from the menu in the sheet, choose "Bookmarks Bar."

▼ **Or:** Open the Bookmarks Window (click the tiny icon on the far left of the Bar). Select the collection on the left that contains a bookmark you want in the Bar. Find the bookmark on the right side of the window, then drag it into the "Bookmarks Bar" collection on the left.

This will *move* the bookmark from the existing collection to the Bar. **To put a copy in the Bar** instead, hold down the Option key and drag.

▼ **Or:** Open the Bookmarks Window, as described above. Find a bookmark in any collection. From the right side of the window, drag the bookmark directly into the Bar itself (as opposed to the collection on the left). This will also put the bookmark into the Bookmarks Bar collection. Option-drag to put a copy in the Bar.

▼ **Or:** Open the Bookmarks Window (click the tiny icon on the far left of the Bar). Drag any **folder** from the Collections pane on the left and drop it directly in the Bookmarks Bar *or* into the Bookmarks Bar collection.

The Bookmarks Bar.

*If you put a **folder** in the Bookmarks Bar, you will have access to every bookmark in the folder. This example shows a folder with subfolders stored in the Bookmarks Bar.*

To rearrange the bookmarks in the Bar:

▼ Drag the bookmarks left or right in the Bar.

*Control-click on any bookmark in the Bar to get this **contextual menu** where you can **edit** the name or address, **delete** the bookmark, or **open** it in a new, separate window.*

To REMOVE a bookmark from the Bar:

▼ Drag the bookmark off the TOP of the bar (not sideways or down). **IMPORTANT NOTE:** This will **DELETE** the bookmark, not just remove it from the Bar! If you drag a folder off the Bar, *it will delete every bookmark in that folder!*

▼ **To remove an individual bookmark** from the Bookmarks Bar and still **KEEP THE BOOKMARK,** open the Bookmarks Window. Select the Bookmarks Bar collection on the left, then drag the bookmark you want to remove and drop it into any other collection.

To remove a bookmark folder, open the Bookmarks Window, select the Bookmarks Bar collection, drag the folder from the right side of the window, and drop it into the Collections pane on the left.

The History Menu

The History menu keeps track of every web site you've visited for the past week: use the History menu or the Bookmarks Window, as shown below. Click any History page like a bookmark to go back to that page. After about a week, the pages you've visited will disappear from the History menu.

To clear all the pages out at once whenever you feel like it, go to the History menu and choose "Clear History." **Or** in the Bookmarks Window, select the "History" collection, click in the Bookmark pane on the right, press Command A to select all, then hit the Delete key.

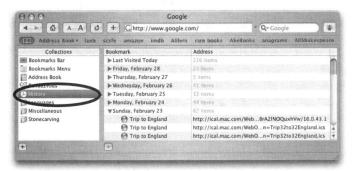

To save any History page as a permanent bookmark, drag it from the right side of this window and drop it into a collection on the left.

Import bookmarks from Internet Explorer

If you've been using **Internet Explorer** as your browser, any "Favorites" you made in that program will automatically be imported into Safari. You'll find them in the Bookmarks Window, in the Collections pane; there will be a folder called "Imported IE Favorites."

As explained on pages 261–263, folders in the Collections pane will not appear in the Bookmarks Menu. You can either move the bookmarks from this folder into the "Bookmarks Menu" collection, as described below, or double-click on any link in the Bookmarks Window to go there.

To move Internet Explorer bookmarks into your Bookmarks Menu:

1. Open the Bookmarks Window (click on the tiny book icon in the Bookmarks Bar *or* press Command Option B).

2. Click once on the folder in the Collections pane named "Imported IE Favorites." Its bookmarks will appear on the right.

3. Drag the bookmarks from the right side of the window and drop them into the collection of your choice on the left side.

   To make all of these imported bookmarks appear in the menu at the top of the screen: click on the right side of the Bookmarks Window, press Command A to select all, then drag them all into the "Bookmarks Menu" collection.

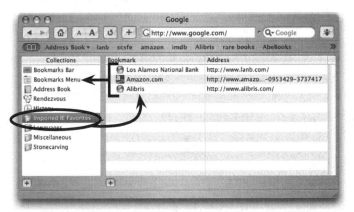

Drag these bookmarks either to the "Bookmarks Menu" or to another Collection folder. Once the IE Favorites folder is empty, select it and hit the Delete key to remove it.

Import bookmarks from other browsers

Importing bookmarks from browsers other than Internet Explorer is not as straightforward as described on the opposite page. You can use the method below, however, to get your bookmarks from Netscape into Safari:

1. Find your bookmark file; it should be in the path shown below.

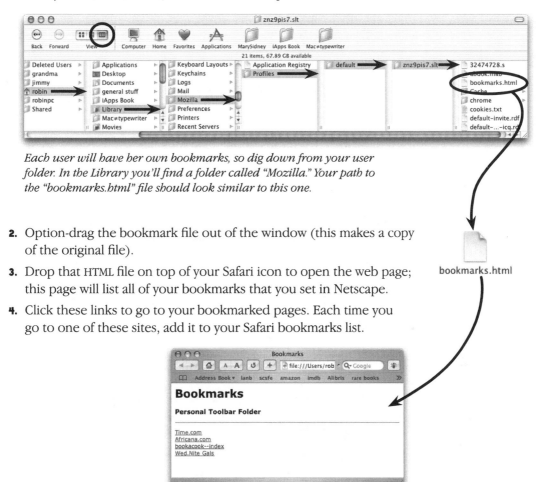

Each user will have her own bookmarks, so dig down from your user folder. In the Library you'll find a folder called "Mozilla." Your path to the "bookmarks.html" file should look similar to this one.

2. Option-drag the bookmark file out of the window (this makes a copy of the original file).

3. Drop that HTML file on top of your Safari icon to open the web page; this page will list all of your bookmarks that you set in Netscape.

4. Click these links to go to your bookmarked pages. Each time you go to one of these sites, add it to your Safari bookmarks list.

SnapBack

This is the icon you'll often see in the Address field or in the Google field.

SnapBack

The **SnapBack** button is a great feature. How often have you gone to a page you enjoyed, wandered off the path into the wilderness of the Internet, then tried to find that original page again? SnapBack can take you right back to where you started. Keep in mind that SnapBack is a *temporary* marker.

There are three ways to use SnapBack:

▼ **Google search results:** When you do a search in Google, the search results page from which you choose a link is set as the SnapBack page. That is, you might click a link on the *first* page of the search results, then wander through four or five pages. The SnapBack icon in the Google field will take you back to that *first* page.

If you go to the *fourth* page of Google results and click a link from there, the SnapBack icon will take you back to that *fourth* page.

Note: If you open different windows to use Google, the SnapBack button in each window will return you to the search results *for that window.*

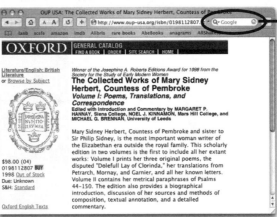

Because I got to this web page by following links from the Google search results page, this SnapBack will return me to the original results page, above.

▼ **Choose a page:** When you type a new URL (web address), **or** choose a bookmark, **or** choose a page from the History menu, **or** open a new window, *the SnapBack is applied to that page.*

You won't see the SnapBack button until you leave the marked page and go to another.

As soon as you leave the marked page, the SnapBack button will appear. It will stay there, linked to that page, until you enter a new web address, choose a different book-mark, or choose a page from the History menu.

***If you open a new window,** the new page in that new window will have its own SnapBack button. **The SnapBack in the previous window will remain active** for the contents of that window.*

▼ **Assign SnapBack to a page:** You can go to the History menu and choose "Mark Page for SnapBack" for any open page (or press Command Option M). This will override the automatic SnapBack that was applied to a page.

This assigned SnapBack **will only last** until you do one of the things mentioned above: enter a new URL, choose a bookmark, choose a page from the History menu, **or** click the Back or Forward button.

If a link opens to a new window, you lose the SnapBack because it belongs with the other window.

Safari Preferences

The preferences for Safari are pretty simple and self-explanatory. Click each item in the toolbar to set preferences for that feature.

*If you have a **web page style sheet** you like, you can choose to override a web site's style sheet with one of your own. Do this in the Appearance pane of Preferences.*

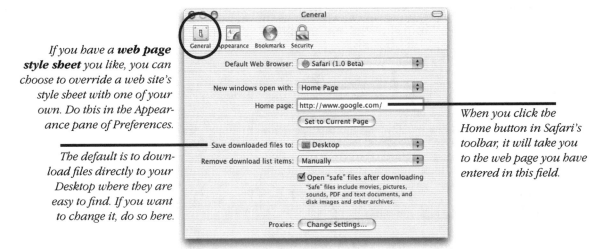

When you click the Home button in Safari's toolbar, it will take you to the web page you have entered in this field.

The default is to download files directly to your Desktop where they are easy to find. If you want to change it, do so here.

Shortcuts in Safari

Scroll around a web page: Either click in the web page or hit the Tab key until the *page* (as opposed to the Address field or Google field) is selected. Then use the **arrow keys** to go up, down, or sideways.

Scroll farther: Use Option Arrowkeys.

Scroll DOWN a window screen at a time: Hit the Spacebar.

Scroll UP a window screen at a time: Press Shift Spacebar.

To bookmark a page *without* displaying the drop-down sheet asking you to rename and file it, press Command Shift D.

Rendezvous

Eventually Safari will be able to use **Rendezvous** to find web addresses for things like printers, routers, webcams, or administrative sites that may be set up on your local network. As we write this, the technology is not quite ready. If you find you have a use for it, use the directions above to put Rendezvous in your Bookmarks Bar or Menu, then choose "About Rendezvous" from its menu. Or go to **www.apple.com/rendezvous.**

Section *three*

.Mac apps

.Mac (pronounced "dot Mac") is a collection of tools and services that are available if you subscribe to a one-year .Mac membership for $99.95. For most people, the value of a .Mac membership far exceeds the price tag.

Each .Mac membership includes the software and services explained in this section: an **email account** with 15 megabytes of email storage space; **WebMail** for access to your email account and Address Book from any Mac or PC in the world; **iDisk** storage, 100 megabytes of personal storage space on Apple's servers; **HomePage,** web-based software for creating and publishing web pages; **iSync** to synchronize Address Book and iCal calendar information between multiple computers; **Backup** software to archive important files to discs or to your iDisk; **Virex** software for virus protection; **Slides Publisher** to publish your own slideshows over the Internet; and personalized **iCards** (electronic greeting cards) using your own photos. Membership also gives you access to a members-only technical support service.

Go to **www.mac.com** and click "Join Now." Or sign up for a 60-day free trial, complete with an email address, to help decide if you should join.

This membership is also referred to as a **Mac.com account** (pronounced "Mac dot com). People use both terms, so don't get confused.

iDisk

When you become a .Mac member, you have instant access to your **iDisk**—100 megabytes of personal storage on Apple's servers. You can upgrade your iDisk storage capacity at any time (for a fee), up to 1000 megabytes.

Your .Mac account relies on iDisk to make its best features a reality: creating web pages, backup protection of important files, synchronization of address books and Macs, customized iCards, online calendars, slideshow screensavers, and whatever else Apple may offer in the near future.

You may want to use your iDisk to store files in a safe, remote location as personal backups, or to store important files so you can retrieve them from any other location. Any files stored on your iDisk are accessible by you or (if you choose) a guest at any time, from almost any computer (Mac or PC).

Sharing files with others is effortless using iDisk Utility, which is a free download from Mac.com. Just set permissions and give someone your .Mac name and password to allow them to upload or download files to your Public folder. The iDisk Utility also makes it easy to monitor your iDisk space, access other .Mac members' Public folders, or purchase additional storage space.

iDisk is a wonderful asset that you'll use more and more as you become familiar with all the ways it can enhance your ever-expanding iLife.

Put iDisk on Your Desktop

You can "mount" your iDisk so it appears on your Desktop just like any other hard disk, then drag and drop files and folders between iDisk and your computer.

To open your iDisk:

1. If you haven't already connected to the Internet, do so now.

2. From the Go menu at your Desktop, choose "iDisk." (If you have more than one account, how does it know which one to open? See the opposite page.)

If you've *never* logged in to your .Mac account before, you might have to enter your member name and password in a login dialog box similar to the one shown below. After a few moments, an iDisk icon labeled with your member name appears on your Desktop, as shown to the left.

roadrat

If you've logged in to your .Mac account before, when you choose "iDisk" from the Go menu, a window opens that displays your iDisk, as shown below. Amazing. Don't get confused with these folders *that are named exactly the same as the folders in the Home window* on your computer. The icon in the title bar (the iDisk crystal ball) indicates you're looking at folders on Apple's servers.

If this icon appears on your Desktop but no window, double-click the icon to open its window, revealing the folders inside.

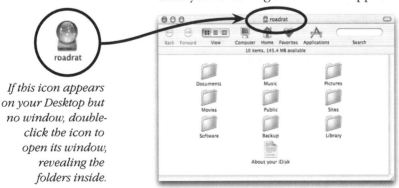

How does it know?

How does your Mac know which iDisk is yours? Once you have set up an account, your member name and password appear in the Internet System Preferences: click the System Preferences icon in your Dock, then click the Internet icon. You can see below the member name and password.

If you have more than one .Mac account, you can quickly and easily go to another account by first changing the member name and password in this Internet preference pane. The Go menu goes to whatever is entered here.

If you open your other account regularly, it will be easier for you to use the iDisk Utility, as explained on the following pages.

To quickly and easily open another iDisk account, change the name and password here.

Other ways to open your iDisk

▾ **Put an iDisk icon in your window Toolbar** (as shown to the right): Control-click on any open Finder window Toolbar, then from the "Customize" sheet that slides down, drag the iDisk icon to the Toolbar. Click "Done." Now you can click that iDisk icon whenever you want to open your iDisk.

▾ **Use iDisk Utility,** as explained on page 279.

iDisk Contents

When you double-click the **iDisk** icon on your Desktop to open its **window,** you're actually looking at files and folders that are on Apple's server, which explains why there may be a delay opening the window (especially if your Interent connection is a phone modem instead of a broadband connection, such as DSL or cable).

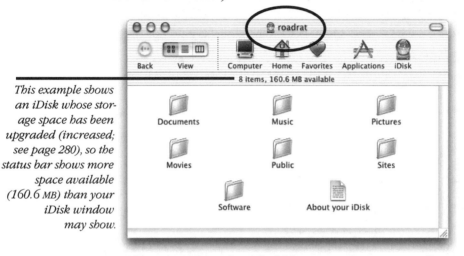

This example shows an iDisk whose storage space has been upgraded (increased; see page 280), so the status bar shows more space available (160.6 MB) than your iDisk window may show.

This is an iDisk window. The folders you see here are actually on one of Apple's servers!

The icon in the title bar is your only clue that you are not in your own Home folder on your Mac— you have been magically transported to a computer (server) at Apple.

All of your iDisk folders are **private** and accessible only to you (or someone who knows your password) except the folder called Public.

Documents folder: Drag into this folder any kind of document that you want to store and make available to yourself over the Internet. This folder is private and only you have access to it.

Music folder: Drag music files and playlists to this private iDisk folder so you can have access to it from anywhere over the Internet.

Pictures folder: Drag individual photos or folder of photos that you plan to use in a HomePage web site into this iDisk Pictures folder so you'll have access to them when you're building the web page.

Movies folder: Drag movies that you might use in a HomePage web site into this iDisk Movies folder so you'll have access to them when you're building the web page.

Public folder: Put files and folders here that you want to make accessible for other people. *Other people can access files that you drag to your iDisk Public folder, if they have your .Mac member name.* Or you can open any other Public folder if you have another person's .Mac member name.

Sites folder: The Sites folder stores any web pages that you've created using HomePage. You can also store sites here created with any other web authoring software.

Software folder: The Software folder contains software provided to you by Apple, as well as Mac OS X software that you can download by dragging files to your computer. There's also a folder named "Extras" that contains royalty-free music files you can use in your iMovies. If you see anything you want in these folders, drag it to your Desktop.

The contents of this folder do not count against your iDisk storage space allotment.

Backup folder: When you use **Backup,** Apple's software for .Mac members (see Chapter 13), this is where the archived files are put.

Library folder: This folder contains application support files. Anything that needs to be in this folder will automatically be placed there.

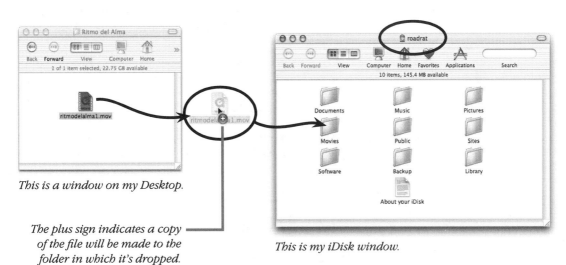

This is a window on my Desktop.

The plus sign indicates a copy of the file will be made to the folder in which it's dropped.

This is my iDisk window.

Drag files or folders from your computer to one of the folders in the iDisk window. To copy files from your iDisk, drag them from the iDisk window to your Desktop.

It's Easy to Get Confused!

When you open your iDisk, you may notice that it looks almost exactly like your Home window. You can tell it's your iDisk, though, because of the name of the window and the icon in the title bar, as shown on the previous pages.

But as soon as you open any folder, the iDisk icon in the title bar disappears and you can no longer tell if the Pictures folder you have opened is the Pictures folder on Apple's server or your own folder on your hard disk!

Here is how you can check: Hold down the Command key and press on the title bar of any window—it will drop down a menu that tells you where that folder/window is stored.

Is this folder on your hard disk or your iDisk?

Command-click on the title bar to see where the open folder is actually located.

Save Directly to Your iDisk

You can save any document or photo in any application directly to your iDisk: Choose Save from the File menu, then from the "Where" menu, choose your iDisk and the folder you want to save it into, as shown below.

Keep in mind that if you continue to work on a file that you save to your iDisk, *you are actually working directly on Apple's computers.* It's best to save to the iDisk when you're finished with a file.

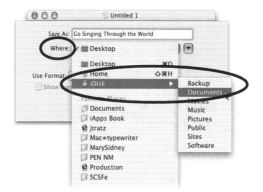

Manage Your iDisk with iDisk Utility

The **iDisk Utility** is the easiest way possible to open your iDisk—and it's free if you have a .Mac account. In addition, with iDisk Utility you can open other .Mac members' Public folders (if you have their passwords), open your other accounts without changing your Internet settings, set access privileges for your iDisk, set password protection for your Public folder, monitor your iDisk storage capacity, and add extra storage to your iDisk.

iDisk Utility

To download iDisk Utility from the .Mac web site:

1. Go to www.mac.com.

2. Click the iDisk icon in the web site toolbar, then log in to your .Mac account with your member name and password.

3. Click the "Downloads" link to open a page of software links.

4. Click the "iDisk Utility.dmg" link to download the software.

5. Follow the instructions in the installer window that opens. iDisk Utility is installed in the "Utilities" folder, which is located in the "Applications" folder.

6. Double-click the iDisk Utility icon. Its window opens, as shown below.

Tip: For convenience and easy access, keep the iDisk Utility in the Dock: while the iDisk Utility is open, Control-click (or press and hold) its icon in the Dock to show the contextual menu, then choose "Keep in Dock."

To open another account of yours or another member's iDisk:

1. Open iDisk Utility as explained above.

2. Click "Open Public folder," then enter your or another member's "Member Name" in the field. Click "Open."

3. An icon representing your other account or another member's Public folder appears on your Desktop, as shown to the right. Double-click this icon to open their Public folder into a window from which you can access the folders and files you find there.

dearrobin

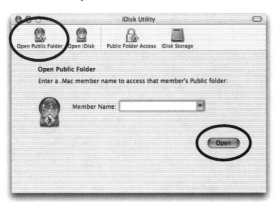

Open iDisk pane

Tip: If you or anyone you know needs to access an iDisk from a machine running **Windows XP,** download the free **iDisk Utility for Windows XP.** Installation instructions are included with the download.

You'll find it in the iDisk section of Mac.com.

In the iDisk Utility, click the "Open iDisk" icon to access an entire iDisk for which you have a member name and password.

Public Folder Access pane

Use this pane to set access privileges or to set password protection for your Public folder.

iDisk Storage pane

Use this pane to keep track of how much iDisk storage space you're using. If you need more, click "Buy More" to see available options and prices and to purchase more storage.

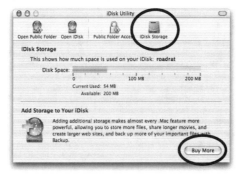

iCards

If you've never had the urge to send an email postcard to friends, **iCards** could change your attitude. This always-changing collection of beautiful, eye-catching, images are a notch or three above what you usually get from other online greeting card services. A great-looking card with a postmark captures attention more effectively than a plain old email message. You can even use one of your own photos that you've copied to your iDisk, instead of a photo from the iCard image library. Because iCards are such a great way to announce events, HomePage uses it to announce newly created web sites. So start uploading your favorite photos to the Pictures folder in your iDisk. If you haven't signed up for a .Mac account yet, you're missing a powerful lot of *fun.* And a lot of *powerful* fun.

Send an iCard

Anyone can send **iCards** to friends and family, even without a .Mac account, but to send an iCard *using your own photo,* you do need a .Mac account. An iCard is simply an electronic postcard you can send to anyone on any computer. iCard is far better than most Internet postcards for two reasons: The quality of the graphics is superior, and iCards are sent straight to the recipient instead of requiring a visit to a web page to "pick up" a card.

To send an iCard from the iCard Image Library:

1. Go to **www.mac.com** and click the iCards tab.

2. Click the "iCards" button.

3. On the iCards welcome page, shown below-left, click on a category.

4. Then click on a specific iCard thumbnail, circled above, to open a full-sized, editable version (next page).

5. On the editable iCard version that appears (shown right), write a message and select a font, then click the "Continue" button.

6. The next page previews your card and lets you address the card to as many recipients as you like.

   Enter your name and email address in the "Name" and "Email" boxes.

   If you want to receive a copy of the email, check the "Send a copy to myself" box.

   To protect the privacy of recipients, you can hide their email addresses if you check the "Hide distribution list" box. The contents of the "To:" field of the email will contain the words "Apple iCards Recipients" instead of recipients' email addresses.

   Enter a recipient's email address in the text box. To add multiple addresses, click the "Add Recipient" button after each address entry. All recipients will appear in the "Recipient List."

7. Click the "Send Your Card" button in the bottom-right corner.

8. A "Thank you" page opens, with the options of "Send same iCard" to someone else or "Return to Categories" to choose another photo (shown below).

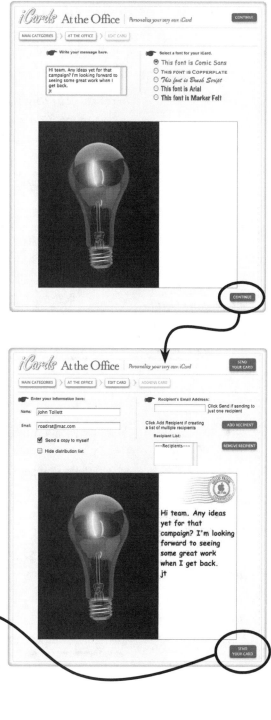

Create Your Own iCard

Apple's iCard images are beautiful, but you probably have photos of your own that you'd like to use. That's easy if you've already copied some photos to the Pictures folder on your iDisk (see Chapter 9 to learn about iDisk).

To create your own iCard:

1. On the iCards welcome page, click the "Create Your Own" icon in the bottom-right corner.

In the "Members' Portfolio," .Mac members can upload photos to be added to the collection for others to use.

2. Choose a photo from the "Pictures" pane. This pane shows the contents of the "Pictures" folder on your iDisk.

3. When you see the picutre you want, click "Select This Image."

To show the contents of a folder, select it, then click the "Open" button. Or, you can double-click the folder name in the list.

*To see a photo's **preview**, select it, then click the "Preview" button. Or, you can double-click the photo name in the list.*

Tip: If you can't see the contents of your Pictures folder, click the "Update Folder" button. Or, try using a different browser.

Click to choose an image.

The "Pictures Folder Images" pop-up menu lets you navigate back to the "Pictures" folder after you've drilled down to sub-folder levels looking for an image.

4. Type your message in the text box (circled below).

5. Select a font to use on the iCard.

6. Click the "Size to Fit" box to trim your photo to fit iCard's aspect ration. If don't like the results, uncheck the box and compare the two settings.

7. Click the "Continue" button.

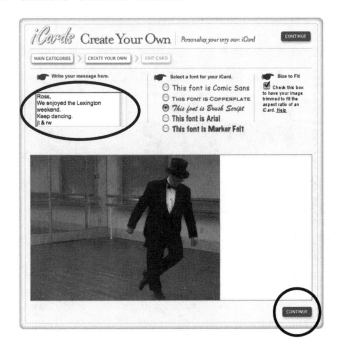

—continued

8. This page previews your card and lets you address the card to as many recipients as you like.

> **Enter your name and email address** in the "Name" and "Email" boxes.
>
> If you want to recieve a copy of the email, check the "Send a copy to myself' box.
>
> **Enter a recipient's email address** in the text box.
>
> **To add multiple addresses,** click "Add Recipient" after each address entry. All recipients will appear in the "Recipient List."

9. Click the "Send Your Card" button in the bottom-right corner.

> In the "Thank You" page that opens, choose to "Send same iCard" to someone else, or "Return to Categories" to create another card.

Click here to go back and make changes to your card.

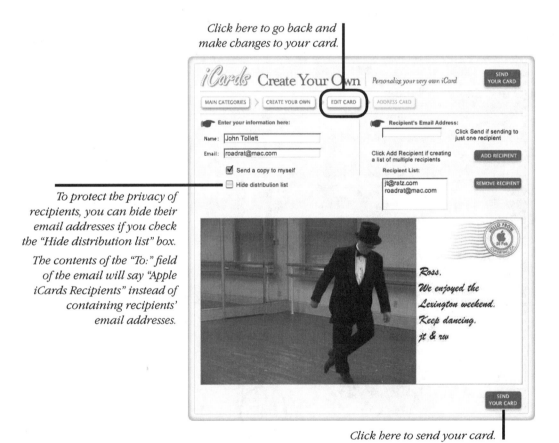

To protect the privacy of recipients, you can hide their email addresses if you check the "Hide distribution list" box.

The contents of the "To:" field of the email will say "Apple iCards Recipients" instead of containing recipients' email addresses.

Click here to send your card.

HomePage 11

While some people complain that a .Mac account costs $99 a year, I think this one feature called **HomePage** is worth many times more than the price tag, even if it didn't include all the other powerful tools and features. Speaking as a professional web designer, I'd say the templates that come with HomePage are the best-looking template-based web page authoring solutions you'll find anywhere. Being able to publish a collection of photos or streaming QuickTime movies on a great-looking page within minutes is not just convenient, it's amazing. And fun. The flexibility to easily update and rearrange pages makes web site management enjoyable rather than a time-consuming headache.

The ability to publish photos, text, and movies in a professionally designed environment will inspire your creative thinking. If you're a creative professional, the simplicity and elegance of HomePage will inspire ideas for more efficient communication with your clients and associates.

Add Photos and QuickTime Movies to iDisk

HomePage accesses all photos and movies from three folders on your iDisk: the Pictures folder, the Movies folder, and the Library folder.

To make photos available for use in HomePage, log in to your iDisk (see Chapter 9) and drag individual photos or an entire folder of photos from your computer to the **Pictures** folder on your iDisk.

If you plan to use movies on your HomePage, drag QuickTime movies from your computer to the **Movies** folder on your iDisk.

Use images from Apple's Image Library

Some Themes, such as "Newsletter," offer access to Apple's Image Library in case you don't have pictures of your own to use. You can select from those that Apple provides in iDisk's **Image Library** folder. When you see a photo box in a template with the "Choose" button, click the button and select one of your own photos or select the "Image Library" folder to choose an image.

Click a template photo's "Choose" button to access the Image Library folder.

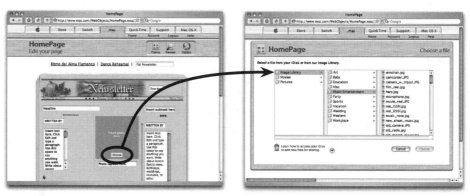

A file-size reminder

When you drag photos to the Pictures folder on your iDisk, you can use those photos on web pages. But make sure the images you place in the Pictures folder are reasonable file sizes—the smaller an image is, the faster it will download to a web browser. HomePage automatically creates small thumbnail versions of photos for most pages, but those thumbnails link to the original full-sized photo that you put in the Pictures folder. If the original photos in the Pictures folder are unnecessarily large, some of your web pages will be painfully slow to download, plus you'll fill up your allotted server storage space very quickly.

Ideally, photos destined for a web page should be saved in a JPEG format, have a resolution of 72 ppi, and a maximum size of 640 x 480 pixels.

Build a Web Site with HomePage

With **HomePage** you can easily create and publish a single web page, an entire web site, or several sites. Choose from a variety of beautiful themes that are designed to display photo albums, QuickTime movies, résumés, newsletters, invitations, and more.

1. From the .Mac web page (**www.mac.com**), click the "HomePage" icon.

2. Enter your Member Name and Password in the .Mac login window (immediately below) to access the HomePage opening page, from which you can build a single web page or a collection of pages.

The login window.

Click one of the theme tabs that seems to be a good fit with the type of web site you want to create. Each theme provides multiple design styles for you to choose from.

Choose a design style to use with your theme.

—continued

3. When you choose a design style from the Photo Album theme, the "Choose a folder" window opens. This window shows the photos in the Pictures folder of your iDisk. Choose a folder of photos to place in your new HomePage Photo Album, then click "Choose."

   If no folders of photos are showing, it means you have not yet copied any from your computer to the Pictures folder on your iDisk.

   See Chapter 9, or click the small button in the bottom-left corner to "Learn how to access your iDisk."

This folder is automatically on my iDisk.

The middle column shows the folder I copied to my iDisk.

The far-right column shows the contents of the folder.

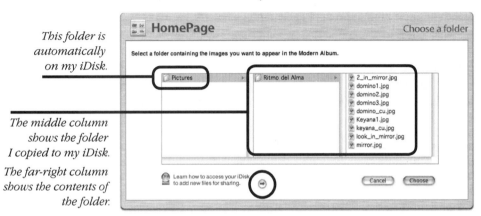

4. A page based on your theme choice opens (below). Click the "Edit" icon to open an editable version of the page (next page).

5. Edit the headline, text, or captions. You can also choose between a two- or three-column layout, change the Theme, or Preview the page. When you're satisfied with the results, click the "Preview" or "Publish" icon.

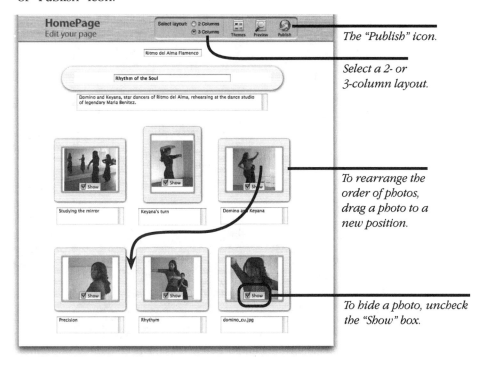

The "Publish" icon.

Select a 2- or 3-column layout.

To rearrange the order of photos, drag a photo to a new position.

To hide a photo, uncheck the "Show" box.

After you click "Publish," the message below opens to give you the web address of your new site. Click the iCard button to send announcements to friends.

6. Click "Return to HomePage" to add more pages or sites (next page).

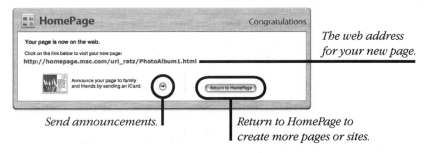

The web address for your new page.

Send announcements.

Return to HomePage to create more pages or sites.

—continued

7. Return to HomePage and you'll see it looks different now. The Photo Album we just created is listed in the "Pages" pane.

You'll certainly want to add more pages to your site. To add another page, Click the "Add" button beneath the "Pages" pane.

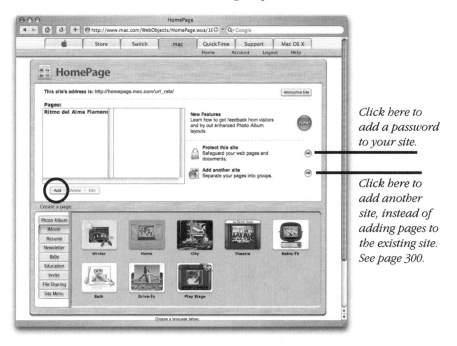

Click here to add a password to your site.

Click here to add another site, instead of adding pages to the existing site. See page 300.

Add another page

For this example, the next page we add will contain a QuickTime movie. If you haven't copied a QuickTime movie you want to use to the Movies folder on your iDisk, do so now. (See Chapter 3 for information on editing movies and exporting as QuickTime for the Internet.)

1. From the Theme window that opens (below), select a theme and design style. When you click the design style icon, the new page template opens (next page).

The "iMovie" theme is chosen. Click on a design style.

2. Click the "Edit" icon to open an editable version of the page.

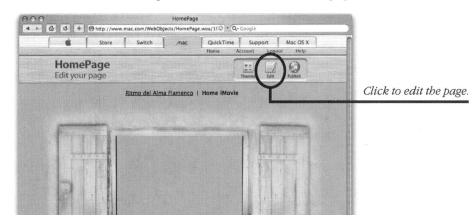

Click to edit the page.

3. Click the "Choose" button (below) in the QuickTime window to select a QuickTime movie (next page). Type new text in the text boxes.

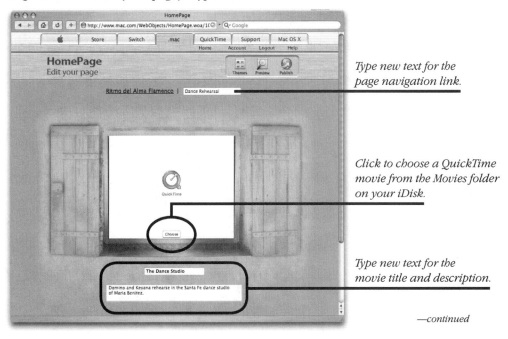

Type new text for the page navigation link.

Click to choose a QuickTime movie from the Movies folder on your iDisk.

Type new text for the movie title and description.

—continued

4. From the "Choose a file" window, choose a QuickTime movie that has been copied to the Movies folder on your iDisk. Click "Choose" to place the selected movie on the iMovie page.

A preview of the selected QuickTime movie.

No movies in the Movies folder means you have not yet copied any from your computer to the Movies folder on your iDisk.

See Chapter 9, or click the small button in the bottom-left corner to "Learn how to access your iDisk."

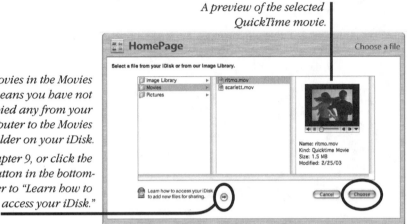

5. After the QuickTime movie is selected, a preview window opens (below). Click the "Edit" icon to make additional changes, or click the "Publish" icon to publish the page on the Internet.

Click "Edit" to make additional changes.　　*Click "Publish" to publish to the Internet.*

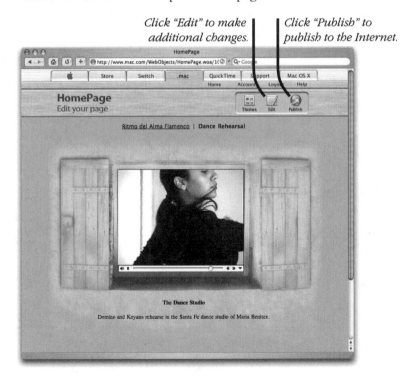

▼ After you click "Publish," a dialog box will open asking you whether you want to visit the new page or return to HomePage.

▼ Return to HomePage and notice the "Pages" pane has added the new page to the list (below). As you add pages, you can change which page is the first page of the site (the Start page) by dragging a page name to the top of the list. The bold text indicates the Start page.

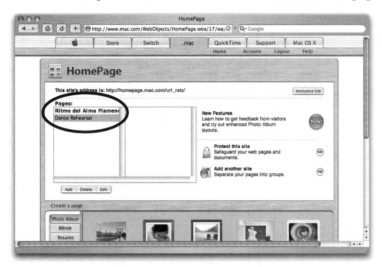

Add password-protection to a site

You can enable password protection to restrict who can visit your site.

1. Select a site in the "Sites" list of HomePage, as shown above and on page 292.

2. Click the small arrow button next to the padlock icon.

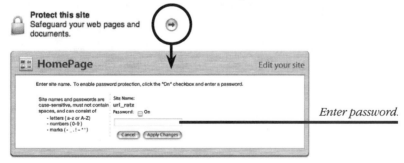

Enter password.

3. Click the "Password: On" checkbox.

4. Enter a password, using the rules listed in the window.

5. Click "Apply Changes."

Create a Site Menu for Your Existing Pages

After you've made a couple of individual pages, you can create a **Site Menu** page. The Site Menu page contains a link for each page you've ceated (photo albums, movie pages, newsletters, etc.). It provides an overview of the entire site's content. Sounds complex? No, it's incredibly easy.

1. In the main HomePage window, click the "Site Menu" tab (shown below).

2. Click one of the design style icons (circled below) to open "Edit your page," a page that contains an image link for each page of the selected site.

   In this example, the two pages we've created are considered a "site." Later we'll explain how to create new sites (see page 300).

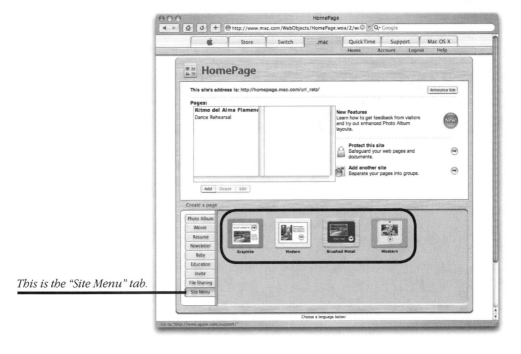

This is the "Site Menu" tab.

3. To customize the text, to add more items, or to delete items from this site menu page, click the "Edit" icon (shown below).

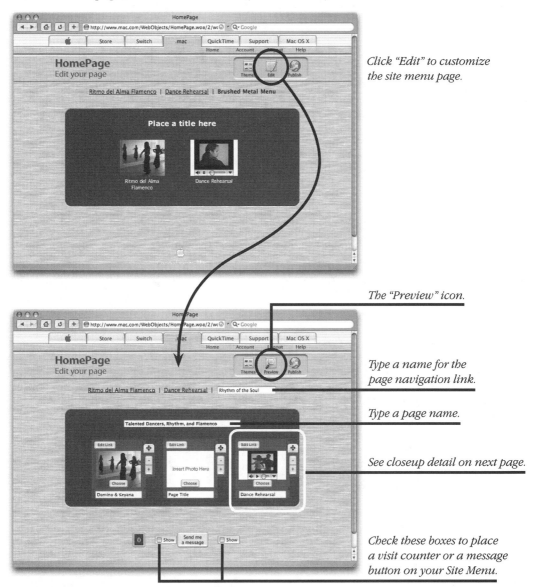

Click "Edit" to customize the site menu page.

The "Preview" icon.

Type a name for the page navigation link.

Type a page name.

See closeup detail on next page.

Check these boxes to place a visit counter or a message button on your Site Menu.

4. After making your edits, click the "Preview" icon (above) to see the final page design. This example has just three image links, but you can add as many as necessary. Keep in mind that too many images on the Site Menu page creates a slow-loading, long-scrolling page.

—continued

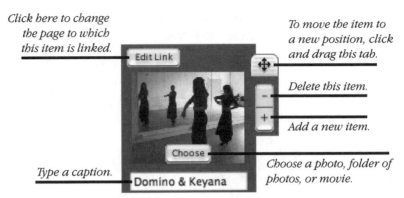

Click here to change the page to which this item is linked.

To move the item to a new position, click and drag this tab.

Delete this item.

Add a new item.

Type a caption.

Choose a photo, folder of photos, or movie.

Closeup view from previous page.

5. Before you click the "Publish" icon, you need to set this page as the Start page. It has links to all the pages of the site, so it makes sense that it should be the first page you see.

Click the "HomePage" link in the top-left corner to open HomePage (shown below).

The "HomePage" link.

Click here to return to HomePage, as shown on the next page.

6. Locate the name of the site menu page in the "Pages" pane, then drag the name to the top of the list. The name will change to bold type, indicating it is now the Start page.

7. To publish the page, click the "Edit" button beneath the Pages pane, then click the "Publish" icon on the "Edit" page that opens.

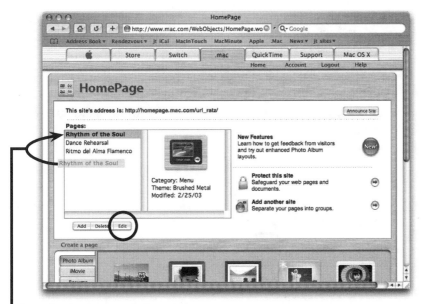

Drag the site menu page just created to the top of the list to make it the Start page.

Create another Site

You can add a variety of unrelated pages to your site, but it's much better to organize your pages into related groups, called Sites. When you create a new Site, HomePage changes to show both a "Sites" pane and a "Pages" pane, as shown on the next page.

To create a new site:

1. Go to HomePage.

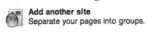

2. Click the small arrow button next to "Add another site."

3. Enter a site name in the "Create a site" window. To include password protection, click the "Password: On" box.

4. Click "Create Site."

5. The top section of HomePage now includes a "Sites" pane in addition to the "Pages" pane, as shown below.

6. To add pages to the new site, select the site name, then click the "Add" button under the "Pages" pane.

Select a site.

Click "Add" to add pages to the site.

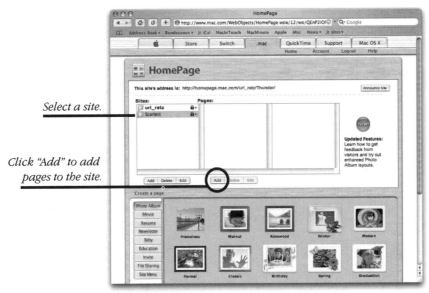

Site management

HomePage makes it easy to manage your sites. Use the buttons beneath the "Sites" pane and the "Pages" pane to add, delete, and edit pages or sites. Change themes or page designs whenever you want. Rearrange the order of pages in a site, or move pages from one site to another site.

- ▼ **To add pages** to the new site, select the site name, then click the "Add" button under the "Pages" pane and create new pages. As you add to the new site, the page names are added to the "Pages" pane.

- ▼ **To delete pages** from a site, select the page name, then click the "Delete" button beneath the "Page" pane.

- ▼ **To move pages** from one site to another, select a page in the "Pages" list and drag it to a Site folder in the "Sites" list.

- ▼ **To add new sites,** click the "Add" button beneath the "Sites" pane, as explained on the opposite page.

- ▼ **To delete a site,** select its name and click the "Delete" button beneath the "Sites" pane.

- ▼ **To add, change, or remove a password** for a site in the "Sites" pane, click the "Edit" button beneath the "Sites" pane.

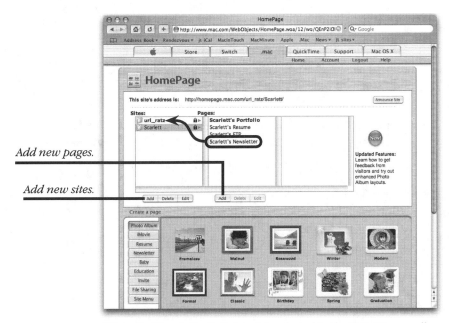

Add new pages.

Add new sites.

When the "Scarlett" site (above) is selected in the "Sites" pane, all the pages associated with that site are shown in the "Pages" pane. This example shows how a page can be dragged from its current location (in the "Scarlett" site) to another site (the "url_ratz" site).

This is a final page published on the Internet. To add more content later, log in to HomePage, select the page in the Pages list, then click the "Edit" button.

Buy More iDisk Space

You can create multiple sites with HomePage, limited only by the amount of your iDisk storage space on Apple's servers. You can **purchase** up to one gigabyte of **iDisk storage** in addition to the 100 megabytes provided with your .Mac membership.

To upgrade your iDisk storage, go to the .Mac web page and click the "iDisk" icon at the top of the page. Click the "Upgrade" button to open a web page in which you can buy more iDisk storage space.

You can also use a very handy utility called **iDisk Utility.** If it's not on your computer you can download it from the .Mac web site at **www.mac.com.**

At the moment, extra storage costs this much:

300 MB:	*$100/year*
500 MB:	*$180/year*
1000 MB:	*$350/year*

For full details on iDisk and iDisk Utility, see Chapter 9.

1. Open iDisk Utility, then click the "iDisk Storage" icon in the toolbar.

2. Click the "Buy More" button in the bottom-right corner to open a page in which you can buy more iDisk storage space.

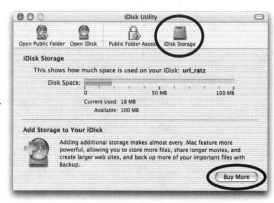

WebMail

Your .Mac account includes a **WebMail** account that enables you to check your mail or send mail from any computer with an Internet connection anywhere in the world. You can check your .Mac email account, or set up WebMail to check any other email accounts you have.

WebMail's Address Book can give you online access to all your contacts if you use iSync to synchronize with the Address Book on your computer.

This chapter walks you through how to set up your .Mac WebMail account, check your email, send new messages, sync Address Book, set preferences for WebMail and Address Book, and more.

Apple's documentation sometimes refers to WebMail as Mac.com WebMail, and at other times as .Mac (dot Mac) WebMail. We've decided to use "Mac.com" because that's what you see on the official icon (above). *But* sometimes we have to use .Mac when we refer to that term as it's used in a window or dialog box. Just keep in mind that .Mac and Mac.com are the same thing.

Call it what you will, WebMail is still another good reason your .Mac account is such a great value.

Mac.com WebMail

When you sign up for a .Mac account, you get a Mac.com **email** account with fifteen megabytes of storage space for your email messages (which is a lot of email). See the Mail chapter (Chapter 5) for details about your .Mac account and how to set it up to send and receive email—it's great. **The advantage of WebMail** is that you can check all your mail from all of your accounts from any web browser on any computer anywhere in the world.

It's easy to start using Mac.com WebMail:

1. Go to the Mac.com web site, then click the "Mail" icon in the toolbar.

2. Log in to your .Mac account with your member name and password.
3. Your personal Mac.com WebMail page opens, as shown below. From this web page and other linked pages you can perform all your email tasks just like at home, even if you happen to be in Ankara.

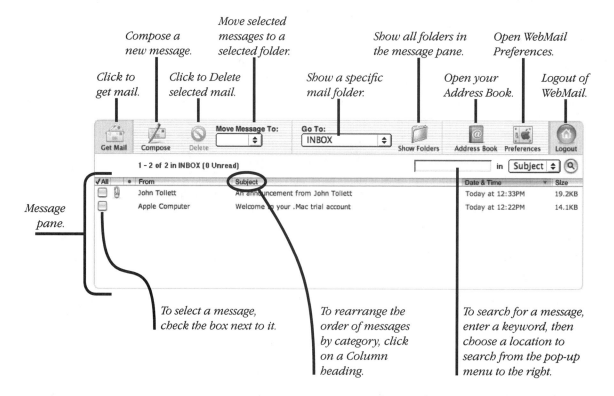

Compose a new message.

Move selected messages to a selected folder.

Show all folders in the message pane.

Open WebMail Preferences.

Click to get mail.

Click to Delete selected mail.

Show a specific mail folder.

Open your Address Book.

Logout of WebMail.

Message pane.

To select a message, check the box next to it.

To rearrange the order of messages by category, click on a Column heading.

To search for a message, enter a keyword, then choose a location to search from the pop-up menu to the right.

Get your Mail and Read It

1. Click "Get Mail" to collect any new messages and show them in the "Inbox" message pane, along with any other existing messages.

2. Click on a message in the list to open it in its own page.

Compose and Send a Message

1. Click the "Compose" icon to open a new message page.

2. Type an email address in the "To" field.

    Or choose an addressee from the "Quick Addresses" pop-up menu. The names that show up in this menu are set in "Address Book" by putting a check in the "Quick Address" column to the right of a name, as shown to the right. You can store up to ten names in the "Quick Addresses" pop-up menu.

The email addresses that you check appear in the "Quick Addresses" pop-up menus.

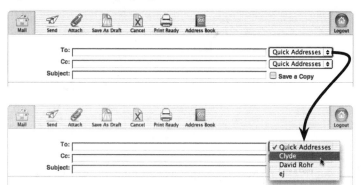

Choose a name to automatically place the email address in the "To," "Cc," or "Bcc" field.

Or click the "Address Book" icon in the toolbar. Address Book opens, and shows pop-up menus in the "Destination" column. Click one of the pop-up menus and choose one of the address field options to have that person's email address automatically entered into the selected address field (To, Cc, or Bcc). You can set multiple pop-up menus to automatically enter email addresses into the various address fields of an email. When you go back to the Composition page, your selections are shown in the various address fields of the email form.

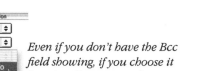

Even if you don't have the Bcc field showing, if you choose it here it will appear in the message.

Cc stands for Carbon Copy, or Courtesy Copy.

*Bcc stands for Blind Carbon/Courtesy Copy. Any name you put in the Bcc field **will not** be visible to anyone else receiving the message.*

Attach a File to a Message

Below are instructions for attaching a file that's on your own computer.

1. Click the "Attach" icon in the toolbar to open the "Attach" page.

2. Click "Browse," use the "Open" window to navigate to a file on your computer you want to attach, then click "Open."

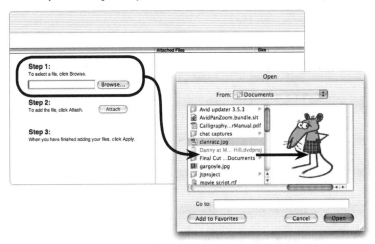

3. Click "Attach" to add the file to your message. Repeat steps 1 and 2 to add additional files. The name of the attached files appear in the "Attached Files" column. **To remove a file,** click the "Remove" button. To finish adding the attachments, click "Apply" to return to the "Composition" page.

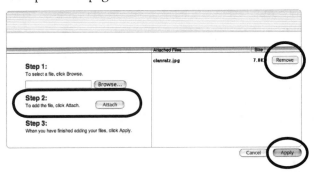

4. Your email header shows a list of attached files. Address the email, type your message, then click "Send."

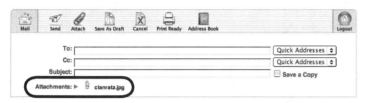

The email with its attachment, as received in Mac.com WebMail's Inbox.

The "Go To" Pop-up Menu

The "Go To" pop-up menu in the main toolbar of WebMail lets you choose which folder's content shows in the message pane, such as INBOX, Deleted Messages, or Sent Messages. If you've set the option in Preferences to "Check Other POP Mail" (as explained on the following page), the other POP email account will be available from this menu.

Set WebMail preferences

On the WebMail page, click the "Preferences" icon to open the Preferences page, as shown below. Set the various options for viewing and sending messages. While most are self-explanatory, here are a few clarifications.

Composing: Add Bcc Header adds a Blind carbon copy field to the address section of a new message. The identity of those in a Bcc field is hidden from all recipients.

Viewing: Show "All Headers" Option shows all the email header information that is available. The header information is usually edited to show only the most relevant information.

Account: Email Forwarding lets you designate an email address to which your mail for this account is forwarded. **Auto Reply** lets you set an automatic response to emails. **Check Other POP Mail** enables you to check other mail accounts from WebMail.

WebMail's Preferences page lets you monitor how much email storage is available in your Mac.com account.

To create a custom signature that accompanies every message, choose a photo and type a signature message.

Forward email sent to this account to any other email address you choose.

The "Incoming Mail Server" is the service through which you get this mail. For instance, your email account at attbi.com would come through mail.attbi.com. Check with your provider if "mail.domain.com" doesn't work for you.

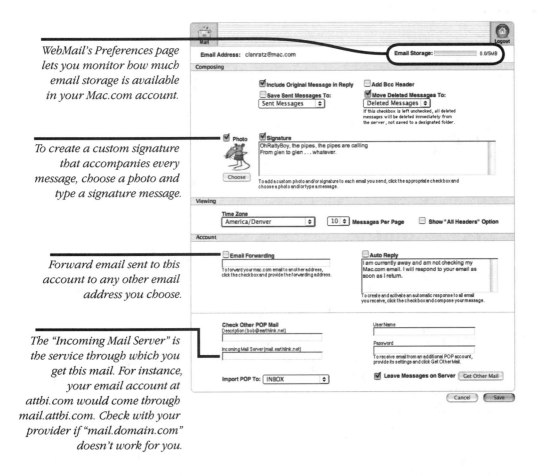

Sync Your Address Book

In addition to receiving or sending messages, WebMail includes Address Book to provide online access to all your contacts. Using iSync, you can sync the WebMail Address Book to the Address Book on your Desktop so you always have access to current contact information, no matter where you are. See Chapter 14 for details about iSync.

To sync your Address Book (part 1):

1. Click the "Address Book" icon on the WebMail page.

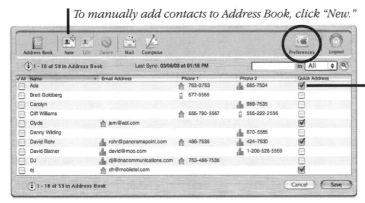

To manually add contacts to Address Book, click "New."

To show a person's name in the "Quick Addresses" pop-up menu when you compose a new message, click her checkbox.

2. Click the "Preferences" icon on the Address Book page, circled above, to get the page shown below.

3. Click the checkbox to "Turn on .Mac Address Book Synchronization."

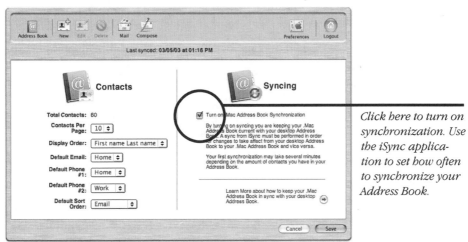

Click here to turn on synchronization. Use the iSync application to set how often to synchronize your Address Book.

—continued

To set up synchronization (part 2):

You must download the software iSync to complete the process, and then you have to "register" your Mac to the .Mac synchronization server (if you need more details than what is provided below, please see Chapter 14).

4. Download iSync from the Mac.com site, if you haven't already.

5. Make sure you are connected to the Internet. Open iSync.

6. Click the ".mac" icon on the iSync panel to expand the window and show the available options.

7. If you have not yet registered your Mac, click the button to "Register" (not shown below), name your computer, and in a minute it's done. You'll see the window shown below.

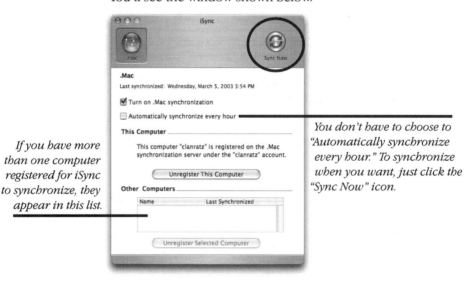

If you have more than one computer registered for iSync to synchronize, they appear in this list.

You don't have to choose to "Automatically synchronize every hour." To synchronize when you want, just click the "Sync Now" icon.

8. Check "Turn on .Mac synchronization" if it's not already checked.

9. Click the "Sync Now" icon, up at the top-right.

The synchronization takes a few moments, depending on the size of Address Book on your Mac. When iSync is finished, the WebMail Address Book is a duplicate of the version on your computer.

Backup

Sooner or later, every computer user learns (usually the hard way) the wisdom of regularly backing up important files. It's a simple concept, but most of us suffer from a human operating system bug called "optimism." We think our data is safe. Instead, we should assume the worst is going to happen—corrupted files, theft, fire, lost files, accidentally trashed files, mistakenly overwritten files—and prepare accordingly.

A Mac.com membership includes **Backup,** your personal software for effortlessly backing up the files you can't afford to lose. You can back up to removable media, such as CDs and DVDs, to your iDisk, or to both for extra security and peace of mind.

Some files are too large to fit on iDisk, a CD, or even a DVD. Backup can break large files apart and use multiple discs to create a backup copy. When you need to restore such files, Backup rejoins them on your hard disk.

Backup's *QuickPick* feature makes it easy to back up bundles of files, such as all the files on your Desktop, or in the iTunes Library (to include playlists and song files), without having to find the files on your hard disk.

Use Backup to schedule regular, automatic backups to your iDisk for files that change often.

Even if you use other backup solutions for large projects, such as copying files to an external drive, Backup is convenient and ideal for making archival copies of the included QuickPick packages, such as iCal calendars, Address Book contacts, and Keychain passwords.

Important Note about Backups

If you have very important files, **don't rely on one backup.** Make at least two, and store them in different locations. People have had their offices broken into and all of the computers stolen, plus all the backup disks. A fire has the same result. So make at least two backups and send one to your mother or your bank vault or your east-coast office.

Download and Install Backup

Before you can start using Backup, you must first **download** it from Apple's Mac.com web site.

1. Go to the Mac.com web site (**www.mac.com**) and click the "Download" icon (the red umbrella) on the web page's toolbar.

2. You'll be asked to log in using your Mac.com membership name and password.

3. From the "Backup" page that opens, click the "Download Backup" icon (shown below) to open the "Download Backup" page.

Note: Turn off Energy Saver before you use Backup, or Sleep might interrupt the process.

4. Click the Download *link* for the version of Backup that is compatible with your version of Mac OS X, circled below.

5. After downloading is finished, install the software as usual (double-click the .dmg or .pkg file and follow the directions).

6. Find the Backup icon in the Applications folder, then double-click its icon to open the Backup window, as shown on the next page.

The Backup Window

The main **Backup window** puts a lot of information and functionality into a compact space.

▼ From the **pop-up menu,** choose the location to which you want to save backed-up files. **Or** choose to "Restore" backed-up files and copy them to your hard disk.

▼ The **QuickPick** items in the "Items" column (package icons) are *groups* of files that are all backed up at once.

▼ When you choose "Back up to iDisk" in the pop-up menu, the **status bar** shows how much space on your iDisk is used and how much space is available.

▼ Items that are *checked* in the **Back Up** column will be copied when you click the "Backup Now" button, or when a backup is scheduled.

▼ Click the **Show Toolbar** button (upper-right of the window) to reveal several additional tools (see page 316).

Tip: The pop-up menu allows you to choose to save files to your iDisk or to a removable disc (CD or DVD).

When **Backup to iDisk** is selected, the *iTunes QuickPick package* includes only *playlists,* due to the limited storage space that is available with iDisk storage.

When **Backup to CD/DVD** is selected, the *iTunes QuickPick package* includes the entire *Library* of song files.

The *disc spanning* technology that Backup uses to copy large files to multiple discs means virtually unlimited storage.

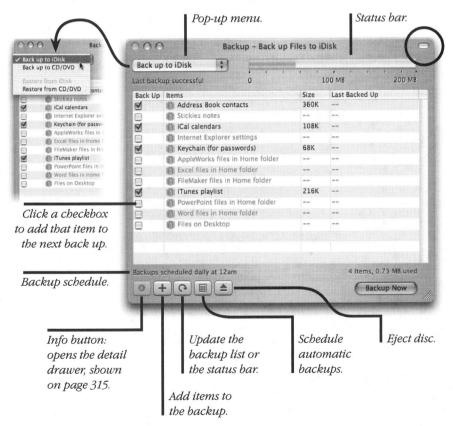

Pop-up menu.

Status bar.

Click a checkbox to add that item to the next back up.

Backup schedule.

Info button: opens the detail drawer, shown on page 315.

Add items to the backup.

Update the backup list or the status bar.

Schedule automatic backups.

Eject disc.

Add Items to the List

The easiest way to **add files or folders** to the backup list is to *drag* them to the Backup window. You're not actually moving the files yet, just creating a list of the files you want to backup.

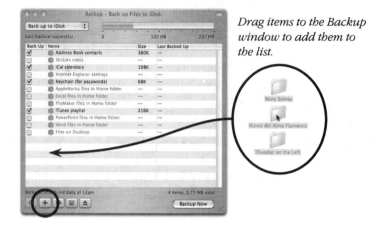

Drag items to the Backup window to add them to the list.

Or click the "Add items" button (the plus sign, circled above) to make a Finder sheet slide down from the top of the window (shown below). Find a file or folder you want to add to the list, then click "Choose."

Delete items from the backup list

To remove an item from the backup list, select a file, then press "Delete." QuickPick items (the package icons) cannot be removed.

The Details Drawer

To open the **Details drawer,** select a file or folder in the backup list, then click the "Info" button (the icon with the letter "**i**"). The Details drawer slides open to show information about your selection. If you selected a **folder,** the drawer shows the contents of the folder and any subfolders that may be present. If you selected a *QuickPick* item (one with a "package" icon) the drawer shows the contents of the QuickPick package.

From the "Show" pop-up menu, choose "General Information" or "Backup Information."

Exclude individual items from the backup

To exclude items *in a folder* from being backed up:

1. Select a folder in the backup list called "Items," as shown to the right.

2. Click the "Info" button to open the Details drawer.

3. In the Details drawer, uncheck the items you don't want to back up.

To show the contents of a selected (highlighted) item in the list, click this "Info" button.

A dash indicates some items in the folder are not checked and will not be included in the backup.

Show Additional Tools

To show a hidden toolbar with **additional tools,** click the small button in the upper-right corner of the Backup window.

Click this button to hide or show the toolbar.

▼ **Find:** Open a "Search" window in which you can search for files or folders you want to back up. From the "Search Results" window, drag the desired file to the Backup window.

▼ **Preferences:** Turn "Mirroring" on or off.

When Mirroring is **on,** every time you backup to your iDisk, Backup will check the existing files on your iDisk for matching files on your hard disk. If it does not find matching files because you deleted them from your hard disk (or changed their names), those same files will be removed from the Backup folder on your iDisk. In other words, it will "mirror" what it sees on your hard disk.

Be careful with this option, especially if you have automatic backup turned on (page 319), because if you accidentally throw away a file from your hard disk or it becomes corrupted and you toss it, Backup will delete it from your iDisk as well, defeating the purpose of having the backup file.

▼ **Log:** Open a text file record of your previous backups.

▼ **Buy Media:** Open the Apple web site to buy CDs or DVDs and have them delivered to your home or office.

Back up to Your iDisk

When you're ready to backup files, you can choose your **iDisk** location to save files into, depending on how much space is available. If there's not enough room on your iDisk, the status bar is colored red. If necessary, click the "Buy Storage" icon in the toolbar to buy more space (it's an annual fee).

See the following page for backing up to a CD or DVD.

The best reason to backup files to your iDisk is so you can access them anywhere in the world. Everything will go into a folder called "Backup."

1. From the pop-up menu, choose **Back up to iDisk** to save your files to the Backup folder on your iDisk.
2. Select the items in the backup list you want to back up.
3. Click "Backup Now."

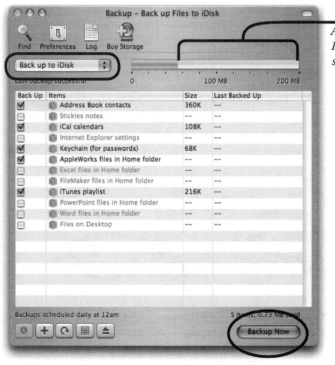

Available iDisk space. *I upgraded my disk space to 200 megabytes.*

Tips:

To select all items in the backup list, from the Edit menu choose "Select All."

To check all checkboxes in the backup list, from the Edit menu choose "Check All."

To **uncheck all** items in the backup list, from the Edit menu choose "Uncheck All."

4. A window tracks the progress of items as they upload to your iDisk.

Back up to a CD or DVD

*See the previous
page for backing up
to your iDisk.*

You must have an internal CD-RW drive or a SuperDrive to use this option.

There are several reasons why you might want to choose to back up files to an optical disc (CD or DVD) instead of to your iDisk: You may not always have access to an Internet connection and your iDisk; your iDisk probably doesn't have enough space to hold all your backups; many files (especially iMovie and iDVD files) may be too large for even the largest iDisk configuration. You can buy up to one gigabyte of iDisk space, but movies and DVD projects can be much larger than that.

1. From the pop-up menu, choose **Back up to CD/DVD.**

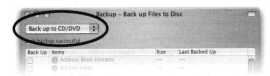

2. Select the items in the list that you want to archive.

3. Check the "Estimate of Required Discs" in the bottom-left corner of the Backup window, circled below, to see how many CDs or DVDs are required to backup the selected items.

*Backup's estimate as to how
many discs you'll need
is just an estimate.*
**Make sure you have extra
discs available,** *just in case!*

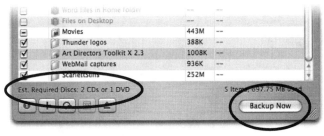

4. Click "Backup Now."

5. Insert a blank CD or DVD into the drive.

6. In the window that opens, name your backup (right).

7. If the backup requires more than one disc, the current disc ejects when finished and a prompt notifies you to insert another disc. **The last disc burned is the "master" disc of the backup set.** Label the last disc of the set as the master disc. When you want to restore the data at a later date, Backup will ask for the master disc to start the restore.

8. Click OK when Backup is finished.

Schedule Your Backups

You can schedule **automatic backups** of files to your iDisk. Of course, you must be connected to the Internet for an automatic backup.

1. Click the "Schedule" button in the bottom-left corner of the window. The schedule sheet slides down into view.

2. **Schedule iDisk Backups:** Choose "Daily" or "Weekly."

3. **Frequency Options:** Choose how often and when. If you chose "Weekly," you'll get an option to choose the day of the week. Click OK.

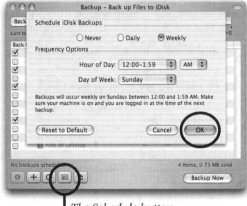

The Schedule button.

Remove Items or Clear Your iDisk

To remove a backed up item from your iDisk, from the pop-up menu, choose "Restore from iDisk." Select the item, then go to the Edit menu and choose "Remove from List." *You cannot go to your iDisk and remove files directly.*

To clear the iDisk Backup folder of its contents, from the pop-up menu, choose "Restore from iDisk." Then go to the Edit menu and choose "Clear iDisk Backup Folder."

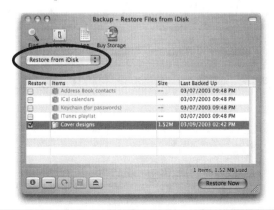

Restore Files from an iDisk

To copy backed-up files from your iDisk back to your hard disk:

1. From the pop-up menu, select "Restore from iDisk."

2. In the "Restore" window, choose items in the list to restore.

3. Click "Restore Now."

From any computer that can log in to your iDisk (use the iDisk Utility, if necessary; see Chapter 9), you can drag files from the Backup folder in your iDisk to your hard disk. This will never remove the original file from the iDisk—it just makes a copy. (You cannot drag files *into* the Backup folder.)

Restore Files from a CD or DVD

To copy backed-up files from a CD or DVD back to your hard disk:

1. From the pop-up menu, select "Restore from CD/DVD."

2. Backup will ask for the master disc of the backup set. Insert it. (If you don't know which one is the master disc, see page 318.)

3. In the "Restore" window, choose items in the list to restore.

4. Click "Restore Now."

*Preparation
works much better
than optimism.*

—John Tollett

iSync

iSync

iSync is an easy and convenient way to keep your iCal calendars and your Address Book information synchronized between multiple Macs. You can also synchronize your iCal and Address Book information between your computer and your Mac.com account.

iSync can even synchronize iCal calendars and contact information with iPods, Palm OS devices, and some Bluetooth-enabled wireless phones.

A Palm OS device is any PDA (Personal Digital Assistant) that uses the Palm operating system. To use iSync with one of these devices, the device must have Palm Desktop 4.0 (or later) installed.

In addition to a Mac.com membership, iSync requires a PowerBook G4, iMac, eMac, or Power Mac G4, all running Mac OS X, version 10.2.2 (or later).

If you can't stand the idea of manually re-entering all your calendar and

contact information on another computer or in your Mac.com account's Address Book, download this free application and get synchronized.

The iSync window shows any devices you have added to iSync.

Download, Install, and Register

To start using iSync, you must download and install it.

1. Go to Apple's iSync web site at **www.apple.com/isync**.

2. Click the "Download iSync" icon.

3. From the "Get iSync" web page, fill out the short registration form for iSync (name and email address), then click the "Download iSync" button.

4. After the download is complete, follow the instructions in the installation window that opens.

5. In the Applications folder, locate iSync and double-click its icon to open it.

6. Register your computer to the Mac.com synchronization server: Click the "Register" button (circled below). In the next pane that appears type a name to identify your computer, then click "Continue."

After iSync installation is finished, you can drag these files from your Desktop to the Trash.

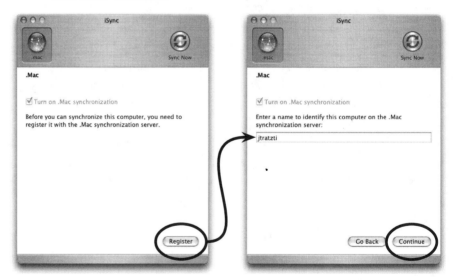

7. When registration is finished, select "Turn on .Mac synchronization," as shown on the next page.

▼ To register more than one computer to a Mac.com account, you must perform the registration process from each individual computer. All computers registered to a specific Mac.com account are listed in the "Other Computers" pane, shown below.

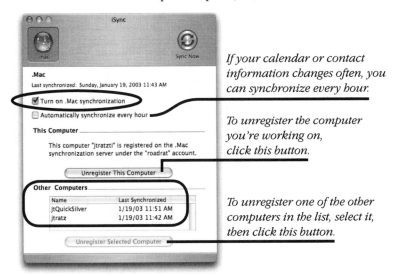

If your calendar or contact information changes often, you can synchronize every hour.

To unregister the computer you're working on, click this button.

To unregister one of the other computers in the list, select it, then click this button.

Mac-to-Mac Synchronization

Many people work on two or more computers; one at the office and one at home, or there may be multiple computers in one office or home. To synchronize all the computers so they have the same Address Book and iCal calendar information, perform a Mac-to-Mac synchronization.

1. Open iSync if it's not already open.

2. Click the "Sync Now" button.

During a sync, the "Sync Now" button changes to the "Cancel Sync" button.

The first time you sync, iSync copies the Address Book and iCal data from the computer you're sitting at to Apple's synchronization server. The next time you click "Sync Now" your computer compares the data to see if changes have been made since the last sync. If changes are detected, you receive an alert like the one below, telling you what changes are to be made and to what device (your computer or the .Mac synchronization server) the changes will be made.

3. Click "Proceed" in the "Safeguard" window (below) to finish syncing.

4. Go to another Mac that you've registered (as described on the previous two pages), open iSync on that computer, then click "Sync Now." The iCal and Address Book information on the .Mac synchronization server is copied to the current computer. If iSync detects changes to a file on the server and on the computer, it will ask you which one to change.

Synchronization Tips

Below are a few tips and techniques that can be helpful when using iSync.

▼ **If you change your mind** after performing a synchronization, you can **revert** to the previous version of files: From the Devices menu, choose "Revert To Last Sync...." In the alert window that opens, click the "Revert to Last Sync" button.

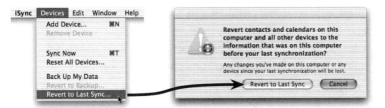

▼ If you want to **replace** the iCal and Address Book information on *all* computers and devices with the information on a *specific* computer or device, you can perform a **one-way synchronization:** From the Devices menu, choose "Reset All Devices...." Then choose the computer or device that you want to use as the source of data to transfer to all other computers and devices that you've added to iSync.

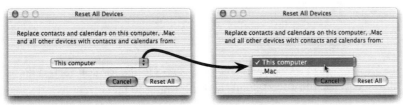

Other devices you've added to iSync show in this pop-up menu.

iSync Preferences

To set your iSync preferences, from the iSync application menu, choose "Preferences...."

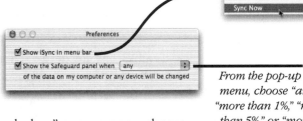

▼ "Show iSync in menu bar" places an iSync icon in the upper-right corner of the menu bar, giving easy access to the "Open" and "Sync Now" commands.

From the pop-up menu, choose "any," "more than 1%," "more than 5%," or "more than 10%."

▼ From the "Show the Safeguard panel when" pop-up menu, choose when the "Safeguard" window (previous page) appears.

Add Other Devices and Synchronize

iSync can also synchronize Address Book and iCal information to several other devices:

▾ **Palm OS devices** such as Palm Tungsten, Zire, the Handspring Treo and Visor, or the Sony Clié models.

▾ **iPod,** Apple's popular MP3 player.

▾ **Bluetooth-enabled wireless phones,** such as the Sony Ericsson T68i. The list of wireless phones that are compatible with iSync and Mac is a small one for the time being. As the popularity of Bluetooth technology grows, the list of options should expand.

For a current list of Bluetooth-compatible devices, visit **www.apple.com/ bluetooth**.

To add other devices to iSync:

1. From the "Devices" menu, choose "Add Device...."

2. The "Add Device" window opens and looks for connected iPods or wireless phones that are within range (30 feet).

3. Double-click any device that is discovered and shown in the pane above to add it to the iSync window.

iPod and iSync

If you previously set up your iPod to act as a FireWire drive and dragged your contact list or calendars to the hard disk, *delete those files before you go through the iSync process*—iSync can only do this correctly if it originally put the files it needs on your iPod.

Tip: To sync iPod, you must have iPod software version 1.2 (or later) installed.

Download the most current iPod software at **www.apple.com/ipod.**

1. Connect your iPod to your computer using the FireWire cable that came with your iPod.

2. Open iSync.

3. If iPod doesn't automatically appear in the iSync window, do this: From the "Devices" menu, choose "Add Device…," then double-click the iPod button in the "Add Device" window to add it to the iSync window.

4. In the iSync window, shown below, click the top checkbox to turn on iPod synchronization.

5. Choose the items you want to synchronize:

   Check the **Contacts** box to sync Adddress Book information.

   Check the **Calendars** box to sync iCal calendar information.

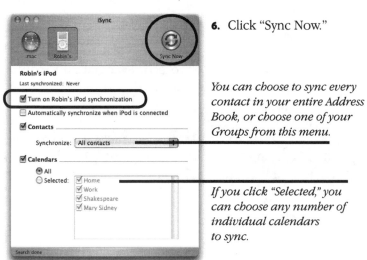

6. Click "Sync Now."

You can choose to sync every contact in your entire Address Book, or choose one of your Groups from this menu.

If you click "Selected," you can choose any number of individual calendars to sync.

—continued

7. The iSync "Safeguard" window alerts you that the synchronization will cause changes to be made to your contacts, and on which device the changes will be made. Because this is an iPod device, all changes are made to the iPod. iSync does not transfer files from iPod to a computer. The first time you sync your iPod, the number of changes may be large if you're transferring all your contacts from your computer to iPod. The number of changes in subsequent syncs may be much smaller if the contact information on your computer has not changed dramatically.

A "Safeguard" window opens for each category you selected in the iSync window ("Contacts" and "Calendars").

Click "Proceed" to continue with the synchronization.

The "Safeguard" window shows to which device changes will be made, and how many files will be added, deleted, or modified.

*This "Safeguard" window shows how many changes are to be made to the **contacts** information.*

*This "Safeguard" window shows how many changes are to be made to the **calendar** information.*

8. After you give permission to proceed, iSync grabs the requested information and transfers it to the iPod.

The synchronization bar shows the sync in progress.

9. When the sync is finished, the iSync status bar confirms with a "Synchronization complete" message.

As shown below, the iSync window now shows a "Last synchronized" date. To perform future syncs to iPod, open iSync, click the iPod button, then click "Sync Now."

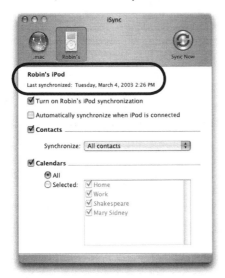

10. If you did *not* set up your iPod to act as a FireWire hard disk, then you can just disconnect it from the FireWire cable. The iPod screen should display a big checkmark and a message that it's okay to disconnect now.

If your iPod is acting as a hard disk (if you can see its icon either on your Desktop or in your Computer window), first **select and eject** the iPod icon, *then* disconnect it from the cable. (The iPod screen will display a warning symbol and a message that it is *not* okay to disconnect, which means you must eject the disk first.)

To determine whether your iPod acts as a FireWire hard disk or not:

Attach the iPod to your Mac.

Open iTunes.

Select the iPod in the "Source Pane."

In the bottom-right of the window, click the iPod button.

Either put a check in the box to "Enable FireWire disk use," **or** choose "Manually manage songs and playlists."

Click OK.

Palm OS devices and iSync

To sync a Palm OS device and computer, make sure Palm Desktop 4.0 (or later) is installed, along with iSync 1.0 Palm Conduit, which is available for download at **www.apple.com/isync**. You also need iCal 1.0.1 (or later).

Tip: You should plan to sync your Palm OS device with only one computer. If you add your Palm device to iSync on more than one computer, the information may not sync correctly.

1. Open the Palm HotSync Manager software.
2. From the "HotSync" menu, choose "Conduit Settings."
3. In the "Conduit Settings" window, double-click the "iSync Conduit," then select "Enable iSync for this Palm device."
4. Click OK. Quit HotSync Manager.
5. Open iSync.
6. Click the Palm OS device icon in the iSync window.
7. Click "Sync Now."

Bluetooth-enabled wireless phones and iSync

To sync a Bluetooth-enabled wireless phone, it must be in "discoverable" mode; the computer you want to sync the phone with must be Bluetooth-enabled or have a Bluetooth adapter connected.

Tip: You can sync your phone with only one computer. If you add your phone to more than one computer, the information may not sync correctly.

1. Open System Preferences, then click the Bluetooth Preferences icon. If you have Bluetooth installed, the icon automatically shows in the System Preferences window.
2. In the "Devices" pane, select your phone in the list, then click "Pair New Device" to pair your computer with the phone. A dialog appears to let you choose which services to use with your phone: select the checkbox labeled "Synchronize your Contacts and Calendar."

Tip: More information about Bluetooth and Bluetooth adapters can be found at **www.apple.com/ bluetooth**.

3. Open iSync.
4. If you don't see your phone icon in the iSync window, from the "Devices" menu, choose "Add Device...."
5. Double-click the phone in the "Add Device" window to add it to iSync.
6. Click "Sync Now."

Slides Publisher 15

Mac Slides Publisher

If you are a .Mac member, you can download a piece of software from www.mac.com called **.Mac Slides Publisher.** This software copies selected photos from your computer to your iDisk and publishes them as a screen-saver slideshow, complete with slow zooms and cross-dissolve transitions. Friends can subscribe to your slideshow and use it on their own computers as a screensaver.

Anyone running Mac OS X version 10.2 or later on their Mac, who is *not* a .Mac member can still "subscribe" to any .Mac member's slideshow—and they don't have to download any software to do it. All it takes is a simple setting in the Screen Effects System Preferences. Then, anytime they're connected to the Internet, they will receive any updates you've made to the the slideshow.

It's just another brilliant feature the Mac provides so you can share your iLife with friends, family, and associtates.

Download .Mac Slides Publisher

To create a slideshow that friends can subscribe to as a screensaver, first download the .Mac Slides Publisher software from the Mac.com web site.

To download the software so you can publish a slideshow for others to use (you must be a .Mac member):

1. Go to **www.mac.com.**

2. Log in with your screen name and password.

3. Click the link called "Downloads."

   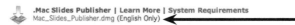

   ### ⬇ *Downloads*

   Get all your software, utilities, and games in one convenient place.

4. This takes you to a web page of downloadable software links. Click "Mac_Slides_Publisher.dmg" link to download the software.

   .Mac Slides Publisher | Learn More | System Requirements
   Mac_Slides_Publisher.dmg (English Only) ◀

Or click the "Learn More" link (shown in the link above) and visit the page shown below. From this page, click the "Download .Mac Slides" button to open the "Download .Mac Slides Publisher" page, as shown on the next page.

As time goes by, the software might be moved to another part of the web site or its name might change! If you don't find it here, poke around the .Mac site.

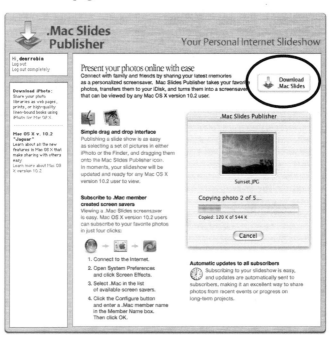

Click on the "Download" line (circled below) to start the download.

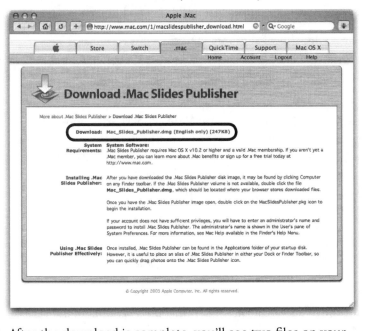

If you use Safari to download .Mac Slides Publisher, you might not see the .dmg file or the disk icon—Safari often takes care of cleaning up for you. You'll find the final file either in the Applications folder or on your Desktop.

5. After the download is complete, you'll see two files on your Desktop: **Mac_Slides_Publisher.dmg,** the compressed file you just finished downloading; and **Mac Slides Publisher,** a white disk icon, which is the version of the file after it has been uncompressed.

6. Double-click the "Mac Slides Publisher" icon, which opens the window shown below.

7. Double-click the "package" called "MacSlidesPublisher.pkg."

Mac_Slides_Publisher.dmg

Mac Slides Publisher

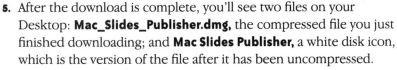

Mac Slides Publisher

8. You will be asked for an Administrator name and password (which is your name and password if you are the only user of this Mac). Provide that and click OK; the Installer window will open and install. To eject the disk image, drag the icon to the Trash.

9. You can throw away the .dmg file and eject the "Mac Slides Publisher" hard disk icon.

Ta da! This is the application that will let you publish slideshows, as explained on the following pages.

Publish a Slideshow

You must be a Mac.com member to publish a slideshow.

To publish a slideshow for others to use:

1. Follow the directions on the previous pages to download the .Mac Slides Publisher software.

2. Connect to the Internet, if you're not already.

3. Position the icon for the "Mac Slides Publisher" where you will be able to see it when you have pictures accessible or iPhoto open. You can drag the application icon to the Dock, into a Toolbar, or make an alias on the side of your Desktop (to make an alias, hold down Command and Option, then drag the application icon to the Desktop).

Mac Slides Publisher

*This is the application icon.
It's in your Applications folder
after you download and install it.*

Note: Every time you drop photos on the Publisher icon, you replace the existing slideshow with the new photos!

4. **To publish a slideshow,** simply drag photographs to the "Mac Slides Publisher" icon and drop them on top.

   ▼ The only files that will work are .JPG or .JPEG files (same things). This is the format a digital camera usually shoots pictures in.

   ▼ You can drag .JPG files from a Finder window (shown below) or from the iPhoto window (shown on the following page).

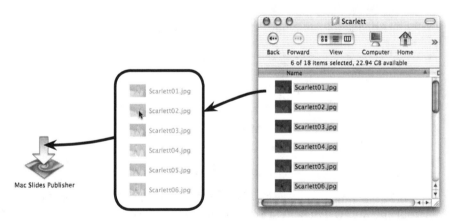

▼ You must drag over all the files you want in the slideshow at once— that is, you cannot drop two photos on the icon, then go get three more, etc. You must select every photo you want in the slideshow and drag them all at once to the icon. You cannot drop a folder on top of the publisher icon.

To select more than one photo, hold down the Command key and click on the images you want to use. Then *let go* of the Command key and drag *one* of the selected files—they will all follow along.

You can drag photos directly from an iPhoto window and drop them on the Publisher icon, as shown here. Notice only nine of the 39 photos have been selected. You can't drag the photo album icon (or a folder) onto the .Mac Slides Publisher icon; *you must select individual pictures.*

This may look like it's dragging only one image, but the number "9" in the shadow image tells you it's really dragging the nine selected images.

Mac Slides Publisher

As soon as you "drop" (let go of) the images, a window opens to display the progress.

When the process of copying the photos to your iDisk is complete, you'll get an opportunity to **announce your slideshow,** shown below.

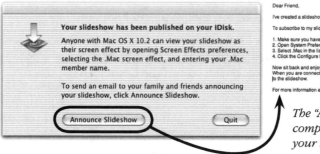

The "Announce Slideshow" email gives complete directions for subscribing to your .Mac Slideshow.

Subscribe to a Published Slideshow

You do not need to be a .Mac member to subscribe to anyone's slideshow.

Tip: When you subscribe to a .Mac slideshow, your Mac will go online to the .Mac member's slideshow every time you connect to the Internet. If it finds new photos, they will be automatically downloaded to your Mac. If you connect with a dial-up modem, you might not want your computer downloading files without you knowing it!
To prevent automatic downloading, uncheck the "Selected" box after you have played the slideshow at least once.

1. Connect to the Internet, if you're not already.

2. Open System Preferences, then click on "Screen Effects."

3. In the list of available screen effects on the left side of the pane, single-click ".Mac."

4. To the right, click "Configure." You'll see the "sheet" (as shown below) slide down from the top of the window.

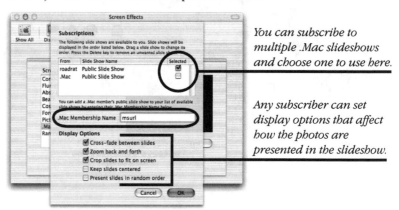

You can subscribe to multiple .Mac slideshows and choose one to use here.

Any subscriber can set display options that affect how the photos are presented in the slideshow.

5. In the center of this sheet, type the screen name of the .Mac member who has published a slideshow to which you want to subscribe.

6. Choose the "Display Options" you'd like, then click OK. As you click OK, the screen name will go to the area at the top of this sheet and its checkbox will be automatically checked.

7. It will take several minutes for the slideshow to download to your Mac. Once it has, you do not have to be online to view the slideshow.

Virex

Virex 7.2

Your Mac.com membership not only gets you a lot of things that are useful, it can also prevent you from getting lots of things that are harmful—like *viruses* and other nasty, disgusting stuff that lurks on the Internet and on seemingly nice people's media that you may need to put in your computer. Traditionally, Macs have had significantly fewer problems with viruses than PCs, but why take chances? Especially when Mac.com offers a free download of **Virex,** anti-virus software from the top-ranked anti-virus research center in the world that employs researchers in sixteen different countries.

Virex automatically checks for updates regularly, providing maximum protection against viruses and other types of code that can harm your computer or your files. Virex can scan individual files, folders, or your entire computer. When a virus or harmful code is detected, Virex can repair or delete the infected file.

It doesn't get any safer or easier than this. Download Virex and breathe easy.

Download Virex from Mac.com

Virex's outward simplicity and ease of use disguises the complex and sophisticated technology behind it.

To download and install Virex:

1. Go to the Mac.com web site (**www.mac.com**) and log in with your member name and password.

2. On the ".mac" web page that appears, click the "Downloads" link.

 Downloads
Get all your software, utilities, and games in one convenient place.

3. On the "Software Downloads" page, click the "Download Virex" link.

Virex® | Learn More | System Requirements
Download Virex

4. After Virex downloads, follow the instructions in the installer window that automatically opens.

5. When installation is complete, you can drag the "Virex.dmg" icon on your Desktop (if you see one) to the Trash.

The installation procedure places Virex in the Applications folder.

Run Virex

1. Double-click the Virex icon in the Applications folder.

2. In the sheet that slides down, enter your administrator password so Virex can perform an automatic "eUpdate" in which it connects to the Internet and checks for the latest virus definition files (DAT files).

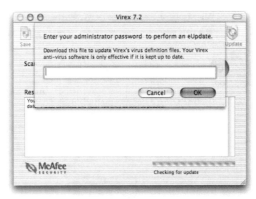

Scan for infected files on your Mac

Virex can scan items on your computer and check them for virus infections. You can select which files, folders, or volumes (partitions or other disks) you want to scan. Scanning an entire disk can take a while, so some scans are better to schedule while you're away or asleep.

1. From the "Scan" pop-up menu, choose one of the items to scan.

   Or click "Choose" in the pop-up menu to open a Finder window in which you can select any folder, file, or volume.

2. Click the "Scan" button, shown above.

Or use this **quick scan method:** select one or more items on your computer, then drag them onto the "Scan" button or onto the Virex icon in the Dock.

See the following page about the "Scan & Clean" button.

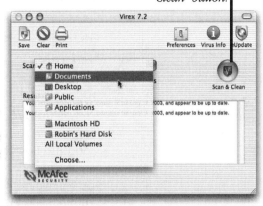

Update the Virus Definitions

Since there are an estimated 62,000 viruses that have been identified, and with more discoveries inevitable, it's recommended that you update Virex's **virus definition files** (DAT files) at least once a week. Virex calls this "electronic" procedure "eUpdate."

▼ **To automatically check** for DAT updates, open Virex. Each time Virex opens it connects to Apple's DAT update web site and checks for new virus definitions.
To prevent Virex from automatically checking for updates, change the setting in the "Virus Update" section of "Preferences" (see figure on page 341).

▼ **To manually check** for DAT updates at any time, click the "eUpdate" button in the toolbar.

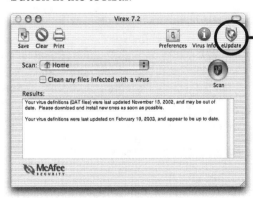

eUpdate does not function if you're using the free trial version of Mac.com.

The Virex Window and Toolbar

The Virex window provides everything you need to keep your computer free from viruses.

Save: Click to save the results of a scan or eUpdate (shown in the "Results" pane) as a text file.

Clear: Click to clear the "Results" pane.

Print: Click to print the contents of the "Results" pane.

Preferences: Click to open the "Preferences" window, shown on the next page.

Virus Info: Click to connect to the *NAI Virus Information Library* (http://vil.nai.com). This web site provides detailed information about viruses, where they come from, how they work, and how to remove them. It also provides information about virus hoaxes, so you can check to see if a virus warning you receive from someone is real or not.

eUpdate: Click to connect to Apple's DAT update web site and check for the latest virus definition files.

Scan pop-up menu: From this menu choose the files, folders, or volumes you want to scan for viruses.

Clean any files infected with a virus checkbox: Check this box if you want Virex to attempt to clean an infected file. When you select this box, the "Scan" button changes to a "Scan & Clean" button. If Virex can't clean an infected file, it *removes* the file from your computer.

*When this box is selected, the **Scan** button changes to **Scan & Clean.***

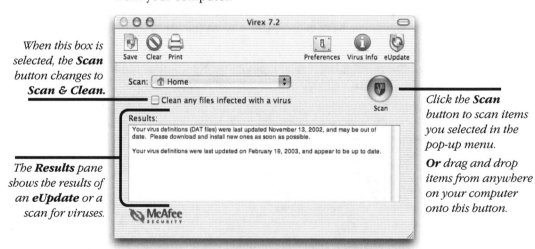

*The **Results** pane shows the results of an **eUpdate** or a scan for viruses.*

*Click the **Scan** button to scan items you selected in the pop-up menu.*

Or drag and drop items from anywhere on your computer onto this button.

Virex Preferences

Click the "Preferences" button in the toolbar to make the "Preferences" sheet slide down, as shown below. The options offered are:

Scan inside compressed (.gz) and archived (.tar) files: Scanning inside compressed files slows scan times, but is much safer than uncompressing files before scanning them. When you uncompress a file that contains an executable malicious virus file, it runs its harmful code immediately upon being uncompressed. You should scan *inside* compressed files.

Archived files are safer, because when you extract them, executable files do not run immediately. To speed up scans of archived files, you can safely *extract* them before scanning.

Automatically scan at login: Scans your *Home* folder each time you log in.

Show detailed results information: Provides additional scan information in the "Results" window during the scanning procedure.

Remove macros from potentially infected files: Attempts to remove infected macros from Microsoft Office files.

Automatically delete infected files: Automatically deletes infected files if cleaning attempts fail.

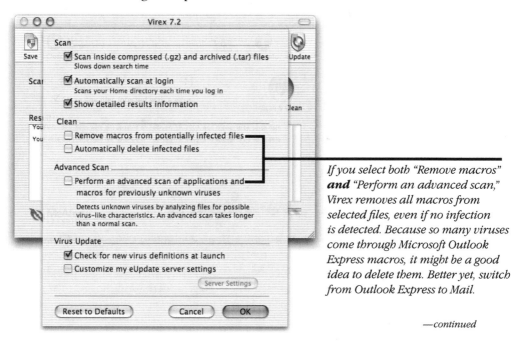

*If you select both "Remove macros" **and** "Perform an advanced scan," Virex removes all macros from selected files, even if no infection is detected. Because so many viruses come through Microsoft Outlook Express macros, it might be a good idea to delete them. Better yet, switch from Outlook Express to Mail.*

—continued

Perform an advanced scan of applications and macros for previously unknown viruses: Analyzes files for unknown viruses. Advanced scans are slower than normal scans.

Check for new virus definitions at launch: Automatically performs an "eUpdate" each time Virex opens.

Customize my eUpdate server settings: When this option is selected, you can click "Server Settings" to open the "eUpdate Server Settings" window, shown below.

▼ The "Type" pop-up menu provides two options: "HTTP" and "FTP."

▼ The default setting is "HTTP" and connects to the Apple DAT update web site. You should not change this setting or the URL (web address) that shows in the "Server URL" text box.

▼ Type your Mac.com account user name and password in the text fields shown.

▼ The "FTP" option is for users who know an FTP server where they can download virus definitions. Some users may have access to virus definition files on their local network and can enter the network address and other necessary information in the "FTP" pane.

Reset to Defaults: Click this button to reset all options to their default settings.

Section four

More Cool apps

In addition to the iLife apps, the Mac OS X apps, and the .Mac apps, you get even more software bundled with a Mac. The additional software that comes with your Mac varies with the particular model you purchase and with Apple's current bundling choices. Some bundled software comes from third-party developers. Because it would take another book to describe all the software possibilities, for this section we've chosen a couple of third-party applications you're likely to have: with **OmniGraffle** you can visualize and organize your great ideas, and **FAXstf** turns your Mac into a fax machine. Also included in this chapter are two of Apple's amazing apps: **AppleWorks,** which includes separate modules for **word processing, spreadsheets, databases, drawing,** and **presentations;** and **Inkwell,** which provides handwriting recognition and Desktop sketching capability (and requires a graphics tablet and stylus).

If some of these apps aren't on your Mac, scan their chapters anyway to see if they could be useful additions to your digital tools collection.

AppleWorks: Word Processing

17

If your Mac is your very first computer, you'll be amazed at the power of "word processing" compared to "typing." This chapter is written in a tutorial style to introduce you to AppleWorks and the power of word processing. If you're familiar with basic computer techniques such as cut and paste or undo, some of the information in this chapter will not be new to you. But even if you're expert with word processing, read page 360, because we see "professionally created" documents every day that look amateurish because the designer didn't know the most basic guidelines for creating professional-level text.

Open the AppleWorks Application

To create a word processing document, you have to open the application AppleWorks because the word processor is one of its components.

1. To open AppleWorks, single-click the "AppleWorks 6" icon in the Dock.

Or open the Applications folder (single-click the Applications icon in any Finder window Toolbar), open the AppleWorks folder (double-click on it), then open the AppleWorks application (double-click on the icon).

2. The first thing you see when you "launch" (that is, "open") AppleWorks is the "Starting Points" palette because AppleWorks integrates several applications into one and you have to choose which one you want.

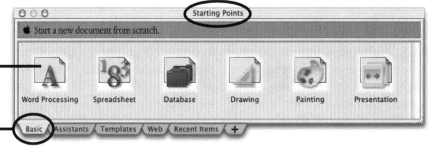

Single-click the "Word Processing" icon.

Click the other tabs to see what they display, but make sure this "Basic" tab is chosen when you want to start a new, blank word processing document.

3. For this exercise, single-click the "Word Processing" icon.

The **tabs** on the bottom of this palette provide easy access to other panes of the "Starting Points" palette:

Basic: Allows you to open a new, blank document in the AppleWorks module you choose (shown above).

Assistants: Contains small utilities that guide you through creating various kinds of files.

Templates: Contains pre-designed templates that you can modify for your own use.

Web: Has several links to web sites.

Recent Items: Holds files that you've worked on recently.

Plus symbol (+): Lets you add custom panes to the "Starting Points" palette.

Create a New Page

So here you are at a blank page! Whenever you create a "new" document on the Macintosh, you will get a clean, blank page, just waiting for you to do something creative to it.

Notice there is a little, flashing vertical bar at the top of the page (circled, below); that's called the **insertion point,** and you will see it everywhere on the Mac. The insertion point is your visual clue that you are in typing mode. When you touch the keys on the keyboard, ***the text will appear wherever that insertion point is flashing.*** That's true not only in AppleWorks, but in every application you'll ever work in, plus at the Desktop of your Mac.

*Open: When you choose the command "Open," it means you want to open a document that has already been created! That is very different from creating a **new**, untitled, clean page, as we're doing now.*

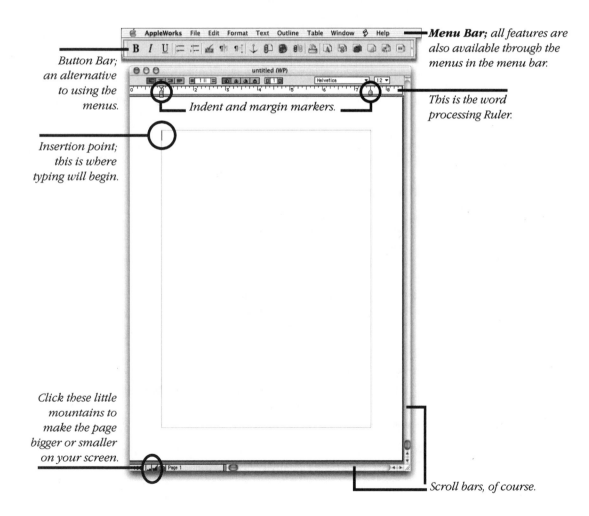

Button Bar; an alternative to using the menus.

***Menu Bar;** all features are also available through the menus in the menu bar.*

Indent and margin markers.

This is the word processing Ruler.

Insertion point; this is where typing will begin.

Click these little mountains to make the page bigger or smaller on your screen.

Scroll bars, of course.

Type Some Text!

Type one space after periods. This is professional-level type you are creating, not typewriter-level. Read The Mac is not a typewriter.

Just go ahead and type. When you get to the end of the line, ***do not hit the Return key!*** Just let the type bump into the right edge; it will "wrap" itself onto the next line all by itself. (That's called a "word wrap.")

After you have typed a *paragraph,* go ahead and hit the Return key. In fact, you can hit it twice if you want more space between the paragraphs.

To fix typos along the way: If you made a typo just a character or so ago, hit the "Delete" key, found in the upper-right of the main section of keys (where the Backspace key is found on typewriters). This will move the insertion point to the left and ***backspace*** over the characters, ***deleting*** them. Make the change and continue typing.

To fix typos somewhere else on the page: If the typo is farther back in the line or in another paragraph, of course you don't have to delete all of the characters up to that point! That would be really boring. This is what to do:

1. Put your hand on the mouse and move the pointer around on the page (don't click the button!). You'll see that the pointer turns into what's called an I-beam when it's positioned over text: ⌶ .

   Notice that if you drag the mouse so this I-beam "cursor" is *outside* of the text area, it turns into a pointer again. *Inside* the text, it's an I-beam.

cursor: A general term for the thing on the screen that moves when you move the mouse, whether it appears as a pointer, I-beam, crossbar, or anything else.

2. Okay. So in the text, position that I-beam directly **to the right** of the character you want to delete, right between it and the next character, like this:

   seremⅠdipity

3. **Click** the mouse button right there. This moves the insertion point from wherever it was and positions it where you click.

   You can't see the insertion point, though, until you move the I-beam out of the way.

   So go ahead and push the mouse to the side (don't hold the button down) so the I-beam floats around somewhere else. What you need is that **insertion point.** It should look like this:

   serem|dipity

   ▾ The flashing insertion point is the important item now, not the I-beam or any other cursor!

4. Now that the insertion point is in position, hit the Delete key to remove the wrong character (the one to the *left* of the insertion point), then type the correct character in its place:

`serendipity`

5. To put your insertion point back at the end of your document so you can continue typing (or to put it somewhere else to correct another typo):

   a. Use the **mouse** to position the I-beam where you want it.

   b. Single-click.

   c. Move the I-beam out of the way. Typing starts at the insertion point, not at the I-beam!

Note: if you like to keep your hands on the keyboard, you can also use the **arrow keys** on your keyboard to move the insertion point around (not the I-beam). Try it.

So type a page. *If you want to remove everything you've done so far and start over,* go to the Edit menu and choose "Select All," then hit Delete.

Try this: Type a headline, then hit two Returns. Type a few paragraphs like the ones shown below. Type a byline at the end ("by" you). Fix your typos. Enjoy yourself. When you've got a few paragraphs, turn the page (of this book) and we'll *format* the text (change the size, the typeface, indents, etc.).

Doll Tearsheet's Answer

Charge me! I scorn you, scurvy companion. What! You poor, base, rascally, cheating, lack-linen mate! Away, you mouldy rogue, away! Away, you cut-purse rascal! You filthy bung, away!

By this swine I'll thrust my knife in your mouldy chaps, an you play the saucy cuttle with me. Away, you bottle-ale rascal! You basket-hilt stale juggler, you!

He, a captain! Hang him, rogue! He lives upon mouldy stewed prunes and dried cakes. A captain! For God's sake, thrust him down stairs; I cannot endure such a fustian rascal.

Doll Tearsheet, from King Henry IV
by William Shakespeare

This is an example of text typed in the word processor of AppleWorks. Yours will look a little different, of course.

Formatting in General

Once you understand the basic rule of changing anything on the Macintosh, you can bumble your way through any program. This is the rule:

Select first. Then do it to it.

That is, the trick is to *select* what you want to change, and *then* go to the menu and make a formatting choice, otherwise the computer doesn't know what you want to change.

In a word processor, select text by pressing-and-dragging over the text:

> Position the I-beam at one end of what you want to select,
> then press the mouse button down, hold it down, and drag
> to the other end. **The text will "highlight," like this sentence.**

Tip: If you miss the last character or two while selecting text, hold down the Shift key, then press-and-drag or tap the arrow keys to select more (or to select less).

Many changes can be made right from the **Button Bar** (shown below) or from the **Ruler,** that strip across the top of the page (shown on the opposite page). You can also choose formatting commands from the **menu** (next page).

To format the text using the Button Bar:

The Button Bar, below, might look rather intimidating, but it will eventually grow useful to you. Many of the commands from the menus are represented by these little buttons so you can click a button instead of having to go to the menu. For instance, which button could you click to make *selected* text **bold?** What if you want to make selected text *italic?*

This is the Button Bar in AppleWorks, and you see the "Help tag" displayed for the "B" button.

As you position your mouse over a button, AppleWorks shows a "Help tag," which is a pop-up message that tells you what that button will do, as shown in the example above.

To use the Button Bar, first select the text you want to change, then click a button. Try making some text bold and some other text italic.

Many of the buttons in the Button Bar will change when you switch to different modules in AppleWorks. If you want to know how to customize this bar, see page 355.

To format the text using the Ruler:

Follow the directions below to use the Ruler to change some of the text.

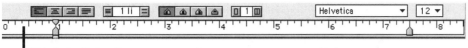

This is the Ruler. Every program that processes text uses a Ruler.

Center the headline

Select the headline, then click in the tiny icon on the Ruler that indicates a centered alignment: ☰ .

(Don't ever center a headline by spacing over with the Spacebar—this is not a typewriter!!)

Justify the rest of the text

Select the rest of the text and click the tiny icon on the Ruler that indicates a justified alignment: ☰ .

Justified text is aligned on both the left and right sides.

Indent one of the paragraphs

Select a paragraph (click once anywhere in it).

In the Ruler, position the very tip of the pointer on the tiny rectangular part of the marker on the left of the Ruler (shown below, left).

Drag that marker to the *right* to create the indent.

Press in the bottom rectangular part of this marker and drag it to the right. Do not press on the triangular parts—they do other things! You might want to experiment.

Drag this marker to move the right margin.

Tip: To make changes to a **paragraph** from the ruler, you don't actually have to select all the characters. Just click once anywhere in the paragraph you want to change.

To make text bold or italic using the menus:

Select the text. Then from the Text menu, choose "Style," then "Bold" or "Italic."

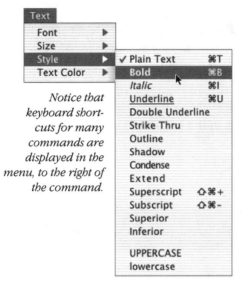

Notice that keyboard short-cuts for many commands are displayed in the menu, to the right of the command.

Or select the text and use the keyboard shortcut. What is the shortcut for the bold style? For the italic style?

Or select the text and use the buttons on the Button Bar.

To change the size of text:

Select the text you want to change (remember, always select first). From the Text menu, choose "Size." Select a size from this menu.

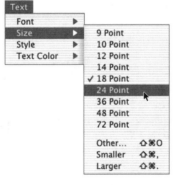

The current size of the selected text is indicated by the check-mark. (If there is no checkmark, there is more than one size of text in the selected portion.)

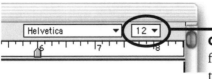

Or *select the text* and choose a size from the Size pop-up menu in the toolbar that is just above the Ruler.

To change the typeface:

Select the text you want to change. From the Text menu, choose "Font" (the current font is indicated in the menu by a checkmark). Select the font you want to use.

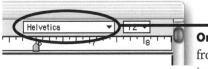

Or *select the text* and choose a font from the menu in the toolbar that is just above the Ruler.

To color the text:

Select the text you want to color. Then, from the Text menu, choose "Text Color."

Choose a color from the palette that appears. You can customize the Button Bar and place a "Text Color" button in the Bar if you want to make it even easier to select text colors; see page 355.

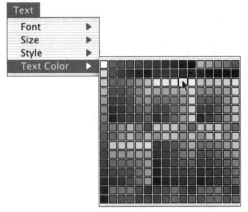

Click on any color to change the selected text color.

To unformat the text:

To remove bold, italic, or any other formatting, *select the text* and choose the same formatting again. This is called a *toggle* command, where the same command turns things either on or off.

Or select the text and choose "Plain Text" from the Text menu to remove all formatting. (What is the keyboard shortcut to change selected characters to Plain Text?)

Example of formatted text

So play around and learn a lot. Below is an example of the same copy you saw on page 349, but with simple formatting applied (the headline is red). If you feel comfortable using a word processor, you will feel comfortable anywhere on your computer.

Doll Tearsheet's Answer

Charge me! I scorn you, scurvy companion. What! **You poor, base, rascally, cheating, lack-linen mate!** Away, you mouldy rogue, away! Away, you cut-purse rascal! You filthy bung, away!

    By this swine I'll thrust my knife in your mouldy chaps,
    an you play the saucy cuttle with me. Away, you bottle-
    ale rascal! You basket-hilt stale juggler, you!

He, a captain! Hang him, rogue! He lives upon mouldy stewed prunes and dried cakes. A captain! For God's sake, thrust him down stairs; **I cannot endure such a fustian rascal.**

Doll Tearsheet, from King Henry IV
by William Shakespeare

Customize the Button Bar

The Button Bar is **customizable.** You can add preconfigured buttons to the Bar or create buttons for specific tasks and name them whatever you like.

To customize the Button Bar:

1. From the AppleWorks menu, choose "Preferences…," then choose "Button Bar…" to open the "Customize Button Bar" window.

Add any of these "Available Buttons," or click "New" and make your own.

2. Double-click a button in the list of "Available Buttons" to add it to the Button Bar, **or** drag it from this window and drop it on the Button Bar in the position you want it.

3. To remove a button, drag it from the Button Bar to the Trash basket icon in the Dock.

To create a whole new button:

Click the "New" button you see in the dialog box above; you'll get the dialog box shown below.

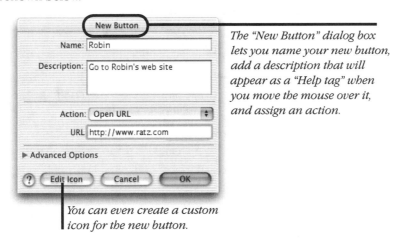

The "New Button" dialog box lets you name your new button, add a description that will appear as a "Help tag" when you move the mouse over it, and assign an action.

You can even create a custom icon for the new button.

Cut, Copy, and Paste

One of the most exciting features of working in a word processor is editing. Never do you have to retype a whole page just to change one paragraph. You can **cut** (remove) text from one place and put it someplace else, or **copy** a favorite sentence and insert it in the middle of another page (or even in another document), etc. It's too much fun. Makes you want to write books or somethin'.

Cut: The cut feature **removes** selected text from the page, just as if you took some scissors and cut it out (except there won't be a hole in the paper).

Copy: The copy feature makes a **copy** of the selected text, and leaves the original text intact.

Paste: The paste feature will **insert** onto the page whatever text you *previously* cut or copied. The text will be inserted *wherever the insertion point is flashing*.

Try it!

Click the button shown below in the Button Bar to make a new, blank word processing page.

So these are the steps to edit your page. Practice on the text you already have on your page, or create a new document (just click on the tiny page icon in the Button Bar at the top of the screen).

To cut text from one place:

1. Select the text by dragging across it (as explained on page 350).
2. From the Edit menu, choose "Cut." Notice the keyboard shortcut is Command X (like Xing or crossing something out).

To copy text:

1. Select the text by dragging across it (as explained on page 350).
2. From the Edit menu, choose "Copy." Notice the keyboard shortcut is Command C (C for copy).

To paste text somewhere else:

Tip: If the Cut, Copy, and/or Clear commands in the Edit menu are gray, that's because nothing is selected at the moment! Remember, select first, then do it.

1. Single-click to set the insertion point (as explained on page 348) at the spot where you want to paste the text into.
2. From the Edit menu, choose "Paste." Notice the keyboard shortcut is Command V (like the caret ^ for inserting something).

Clear and Delete

So have you practiced cutting, copying, and pasting? Let me explain what you did. When you cut or copy, the Mac puts the text (or graphic) into an invisible place called the Clipboard. The Clipboard can only hold one item at a time, so as soon as you copy something else, whatever was in the Clipboard disappears. When you paste, you are actually pasting whatever was on the Clipboard. For instance, if you *cut* three separate pieces of text and then you *paste,* you will paste the *last* item that you cut.

You can paste items forever (well, until you turn off the computer). Whatever you cut or copied will stay in the Clipboard even when you change to a different program or come back in several hours. As soon as the power is turned off, though, whatever was in the Clipboard disappears.

Tip: If you want to see what is currently stored in the Clipboard, go to the Edit menu and choose "Show Clipboard." When you're done, close the Clipboard just like you close any window.

The **Clear** command from the Edit menu, as well as the **Delete** key, will get rid of whatever you had *selected,* but it does *not* go to the Clipboard! Think about this for a minute. Let's say you have a photo of your daughter in the Clipboard because you copied it from one document, and you are pasting it into several different letters. If you want to get rid of some text now, use the Delete key instead of the Cut command so your daughter's photo stays in the Clipboard, ready to paste again—instead of being *replaced* by that text that was *cut.*

Undo

The Undo command is one of the most important things you can learn. Most of the time you can undo the very last thing you did by going to the Edit menu and choosing "Undo." Let's say you wrote a whole letter and then you selected all the text because you wanted to change the typeface. But before you could choose a new typeface, you leaned on the keyboard and all of the selected text turned into "vnm;id." Before you scream, choose Undo from the Edit menu. Memorize the keyboard shortcut: Command Z. Just undo it.

Practice using Undo: Select some text, cut it, then undo it. Paste some text, then undo it.

Save the Document

Rule Number One: SOS: Save Often Sweetheart.

You must "save" every document you create on your computer (unless you never want to see it again). Saving it means you store a copy onto the hard disk. After you save a document, you can open it again, make changes, make a copy, add to it, delete from it, etc. You need to save a document as soon as you begin, and then you need to save changes every couple of minutes as you work. Why every couple of minutes? Because as you work, all of your changes are being held in "memory," which is a temporary storage space. So temporary, in fact, that if the power in your home or office flickers or goes out, or your computer crashes or freezes up, or the cat chews your power cord, everything you had not saved will disappear. Nothing can get it back.

Unfortunately, humans seem to learn best through catastrophes. I can almost guarantee that you won't bother saving often until one very late night when you lose the last two hours worth of work on a report that is due first thing in the morning.

To save your document:

1. With your document open on the screen, go to the File menu and choose "Save As...." You will get the dialog box shown below.

2. Name your document! Name it something you will remember and something that gives you a clue as to what this document is about.

3. Single-click the "Save" button (or hit Return).

4. For right now, your documents will be saved into the "Documents" folder on your hard drive.

Type a name for the file in this edit box.

The folder highlighted here is the one in which your document will be automatically saved. Notice this folder is also displayed in the "Where" menu, directly above.

Always be conscious of where your document is being saved!

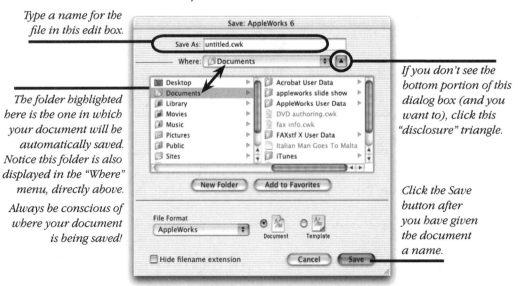

If you don't see the bottom portion of this dialog box (and you want to), click this "disclosure" triangle.

Click the Save button after you have given the document a name.

Close the Document

When you are finished working on a document, you "close" it, which is like removing the page (the document) from the typewriter (the word processor) and putting the page in a filing cabinet.

1. Click the red Close button, just as you would to close any window.
    Or go to the File menu and choose "Close."
    Or use the keyboard shortcut, Command W.

2. If you didn't save the document at the last minute, you will get a dialog box asking if you want to save it or not.

Save changes to the document "test.cwk" before closing?

Don't Save   Cancel   Save

Create Another Document or Open an Existing Document

▼ **To create another document,** single-click on the word processing icon in the Button Bar.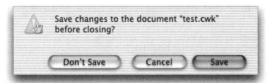

▼ **To open a document you already created,** go to the File menu, choose "Open…," and you should see the document's name in the list. Double-click the name. (Or check the "Recent Items" tab in the "Starting Points palette, as shown on page 346.)

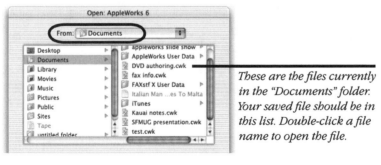

Open: AppleWorks 6

From: Documents

Desktop	appleworks slide show
Documents	AppleWorks User Data
Library	DVD authoring.cwk
Movies	fax info.cwk
Music	FAXstf X User Data
Pictures	Italian Man …es To Malta
Public	iTunes
Sites	Kauai notes.cwk
Tape	SFMUG presentation.cwk
untitled folder	test.cwk

These are the files currently in the "Documents" folder. Your saved file should be in this list. Double-click a file name to open the file.

Tip: You don't have to close one document before you open another! You can have dozens of documents open at the same time. They will all be listed in the Window menu in AppleWorks.

If You Made a Terrible Mistake

If you did something terrible to the document, like perhaps you selected everything and accidentally deleted it, do this:

> From the File menu, choose "Revert." This will revert the document back to the way it was the last time you saved it. That means if you didn't save the document recently, you are out of luck. Save often, sweetie.

A Few Guidelines for Creating Professional-Level Text

Here are some basic rules for creating type on your Mac. These are the tried-and-true techniques that professional typesetters have used for centuries.

▾ One space after periods. Really.

▾ One space after colons, semicolons, question marks, exclamation points, and all other punctuation.

▾ Periods and commas always go inside of quotation marks. Always. (In America.)

▾ Question marks and exclamation points go inside or outside quotation marks depending on whether or not they belong to the phrase inside the quotes.

▾ Professional type does not use the half-inch or five-space indent that we used on typewriters. The correct space is equivalent to about two spaces.

▾ Use an indent for new paragraphs, **or** use space between the paragraphs, but not both.

▾ Learn to use your software to set about a half-line space between paragraphs, instead of hitting two Returns.

▾ Read *The Mac is not a typewriter.*

▾ If you discover you like this typesetting stuff and want to learn much more about how to make your type beautiful and sophisticated, read *The Non-Designer's Type Book,* by me.

AppleWorks:
Database

A **database** is like a really fancy recipe card box, like the kind in which you might store recipes, addresses, baseball cards, or dues-paying membership information. But in a database you can do a lot more with the information than you can with the recipe cards.

In this chapter we're going to create a new, blank database to serve as an address book. Just follow the steps in this chapter and in a couple of minutes you'll have an address book you can use for years. If you like working in a database, there are entire books that will teach you much more, and you can build directly on the database you create right here. Even without reading anything else, you'll be able to make another database for any other collection of information you happen to have, such as research data, personal possessions, scout troop members, etc.

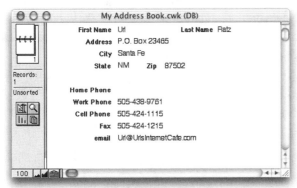

This is a very simple database that took about five minutes to build. You can add to it, change it, rearrange the layout, search it, print labels with it, and much more.

Get Ready to Make a Database

Now, you might be in one of four different situations, depending on whether you've been following along or not. Choose the situation you're in and follow the directions:

A. You just finished the word processing exercise and the letter is still on your screen.

  1. Save this letter once again: press Command S.

  2. Click the red Close button in the upper-left corner,
  or use the keyboard shortcut Command W (W for Window).

B. You finished the word processing exercise, saved and closed it, and didn't quit AppleWorks. In the far-left corner of the menu bar, it says AppleWorks (to the right of the blue Apple logo).

✪ You are exactly where you need to be! Don't touch anything. Go to the top of the next page (in this book).

C. You finished the word processing exercise, saved and closed it, and didn't quit AppleWorks. BUT in the far-left corner of the menu bar (to the right of the Apple logo), you see the name of some other application.

  1. In the Dock, find the AppleWorks icon. Single-click it.

  2. After you click the AppleWorks icon, the "Starting Points" palette and the Button Bar should appear at the top of the screen. Go to the next page (in this book).

D. You skipped the word processing exercise, or you turned off your computer and came back later, and AppleWorks is not open on your Mac.

  1. Open AppleWorks just like you did the first time: Single-click its icon in the Dock.

  Or go to the Applications folder, then open the AppleWorks folder. The AppleWorks application is inside the AppleWorks folder! Double-click the AppleWorks application icon.

  2. Click the "Database" icon in the "Starting Points" window.

  3. Go to the next page (of this book), but skip the first step because you just started a new document.

Create a New Database Document

1. If you do not yet have the beginning of a database on your screen (as shown below, under Step 3), single-click the Database button in the Button Bar (circled, below).

AppleWorks Button Bar.

2. When you start a new database, the first thing you see is the "Define Database Fields" window (shown below).

   A database is filled with "fields" in which you will (later) enter information. What you need to do here is name the fields that you plan to include in your address book, such as First Name, Last Name, Address, City, State, etc. When you're done, each of these "Field Names" will have a space in which to enter the appropriate information.

3. So type "First Name" in the Field Name edit box, as you see in the example circled below.

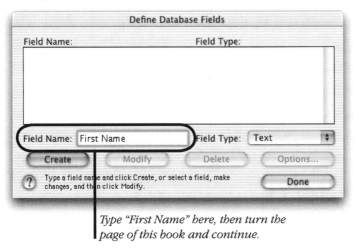

Type "First Name" here, then turn the page of this book and continue.

—continued

4. Click the "Create" button. This puts the field name in the list (shown below), and AppleWorks automatically asks what you want the name of the next field to be. In the next one, type "Last Name," then click "Create."

> **Tip:** You always want to have separate fields for first names and last names because the computer alphabetizes by the first letter in the field. If you have both first and last names in one field (such as "Robert Burns"), you'll get an alphabetized list by first names, which isn't useful very often. If you enter the last name, comma, first name ("Burns, Robert") then your mailing labels will print exactly that, which is kind of dorky.
>
> So always set up one field for first names and one field for last names.

5. Continue adding fields until you have all the ones you need for an address book, until you get to the zip code.

6. When you get to the zip code, do an extra step:

Notice to the right of the "Field Name" is "Field Type" (circled, below). A field type will help you automatically format the data stored in that field. For instance, if you were to choose the field type "Time," the database would automatically enter the time, and it would be formatted to specifications that you can set up.

So for the zip code field, press on the "Field Type" menu (where it currently says "Text") and you'll get the pop-up menu shown below. Choose "Number," since a zip code is always a number.

Tip: Set the phone number Field Type as "Text." If you set it as "Number," you won't be able to use hyphens to separate the numbers. The database software considers hyphens to be text.

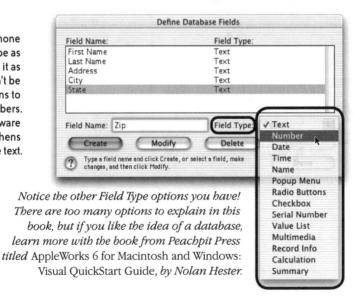

Notice the other Field Type options you have! There are too many options to explain in this book, but if you like the idea of a database, learn more with the book from Peachpit Press titled AppleWorks 6 for Macintosh and Windows: Visual QuickStart Guide, *by Nolan Hester.*

7. Continue to add any other fields you might want in your address book. Make sure you change the "Field Type" back to "Text" (or whatever type you need) for any additions after "zip code."

8. When you have added all the fields you need, click the "Done" button.

   (You can always add, delete, or modify fields at any time, even after you save the database.)

   After you click "Done," you will see the database. It looks like this:

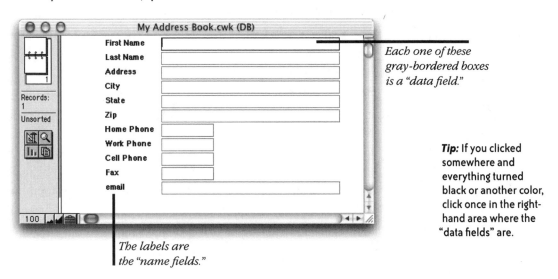

Each one of these gray-bordered boxes is a "data field."

Tip: If you clicked somewhere and everything turned black or another color, click once in the right-hand area where the "data fields" are.

The labels are the "name fields."

9. Before you start entering data (typing information), save this document! Go to the File menu, choose "Save As...," and name this database.

10. Now turn the page of this book and start entering data.

Enter Data into the Database

Your next task in a database is to "enter data," which means to type in the information. It's so easy.

To enter the first address:

1. Click in the "First Name" *field*. You should see the insertion point flashing, which is your visual clue that the computer is ready for you to type. So type the *first name* of the person whose information you want in your database.

2. Now, you *could* pick up the mouse and click in the next field, the one for "Last Name." But the *easier* thing to do is hit the Tab key, which will send the insertion point to the next field.

   So hit the Tab key, type the *last name,* then hit the Tab key again.

3. Continue through the rest of the fields, typing and tabbing. If you don't have information for one of the fields, just skip it (Tab twice). You can always come back next week and fill it in, or change or delete any information.

   After everything is filled in, your database should look something like this:

*Tip: If you accidentally hit the Tab key too many times, **hold down** the Shift key and tap the Tab key; it will move the insertion point **upward** through the fields.*

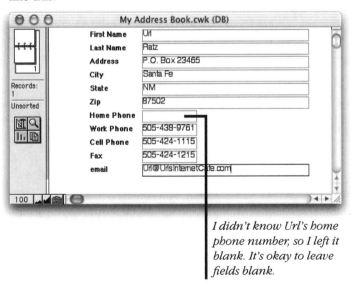

I didn't know Url's home phone number, so I left it blank. It's okay to leave fields blank.

Make More Records

This one collection of fields for one person is called a "record." Your database can have hundreds or thousands of records in it. Each individual record is sort of like one recipe card.

To make another record:

1. Go to the Edit menu and choose "New Record," **or** press Command R.

2. The new record will be added directly after the record you are currently viewing.

Format the Fields

You can change the typeface, size, placement, etc., of any field name or of the data in any individual field. This is called "formatting."

To format the name fields:

1. From the Layout menu, choose "Layout."

2. In the record, click on a field *name,* such as "City."

3. To select the rest of the names, hold down the Shift key and click on any of the other name fields that you want to have the same typeface and size. When you've selected all, let go of the Shift key, but don't click anywhere!

4. From the Format menu, slide down to "Font," then out to the side and pick a font (typeface) you like.

5. Click anywhere to *deselect* the name fields.

   To enter more data: Go back to the Layout menu and choose "Browse."

*This is what a **name field** looks like when you select it.*

To format the data fields:

1. Follow the same directions as above (choose "Layout" from the Layout menu), but this time select the fields themselves: Click on the field *data,* the box where you actually type the text.

2. Hold down the Shift key and click on any of the other data fields that you want to have the same typeface and size. When you have them all selected, let go of the Shift key, but don't click anywhere!

3. Use the Format menu again to format the information.

4. Click anywhere to *deselect* the data fields.

*This is what the **data field** looks like when you select it.*

Enter More Data after Formatting

To enter more data after you've done something like formatting, go back to the Layout menu and choose "Browse." In the Browse mode, you can enter more information.

Change the Layout

You can rearrange the name and data fields, and you can resize them.

1. From the Layout menu, choose "Layout."

2. Press in the *middle* of any field (name or data), and drag it to a **different position.** You can hold the Shift key down and click on more than one field to select a group, then *let go* of the Shift key and move the entire group.

*Press-and-drag in the **middle** of a field to move it.*

3. **Resize any field:** Click once on it, then position the *tip* of the pointer in one of the tiny, square handles that appears. Press-and-drag any handle to resize the field. Try it.

*Press-and-drag the **handle** of a field to resize it.*

Rearrange your database into a more pleasing and sensible order.

This is the "Layout" view.

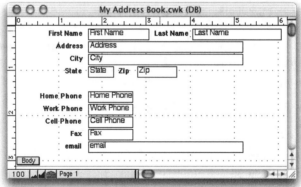

From the Layout menu, choose "Layout" to format text or to rearrange data fields and name fields.

This is the "Browse" view.

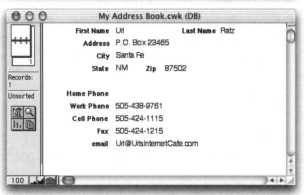

This is a more logical placement of fields than what automatically appears (as shown on page 366).

Make a List of the Records

I find it helpful to view the records as a list be cause then I can see a whole collection at a glance. You can enter data while it is in a list view.

1. From the Layout menu, choose "List."

2. **To rearrange the columns,** press-and-drag any column heading to the left or right, then let go.

3. **To resize the width of any column,** position the cursor directly on the dotted line between two column headings (as shown below). The cursor turns into a two-headed arrow. With this cursor, ✛ press-and-drag to the left or right to widen or narrow a column.

*Press-and-drag in the **middle** of any column heading to move the column.*

*Press-and-drag **between** columns to resize them.*

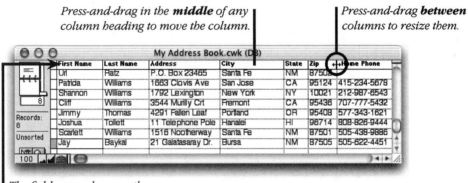

The field names become the column headings.

Sort the Information in Your Database

Tip: If you don't enter data exactly the same way every time, then your sort won't work very well. For instance, if you enter McCoy (no space) or Mc Coy (with a space), the name with the space will be sorted before the name with no space (in computerized alphabetizing, spaces come before letters).

Capital letters are sorted differently from lowercase, also, so Penelope *v*onSchnitzel would come before Abigail **V**onSchnitzel if you sort by last names.

Once your database is set up, you can sort (organize) the information in a number of ways. If you don't have enough records to organize in your file yet, take a moment to add a few more. Then experiment with sorting.

1. From the Layout menu, choose "Browse" or "List."

2. From the Organize menu, choose "Sort Records...."
   You'll get the "Sort Records" dialog box, as shown below.

3. The "Field List" on the left contains every field in your database. Select the field you want to alphabetize by (such as "Last Name"), then click the "Move" button.

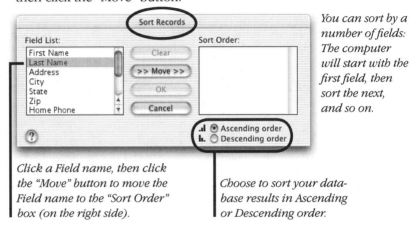

You can sort by a number of fields: The computer will start with the first field, then sort the next, and so on.

Click a Field name, then click the "Move" button to move the Field name to the "Sort Order" box (on the right side).

Choose to sort your database results in Ascending or Descending order.

Maybe you have a lot of people with the same last name, like your entire family. If you move "First Name" over to the "Sort Order" box *under* "Last Name," then the Mac will first alphabetize all the last names, and then alphabetize all the first names within that group. So "Gerald Williams" will be in the list before "Patricia Williams."

4. When you have arranged your sort orders, click OK to go back to your list, which is now organized per your request.

So think of it—you can sort by city, then by last name, then by first name. Your database will then display all of your information organized by city, with people's names alphabetized within each city. The possibilities are amazing. Enter a whole bunch of records and experiment. Enter your entire music CD collection, then organize them by genre, artist, and recording date from oldest recording to newest.

Find Certain Records

Often you will want to select, or find, just certain records. For instance, maybe you want to find the clients who live in a certain city or who owe you money. (Of course, if you want to find the clients who owe you money, you must have set up the database with a field for that information in the first place.)

To search for certain records:

1. From the Layout menu, choose "Find."

2. You see what looks like a blank record (shown below). Type the data you want to find in the field you want to find. For instance, if you want to find all the people with the last name of Williams, type "Williams" into the "Last Name" field.

   If you want to find all the people named Williams who live in the city of Santa Rosa, type "Williams" in the "Last Name" field, and type "Santa Rosa" in the "City" field.

   (If you want to find all the people who owe you more than $150 and you previously set up a formula field to figure that out, use the "Match" feature, under the Organize menu.)

   You can fill in as many fields as you need to narrow the search down to just what you want to find.

3. On the far left, click "All" if you want to find records within your entire database, or click "Visible" if you did a previous search or match and want to find files *within* that selection.

4. After you do a search, you probably want all of your records back. From the Organize menu, choose "Show All Records."

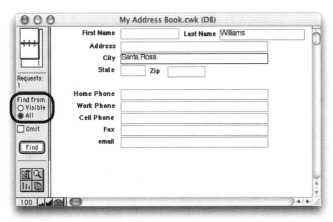

This is how you "find" a selection of records in your database.

Print Your Database

Of course you can print any of the information in your database. Often you will want to limit the records you print by first finding or matching certain criteria. When you print, only the visible records (the ones you found or matched) will print.

1. If you want to limit the records, find or match the ones to print, as explained on the previous page.

2. From the Layout menu, choose "Browse" if you want to print the data as the record displays it, or "List" if you want to print a list.

3. If you're printing a list, the fields might stretch across several pages. To check before you print, go to the Window menu and choose "Page View."

You will get a preview of how your database will look on the printed page. You might need to enlarge the window as large as possible (drag the Resize corner in the bottom-right of the window). *Or* click the little mountain icon (in the bottom-left corner of the window) to reduce the picture on the screen.

Directly in this preview window you can make the columns narrower and rearrange them so things fit on the page better (as you did on page 369).

4. From the File menu, choose "Print…." You might have to experiment with various arrangements in the preview window to get the printed results you want.

AppleWorks:
Spreadsheet

A *spreadsheet* is a very interesting and useful program. It lets you work with numbers and formulas and then play with the possibilities. It can automate just about any sort of scenario you want to create with numbers, such as the various options in a mortgage payment, the variety of discounts and taxable options in an invoice, the ups and downs of your income, and so much more. A spreadsheet is a very versatile program to have on your computer. And it does a lot more than crunch numbers—you can easily make forms, signs, calendars, tables of data, to-do lists, and more.

In this chapter, I'll show you the basics of working in a spreadsheet. Once you get the hang of just a couple of key features, you'll have fun creating all kinds of stuff.

This is an extremely basic spreadsheet that tells you how much money different people still owe you. Even this basic, it's very useful.

Get Ready to Create a Spreadsheet

Now, you might be in one of four different situations, depending on whether you've been following along or not. Choose the situation you're in and follow the directions:

*This is the
"Spreadsheet" button.*

A. You just finished the database exercise and that file is still on your screen.

1. Save this file once again: press Command S.

2. Click the red Close button in the upper-left corner, or use the keyboard shortcut Command W (W for Window).

3. Click the "Spreadsheet" button in the Button Bar.

B. You finished the database exercise, saved and closed it, and didn't quit AppleWorks. You still see the Button Bar.

✪ You are exactly where you need to be!
Click the "Spreadsheet" button in the Button Bar.

C. You finished the database exercise, saved and closed it, and did not quit AppleWorks. BUT you don't see the AppleWorks Button Bar.

1. Find the AppleWorks icon in the Dock. Single-click it.

2. After you click the AppleWorks icon, the "Starting Points" window and the Button Bar will appear at the top of the screen. Click the "Spreadsheet" button.

D. You skipped the database exercise, or you turned off your computer and came back later, and AppleWorks is not open on your Mac.

1. Open AppleWorks just like you did the first time: Single-click its icon in the Dock.

   Or go to the Applications folder, then open the AppleWorks folder. The AppleWorks application is inside the AppleWorks folder! Double-click the AppleWorks application icon.

2. Click the "Spreadsheet" icon in the "Starting Points" window.

3. Go to the next page (of this book).

Create a Spreadsheet Document

Let's make a simple spreadsheet to become familiar with how a spreadsheet functions. It's a little different from other programs you've worked with.

Columns, rows, and cells

What you see on your screen, as shown below, is basically a huge sheet of grid paper.

Across the top are the alphabetic **column headings.**

Down the left side are the numeric **row headings.**

Each tiny block on the page is a **cell.**

Each cell has an **address,** which is the intersection of the column and row. In the example below, the selected cell's address is B2 because it is in column B and row 2.

Column headings.

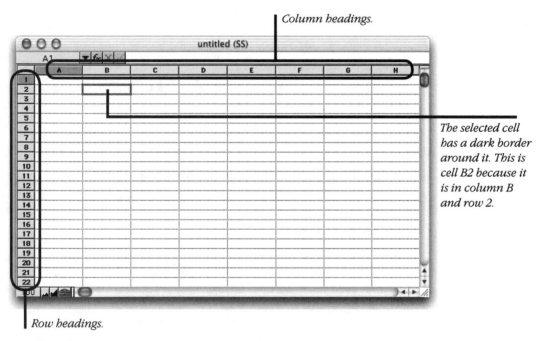

The selected cell has a dark border around it. This is cell B2 because it is in column B and row 2.

Row headings.

When a spreadsheet is open and active, the Button Bar changes to show buttons specific to spreadsheets. Hover the pointer over a button and that button's "Help tag" will appear, as shown above.

Enter Data into the Cells

At first, the oddest thing about a spreadsheet is that when you select a cell and try to type something into it, nothing seems to happen—the text does not appear in the cell. The text you type actually appears in the **entry bar,** *above* the spreadsheet itself, as shown in the example below. Try it: **Click in cell B2,** then type *Frogs R Us Web Design.* The text will appear in the entry bar. *(Make sure you click in cell B2 or the rest of this exercise won't work!)*

This is the entry bar.

This is cell B2.

It doesn't look like the text will fit into that tiny cell, and it won't. But in a spreadsheet, as opposed to a database, the text will just go right through the cell into the next one, as long as the next one is empty.

To make the text appear in the cell, you have to **enter** it: hit the Enter key (on the far-right, bottom end of your keyboard). Then it will look like this:

You still see the text in the entry bar because that cell (B2) is still selected.

Click in any other cell and that thick selection border will move to that cell.

Now experiment with this feature of a spreadsheet: Click on the word "Design," which looks like it is in cell C2. Does the text appear in the entry bar? No, because cell C2 is actually empty. Even though the text spills over to C2, it is *entered* into cell B2, and if you want to change the data, you have to *select* cell B2.

> *Tip:* There are a number of ways to enter the data into a cell, depending on which key you press to enter the data:
>
> **Return key:** Enters data and automatically selects the next cell downward.
>
> **Tab key:** Enters data and automatically selects the next cell to the right.
>
> **Enter key** or click the **checkmark** in the entry bar: Enters data and keeps the same selected cell selected.

Format the Spreadsheet Text

Go ahead and format that text. Just like in the word processor and the database, you have to select the text first, then choose your formatting, right? In a spreadsheet, you select the text by selecting the *cell* in which it is entered.

1. So click once on **B2.**

2. Now go to the Format menu and choose a font, size, and color. For this example, choose the font Impact and the size 24. Oops, it doesn't fit, does it?

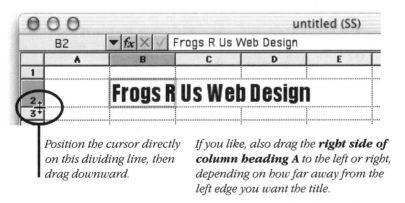

That's okay, let's just open up that row.

3. Position the spreadsheet cursor (⊹) **in the row heading** (*not* on the spreadsheet page) directly on the line dividing two numbered rows, as shown below. The cursor will change to a two-headed arrow. While it's the two-headed arrow, press-and-drag the line *downward* until the text fits in nicely. You might want to leave a little extra space at the top so the title is not too close to the top edge of the cell.

Position the cursor directly on this dividing line, then drag downward.

*If you like, also drag the **right side of column heading A** to the left or right, depending on how far away from the left edge you want the title.*

4. Save the spreadsheet! From the "File" menu, choose "Save As…." Name the file "Frogs R Us." Save the file in the "Documents" folder.

Add a Graphic to the Spreadsheet

1. From the File menu, choose "Show Clippings." You'll get a floating "palette" with a variety of images, called clippings, as shown below.

   Click on a tab at the bottom of the palette to see the different categories of graphics. Scroll up and down to see the images. Drag the title bar to move the palette around.

Click on a tab to display the images in that category.

Click the arrow tab to display more categories.

2. For this exercise, click the "Animals" tab. Scroll down the images and find the frog.

   Press on that frog and *drag* him to your spreadsheet; let go and he will drop right on the page. You'll see "handles" on each corner of the graphic; the handles indicate the graphic is selected.

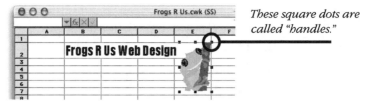

These square dots are called "handles."

3. **Resize the frog:** Hold down the Shift key, then drag a corner handle to make it smaller.

4. **Flip the frog** if you want to: While the frog is still selected (click once on him if it's not), go to the Arrange menu and choose "Flip Horizontally."

5. **Move the frog:** Press in the *middle* of the graphic and drag it into the position shown above.

6. You can put the Clippings palette away now (click the red Close box).

Add Names and Numbers to the Spreadsheet

Now that you've got a fun start, put some numbers in. Let's pretend this is a list of web design clients who owe you money, and you want to see the total of how much money they owe. You need a list of names and amounts.

1. Click in cell **C4.**

2. The entry bar is ready, waiting for you to type. Type the name of someone who owes you money—*but don't hit the Enter key yet!*

3. Instead of using the Enter key, use the **Return key** this time. This will enter the data *and* select the next cell *below* C4. (If you already hit the Enter key, don't worry. Select cell C5 now.)

4. Enter another name, then hit Return. Add three more names this way. It should look something like this:

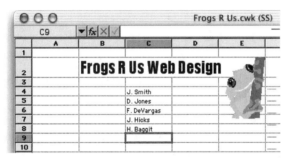

5. Next **align those names to the right** so they will be next to the numbers you are going to enter. To do that, select all the cells with names in them: press-and-drag from the first name to the last name. The selection will look like the example below. You just selected a "range" of cells.

6. From the Format menu, slide down to Alignment and choose "Right."

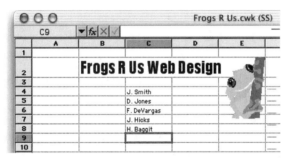

Notice *that when you select a range of cells, only the first cell has a selection border around it, while the rest are highlighted. That's okay—that's what it does.*

Now **enter** the numbers and **format** them.

1. Click in cell **D4.**

2. Type the amount this person owes you, *but don't use a dollar sign or commas.* Type just the number (decimal points are okay).

3. Hit the **Return key.** Enter the next amount. Continue down the column. The numbers should look something like you see below.

If any of your numbers look like this, it just means the column is too narrow to display the number properly. Widen the column.

4. You need to *format* the numbers into dollars. First you must select them. This time, try selecting this way:

Click in the first cell in the number list; *hold the Shift key down;* click in the last cell of that list (then let go of the Shift key). When you hold the Shift key down, everything between the two clicks is selected.

Tip: You can also double-click on any cell (or range of selected cells) as a shortcut to open the "Format Number, Date, and Time" window.

5. From the Format menu, choose "Number…" to open the "Format Number, Date, and Time" window, as shown on the opposite page. You're going to choose to format the numbers as "Currency," which will automatically apply the dollar sign. And you're going to choose how many numbers you want to appear after the decimal point, which is called "Decimal Precision." For instance, if you enter "2" in the Decimal Precision edit box, that means any number in the cell will always display two places after the decimal point. (If you enter more numbers after the decimal point, the computer will round them off to two.)

If you want the currency to display in whole dollars (no cents), change the 2 to 0 (zero, not the letter O!). It's up to you. If you choose zero, any cents that may be in the cells will be rounded off.

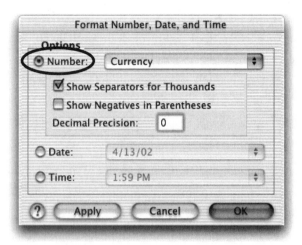

a. Click in the "Number" radio button.

b. Press on the Number pop-up menu and choose "Currency."

c. Check the box to "Show Separators for Thousands," which will add commas in the proper places.

d. Enter "0" (zero) in "Decimal Precision."

e. Click OK.

6. After you click OK, take a look at those numbers!

$1,400
$52,000
$50
$650
$900

View the Spreadsheet without the Grid and Headings

Let's take a quick look at how this looks without all the stuff around it.

1. From the Options menu, choose "Display...."

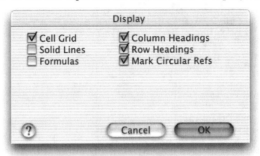

2. Uncheck "Cell Grid," "Column Headings," and "Row Headings." Click OK.

    Your spreadsheet will look something like this:

3. Turn the cell grid and both headings back on so we can finish the project:

    Go back to the "Display" dialog box (choose it from the Options menu) and click those three boxes.

Add a Function

Mathematical formulas and functions (functions are complex formulas) are integral parts of a spreadsheet. They enable you to speculate with the numbers. AppleWorks provides you with a huge number of pre-made functions that you just add the details to. We're going to use a very simple function, called Sum, to total how much these people owe you. (If you want to know more about functions, read the AppleWorks Help file; choose it from the Help menu in AppleWorks.)

You *could* use a simple formula, such as =D4+D5+D6+D7+D8 for your project, but it's faster and easier to use the function that is already set up.

To add a function:

1. First, **format the cell** in preparation for the number you're going to put into it:

   Double-click on the empty cell **D10** to get the number format dialog box.

   Choose "Currency," "Show Separators," and the same "Decimal Precision" you set in the other cells.

   Click OK.

2. Now put the Sum function in the *selected* cell **D10**:

   From the Edit menu, choose "Insert Function…."

   Type "su" to select the Sum function quickly, or just scroll down the list, admiring all the things you could do if you knew what the heck they were. Single-click on "SUM(number 1,number 2…)" to select that function.

3. Click "Insert." *Now don't touch anything!*

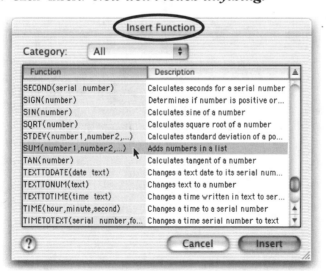

—*continued*

—*continued*

Tip: To enter your own formula, just type an equal sign in the cell. Then click in the cells whose data you want to add to the formula. *Be sure to hit the Enter or Return key as soon as you finish the formula!*

Note: With functions and formulas you can do all kinds of things with numbers.

You could have one cell add the numbers, subtract the percentage you owe your agent, and add the tax. Or you could create a "lookup table" where the cell would look up a chart and add a percentage based on the individual amounts owed, or add penalties daily.

The reason I yelled "Don't touch anything" on the previous page is because once you put a function in a cell or type an = sign to start a formula, *everything you click on becomes part of the formula.* It can make you crazy. So follow these directions carefully. If weird things happen, like strange stuff starts appearing in your entry bar, click the X in the entry bar and start over, selecting cell D10.

If things are going smoothly, you should see the function you selected in the entry bar. You need to substitute the "arguments" in parentheses (the first number, the second number, etc., that are to be added together) with the actual cell addresses that you want to add together.

4. So press-and-drag to select everything between the parentheses, like so:

Select this because you're going to replace it with the cell addresses.

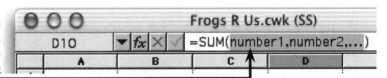

5. While it's selected, *press* (don't click!) in cell D4 and *drag* to D8, which will enter those cell addresses into the formula. The numbers in those cells will be summed. *Before you touch anything else, hit the Enter key* (or click the checkmark in the entry bar). Your entry bar should look like this:

And cell D10 should have the sum total of the money you are owed.

range: A range of cells is any selection of more than one. It is written with two dots between the first and last cell, as you see in your entry bar.

All the cells in a range don't have to be in the same row or column. For instance, you might select a range of cells like C4 ..D10.

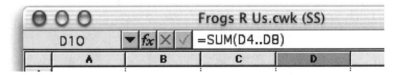

6. Change the amount someone owes you, enter it, and the sum total changes instantly. Try it. If you had made a bar chart or pie chart, the chart would change instantly when you change data.

Move the Data

Perhaps you decided you put all this information in the wrong place. That's easy to fix. Let's move the names and numbers one column to the left.

1. Select the cells you want to move: names, numbers, and total.

2. Hold down the Command and Option keys, and click in cell **B4.**
   Voilà—all the cell data moved over.

Now, click once in cell **C10,** the cell with the formula, and you'll notice that the cell range changed from the original settings of D4..D8 to C4..C8! That's a good thing because there's nothing left in D4..D8.

That formula you originally entered is what's called a **relative** reference, meaning it didn't *really* refer to D4..D8 specifically; it meant, "Sum the cells that are 2, 3, 4, 5, and 6 rows above *me.*" So when the formula moved, you didn't need it to add the cells above *D10* anymore—you need it to add the cells above *C10.* So a relative reference automatically changes the cells the formula refers to, according to the cell that contains the formula. You can also make **absolute** cells that do not change: see the Help file, under the Help menu in AppleWorks, for details.

Apply a Border

The borders feature is what makes creating forms so very easy. You can apply a border to an individual cell or a range of cells; on any one side or on all sides. For instance, you could select cells in a column, such as B4 through B8 and apply a left border to make a vertical line.

For right now, put a border line under the logo.

1. Select all the cells through which the title extends (in my example, that would be B2 through E2), like so:

2. From the Format menu, choose "Borders...."

3. Click "Bottom." Click OK.

The border won't show up clearly while the grid is visible, but take a look at the finished example on the following page.

Change the Color of Cells

Do one more thing to this spreadsheet: color a cell or two. Colored cells can help the organization and clarity of a large spreadsheet.

1. Select the cell with the formula (so the total will stand out).

2. If you don't see a tool palette on the left of the screen, click the little "Tool Palette" button at the bottom-left of the window, next to the scroll bar.

Single-click this button to display the Tool Palette, shown to the left.

3. Single-click the "Color Palette" button and choose a color (below).

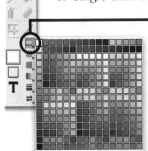

*This is the **Color Palette** button. Click on it and the collection of colors will appear. Click on any color to apply it to the selected cell.*

Or, from the Windows menu, choose "Show Accents." Click on a color in the "Accents" palette to apply it to the selected cell (below).

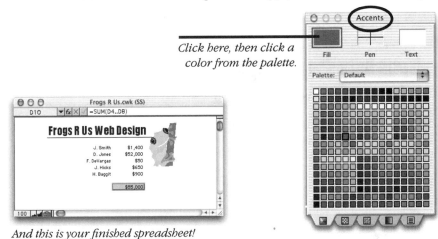

Click here, then click a color from the palette.

And this is your finished spreadsheet!

AppleWorks:
Painting

Paint programs are too much fun. Don't worry if you think you can't draw or paint—this is a fun exercise to walk through, even if you never plan to use this part of the application. Paint a monster because then no one can say it doesn't look like a monster, whereas if you try to paint a rose, you might not be very happy with your results (unless of course you really are a painter).

So don't be intimidated; jump right in and follow the directions. Whether you ever plan to paint things or not, you will learn a lot more about your computer, and you will feel more comfortable and powerful.

If you like painting like this, explore more on your own. I can't tell you *everything* about this program in this short chapter, but AppleWorks has a great Help section: While the program is open, go to the Help menu and choose "AppleWorks Help." Click on the topics you want to learn more about, or type in the name of a topic you are looking for.

Get Ready to Paint

Now, you might be in one of four different situations, depending on whether you've been following along or not. Choose the situation you're in and follow the directions:

This is the Painting icon.

A. You just finished the spreadsheet exercise and the spreadsheet is still on your screen.

1. Save your spreadsheet (if you want): press Command S.

2. Click the red Close button in the upper-left corner, or use the keyboard shortcut Command W (W for Window).

3. Go to the next page in this book.

B. You finished the spreadsheet exercise, saved and closed it, and didn't quit AppleWorks. You still see the Button Bar.

✪ You are exactly where you need to be! Go to the next page.

C. You finished the spreadsheet exercise, saved and closed it, and didn't quit AppleWorks. BUT you don't see the Button Bar.

1. Find the AppleWorks icon in the Dock. Single-click it.

2. After you click the AppleWorks icon, the "Starting Points" palette and the Button Bar will appear at the top of the screen.

3. Go to the next page in this book.

D. You skipped the spreadsheet exercise, or you turned off your computer and came back later, and AppleWorks is not open on your Mac.

1. Open AppleWorks just like you did the first time: Single-click its icon in the Dock.

   Or go to the Applications folder, then open the AppleWorks folder. The AppleWorks application is inside the AppleWorks folder! Double-click the AppleWorks application icon.

2. Click the "Painting" icon in the "Starting Points" palette.

3. Go to the next page (of this book), but skip the first step because you just started a new document.

Open a New Paint Document

▼ To open a new, blank paint document, use the Button Bar: click on the "Painting" button with the little palette.

The Paint Tool Palette.

AppleWorks 6 Painting button is in both the Button Bar and the "Starting Points" palette.

Check out the Painting Tools

Along the left side of the screen you now have special painting tools. Try this:

1. **Click once** on the paintbrush tool (circled, on the right).
2. Now position your pointer on the blank document page.
3. Press-and-drag the mouse around to draw any sort of shape.
4. If you want to undo the last thing you did, press Command Z for Undo.

Before you make an ugly monster, play with some of these paint tools. They're easy, and they teach you a lot about how other programs work. Follow along on the next several pages to experiment.

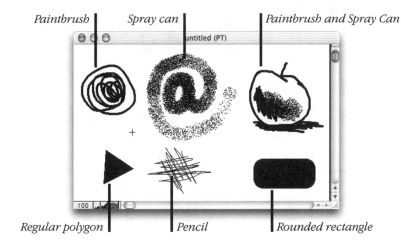

Paintbrush   Spray can   Paintbrush and Spray Can

Regular polygon   Pencil   Rounded rectangle

Erase Anything or Everything you Just Scribbled

▼ To erase part of your image, **single-click** on the eraser tool. Move the mouse over to the document, and press-and-drag over the area you want to erase.

▼ To erase everything on the page, **double-click** on the eraser tool.

The eraser tool in the Tool Palette.

The paintbrush tool in the Tool Palette.

Dip Your Paintbrush in a Bright Color

From the Window menu, choose "Show Accents" to get the palette shown below; click each of the tabs to see the wide variety of textures, patterns, colors, and gradients you can paint with. (The fifth tab is for use with the line tool.) Click a color or texture to paint with it.

To move the Accents Palette, drag its title bar. To close it, click the Close button in the upper-left corner.

Close button

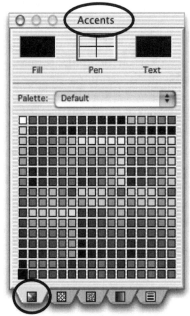

Each tab displays a different pane that contains its own collection of colors, patterns, or textures.

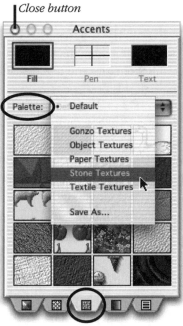

Click on a tab to see another palette. Be sure to check the "Palette" pop-up menu, as shown, to see what else is available in each pane.

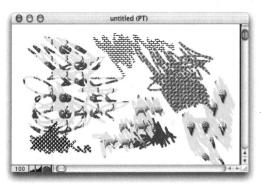

Experiment! Click various tabs in the Accents Palette; choose a color, pattern, or texture; then scribble away with the paintbrush.

Get a bigger paintbrush

1. **Double-click** on the paintbrush tool.

2. **Single-click** on any of those different "brush shapes," as shown below, then click OK.

3. Paint with that new brush: press-and-drag on the page.

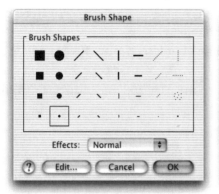

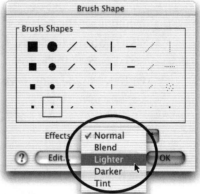

Click any of these brush shapes to choose it. Click "Edit…" to change the shape of the selected brush.

Choose an "Effect" here, then draw on top of something else. The effect will remain in the paintbrush until you change it back!

The trick to painting with your chosen fill and border colors

Experiment with using these colors and patterns! ***The trick is you must choose the color and/or pattern BEFORE you paint something.*** So choose a fancy fill texture and then paint on the page. Then experiment with painting over other items, changing the brush pattern and effect, spray painting, etc.

You can also **choose more than one color and pattern.** Select one of those black-and-white fill patterns, like this: ▨ , then choose a color that you want that pattern to appear in. (You can't change the color of the fancy textures or gradients.)

The shape tools.

The Fill and Pen buttons.

Fill

Pen

Paint using the shape tools

1. You're not limited to using the paintbrush. Choose one of the shape tools near the top of the Tool Palette, as shown to the left.

2. Click on the "Fill" button (shown to the left), then choose a pattern, color, texture, or gradient for the **inside** of the shape.

3. Click on the Pen button, then choose a pattern, color, texture, or gradient for the **border** of the shape.

   Also choose a **thickness** for the border: click on this symbol ▤ and choose a thickness.

4. With the shape tool, *press* on the page and drag diagonally to create a shape. Amazing.

Try these special tools

The regular polygon tool.

▼ Click on the **regular polygon tool**. Press and drag—a shape will appear, and it will rotate around as you move your mouse. Let go of the mouse button to put the shape on the page. Try it.

Double-click the polygon tool to get a dialog box in which you can choose the number of sides you want in the shape.

The irregular polygon tool.

▼ Click on the **irregular polygon tool** shown to the left (I call this the spiderweb tool). On the page, ***don't press-and-drag***—instead, click once, then move the mouse and click somewhere else, then click somewhere else, etc. Cross over the existing lines, if you like. When you have created a shape, *single-click* directly on top of the first point you made, or *double-click* anywhere and the shape will close itself up. It will fill with the pattern or texture you had last chosen.

Remember, to stop the spiderweb tool, click directly on top of the first point you made, or double-click anywhere.

Use the Spray Can

I'll bet you know what to do: choose the **spray can tool.** Choose a color and/or pattern, then press-and-drag on the page.

In the Tool Palette, double-click the spray can tool to open the "Edit Spray Can" window and change the spray.

The spray can (airbrush) tool.

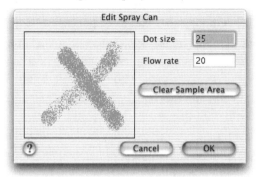

Pour Paint into a Shape with the Paint Bucket

1. Before you can pour paint, you need a shape to pour it into. So first:

    a. Double-click on the **paintbrush tool.** Choose any brush and the "Normal" effect, and click OK.

    b. Then choose a **solid color** from the color palette, and a **solid pattern** from the Pattern palette.

    c. Paint a shape, like a monster head. It is extremely important that the shape be entirely closed (no holes anywhere) because *if there is the tiniest hole, the paint from the bucket will spill out of the hole and spread all over the entire page.*

2. Now choose the paint bucket tool:

3. Choose any color, pattern, or texture.

4. Position the bucket inside the shape that you want to fill with paint. The paint pours out of the very *tip* of the spilling point so make sure the tip is positioned to pour inside the shape.

5. Then just click and the paint will pour into the shape. If you don't like the color, *immediately* press Command Z to undo (or choose Undo from the Edit menu); choose another color or texture, and click again.

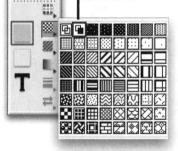

This little icon in the Pattern palette removes any pattern and makes the fill a solid color.

The paint pours out of the very tip.

Transform a Shape

Here's an important technique to experiment with. Take a look at the Transform menu (it's in the menu bar across the top of the screen, not in the Button Bar or any palette). All the commands under Transform are probably gray, correct? That's because you must first *select* a shape that you want to transform (remember, select first, then do it to it). You have two selection tools, as shown to the left: a rectangular tool and a lasso tool.

The selection tools.

The rectangular tool selects a rectangular shape and picks up any background that it encloses. The lasso tool snaps to the exact shape of the object. To see the difference, draw a heart on the page with the brush. Then:

The rectangle selection tool selects the entire rectangular shape.

1. Choose the **rectangular selection tool.** Begin outside of the heart, in the upper-left area, and drag diagonally down to the right.

   Then press the pointer in the center of that selected shape and drag. See, it drags the entire rectangle.

The lasso selects just the object.

2. Now choose the **lasso tool.** Press-and-drag to draw loosely around the heart. When you let go, the lasso snaps to the heart shape. (You don't even have to draw entirely around the shape—when you let go, the lasso will find the other end of itself and snap to it.)

   To drag that selected shape, make sure you see the pointer—when the lasso tool is positioned on a draggable area of the image, it will turn into the pointer. The tool flips back and forth between lasso and pointer, so make sure you have the pointer before you try to move the object!

3. So that's how you select something. Now draw a shape, any shape.

4. Select that shape with either selection tool.

5. From the Transform menu, experiment with the choices. Choose something like "Perspective." Your selected object will display "handles," as shown below. Position the *tip* of the pointer tool in any one of those handles, then press-and-drag. Experiment with other options!

   (You must *re*select the object before you can transform again.)

Tip: Try the "Pick Up" command. First paint a shape. Then select it with the lasso tool. Drag it onto some other shape that has a fancy pattern. While the shape is still selected and sitting on that other pattern, choose "Pick Up" from the Transform menu. Then drag the shape out to a clean part of the page. It will have picked up the pattern. You gotta try it to get it.

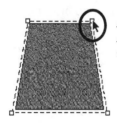

Each corner has a handle. Press-and-drag a handle to reshape the object.

Type Some Words and Color Them

You can also type words onto the page, and you can color those words. But keep in mind that you are painting, not word processing; that is, you won't be able to go back and edit the words or easily change their colors like you can in a word processor. And the text won't print as cleanly as text from a word processor. But it is great fun to do anyway. Follow the directions carefully.

The text tool.

1. Choose the **text tool.**

2. With the text tool, click on the left side of the painting page so you have room for the text to type out to the right. *As soon as you click, you'll see the menu bar change!* Now, while the insertion point is flashing on the page, you have menu items for text.

3. Before you type anything, go to the Text menu and choose the font, size, and color (you'll have to go to the menu three times, one for each choice). Unfortunately, you can't choose any of the patterns, textures, or gradients to type with. But you can choose any solid color.

4. Now type onto the page. Hit the Return key before the type bumps into the right side of the page. If you decide you want a different typeface, size, or color, press-and-drag over the text, then select your new choices. *But don't click outside of the little text box!* The very second you click anywhere outside of that text, the words become paint on the page and you cannot do any sort of editing—if you want to change anything after that point, you'll have to erase it and do it over again. It'll make you a little crazy for a while until you get the hang of it.

5. Once the type is set how you like it, click anywhere outside of the text box. Then you can select it (as described on the previous page) and move it wherever you like, transform it, delete it, etc.

*This is an example of paint text. You can, while typing, choose another typeface, size, and color and whatever you type **next** will be in the new formatting.*

I FOUND BETTER THINGS
IN THE DARK
THAN I EVER FOUND
IN THE LIGHT.

Ross Carter

So Now Paint an Ugly Monster

Use shapes or the paintbrush to create your monster. Use the paintbucket to fill in colors or textures. Paint the forest and the castle. Type a poem about your monster. You can't hurt anything, so experiment with all the tools and options—you'll learn a lot. Just remember to choose the tool, then the color/pattern/fill for the inside and the border *before* you paint.

See, isn't this a stupid-looking monster? So what!
Don't be afraid to paint something dorky—celebrate the dorkiness!

AppleWorks:
Drawing

A **draw program** can be less intimidating than a paint program because you mostly work with lines, boxes, and ovals ("lbo's," affectionately called "elbows"). The things you learn in this exercise will apply to many other programs that have draw tools as part of their features.

It's really a good idea to pair this draw exercise with the preceding paint exercise so you see the difference between a paint program and a draw program. You will not only learn which one to choose for a particular project, but you will feel more comfortable and knowledgeable when you understand the strengths and weaknesses of the two different sorts of applications.

Even if you think you can't draw a thing, go through the exercise and draw a little house. You'll be surprised. Even if your house turns out really silly (it can't be sillier than Robin's drawing), you will have learned a lot.

Remember, if you want to learn more, go to the Help menu in AppleWorks and choose "AppleWorks Help."

Get Ready to Draw

Now, you might be in one of four different situations, depending on whether you've been following along or not. Choose the situation you're in and follow the directions:

This is the Drawing icon.

A. You just finished the paint exercise and the painting is still on your screen.

   1. Save this document (if you want): press Command S.

   2. Click the Close button in the upper-left corner, or use the keyboard shortcut Command W (W for Window).

   3. Go to the next page in this book.

B. You finished the paint exercise, saved and closed it, and didn't quit AppleWorks. You still see the Button Bar.

   ✪ You are exactly where you need to be! Go to the next page in this book.

C. You finished the paint exercise, saved and closed it, and didn't quit AppleWorks. BUT you don't see the Button Bar.

   1. Single-click on the AppleWorks icon in the Dock.

   2. After you click the AppleWorks icon, the "Starting Points" palette and the Button Bar will appear at the top of the screen. Go to the next page of this book.

D. You skipped the painting exercise, or you turned off your computer and came back later, and AppleWorks is not open.

   1. Open AppleWorks just like you did the first time: Single-click its icon in the Dock.

   Or go to the Applications folder, then open the AppleWorks folder. The AppleWorks application is inside the AppleWorks folder! Double-click the AppleWorks application icon.

   2. Click the "Drawing" icon in the "Starting Points" palette.

   3. Go to the next page, but skip the first step, the one that says, "Open a draw document," because you just opened one.

Open a New Draw Document

▼ To open a new, blank draw document, use the Button Bar: click on the button with the document and triangle icon.

This is the Drawing button that appears in the Button Bar and also in the "Starting Points" palette.

Tip: If you see a grid pattern in the background, you can choose to turn it off from the Options menu. Choose "Hide Graphics Grid" to make it go away.

Check Out the Drawing Tools

Along the left side of the screen you have the same Tool Palette, but the Paint tools are grayed out—if you did the painting exercise, you'll notice the paintbrush, spray can, pencil, paint bucket, eraser, and a couple of other tools are not available in the Draw module. So experiment with the Draw tools:

The Draw Tool Palette.

Draw and Resize a Shape

1. Click once on a **shape tool** (indicated at the right).
2. Now move the mouse over so you are positioned on the page.
3. Press-and-drag the mouse to draw a shape. The shape will **fill** with whatever color, pattern, or texture is selected in the Tool Palette.
4. Did you notice when you draw a shape you automatically get "handles" on each corner? (If the handles are gone, click once on any part of the object.) If you press the *tip* of the pointer in any one of those handles, you can alter the shape by dragging the handle. Try it.

*This is the original shape. Notice the handles. When an object is **selected**, you see its handles.*

Press-and-drag on any handle to resize the object.

You can resize any object at any time. It is never permanent.

Fill palettes:
— Color
— Pattern
— Wallpaper
— Gradient

Click this Fill button before you choose from the Fill palettes.

Get Rid of an Object

▼ You've probably noticed you don't have an eraser in this Draw module. That's because each item in this program is seen as a complete object. You must remove an entire object—you cannot remove part of one.
   To delete: Select the item (click once on it with the pointer tool), and when you see the handles on the corners, hit the Delete key.

Change the Fill and Border Thicknesses and Patterns

1. One difference between a Paint program and a Draw program is that in Paint you must choose the fill and the border ("Pen") *before* you create the shape; in Draw you can change it whenever you feel like it.

   Just like in the Paint module, in Draw you have palettes from which to choose the patterns and colors of the *inside* of a shape (the Fill), as well as the border thickness, color, and pattern of the *outside* (the Pen). You can use the buttons in the Tool Palette, or use larger palettes available from the Accents palette.

These are at the bottom of the Tool Palette:

Fill button
(inside shapes)

Pen button
(for lines and borders)

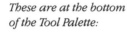
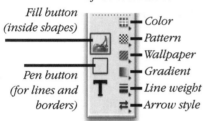

— Color
— Pattern
— Wallpaper
— Gradient
— Line weight
— Arrow style

From the Window menu, choose "Show Accents." The Accents palette looks the same in Paint and Draw.

The tab on the far right is for lines and borders.

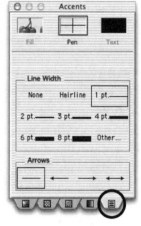

2. At any time—later today, next week, or next year—**click the object to select it,** then change the pattern or color of the inside, the thickness and color of the outside line, the size, or the position of the object. Try these actions (select the object first):

Change the pattern inside the shape (Fill).

Change the thickness and pattern of the border (Pen).

From the Arrange menu, choose "Free Rotate." Then press on any handle, and drag to rotate the object.

Use the Line Tool

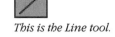

This is the Line tool.

1. Choose the **line tool** by clicking once on it.
2. Press-and-drag on the page to draw a line.
3. After the line is drawn, make sure it is selected (you should see handles on both ends; if not, click once on the line with the *tip* of the pointer), then change the thickness, the color, and add some arrows to one or both ends.

   From the Window menu, choose "Show Accents," then from the Accents palette (shown below, right) select the line attributes (Pen).

   Or use the buttons at the bottom of the Tool Palette: Click any of the small buttons to reveal the pop-up palette.

Draw lines with the line tools.

Click the Pen formatting button so your palette selections will affect the selected line or border.

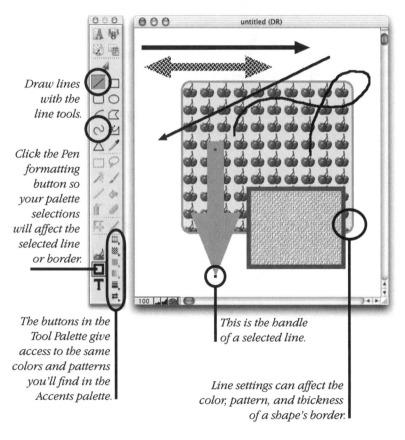

This pane of the Accents palette lets you change line widths, create arrows, and change the border width of a selected shape.

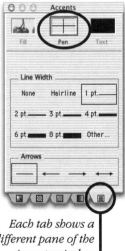

The buttons in the Tool Palette give access to the same colors and patterns you'll find in the Accents palette.

This is the handle of a selected line.

Line settings can affect the color, pattern, and thickness of a shape's border.

Each tab shows a different pane of the Accents window.

Use the Freeform Drawing Tool

So far you have learned how to draw lines, boxes, and ovals (elbows, remember?). But you can also draw freeform shapes, then reshape them, and of course fill them with different colors or patterns, change the line thicknesses, and rotate and flip them to your heart's content.

You have two freeform tools: the freehand tool and something called the bezier tool. First try the freehand tool.

This is the freehand tool.

1. Choose the **freehand tool** from the Tool Palette.

2. Press-and-drag as usual, just like you did in the Paint program or with any other draw tool.

3. Now this is the interesting thing about a freehand form in a Draw program: you can reshape it.

   If the shape doesn't have handles, select it by clicking once on it. Then from the Arrange menu, choose "Reshape."

4. Your cursor changes to a target (⊕), and the freeform shape gets little "points" on it (as shown below).

   Position the *center* of the target cursor on any of the points, press, and then drag. You have to play with it to get the hang of reshaping.

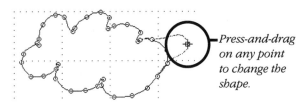

Press-and-drag on any point to change the shape.

Use the Bezier Tool

The Bezier tool (pronounced *bay zyay*), which combines something called "Bezier curves" with a polygon, is another freehand sort of tool.

This is the bezier tool.

1. Choose the **Bezier tool** from the Tool Palette.

2. ***Do not press-and-drag!*** Instead, click once on the page, then move the mouse and click once somewhere else. Keep repeating the click-and-move action to create your shape.

3. When you have the basic shape you want, either double-click to finish the shape, or single-click directly on top of the first point.

4. While the shape is selected, from the Arrange menu, choose "Reshape." You get the same little points you saw with the freehand tool on the previous page.

   But if you click on one of those points with the target cursor, you get "control points" with long handles. Position the center of the target cursor on the end of one of those handles, and drag. Watch the shape change.

   This takes lots of experimenting before you begin to know what to expect when you drag. Try it!

Note: *If you're wondering why curves drawn this way are called Bezier curves: a mathematician named Pierre Bezier invented this technique of drawing curves on a computer. John likes to call them "Pierre curves."*

This is the original shape.

You can either drag the point itself...

...or drag either end of a point's handles.

The outlines display the original shape, plus the new shape, until you let go.

Now Draw a Silly Little House

The tools are pretty easy to use, aren't they? Below are a few guidelines to help you use them. The trick to creating something fun in a drawing program (as in life) is to be creative with what you have.

▼ Keep checking to see which tool is selected. As soon as you draw something, AppleWorks switches back to the pointer tool.

▼ If you need to select an object and it's not getting handles when you click on it, check to make sure you have the pointer tool.

▼ No matter what patterns or colors are currently in the borders or the fills of any object, you can always change them.

▼ Make sure you have the right palette when you try to change a border (line) or a fill.

This is the text tool.

▼ Experiment with the text tool. Choose it, click on the page, and type. Edit the text just like you did in the word processor. The Text menu only appears after you have selected the text tool and clicked on the page!

▼ To select any object and send it behind the other objects or bring it in front: select the object, then use the Arrange menu.

I used the "spiderweb" tool to create the sun's rays, the tree trunk, and the roof.

I drew one cat, then used the pointer tool to drag around all of the different objects that make the cat—this selected all the pieces. Then I held down the Option key and dragged to create a copy of the cat.

To create perfect circles and squares, hold the Shift key down while using the oval or rectangle shape tool.

**Our house
is a very very fine house.**

After I drew this chimney, using the brick fill pattern and a brown color, I sent it behind the roof.

I used the freehand tool to create the cherry tree top and the chimney smoke.

*Text in the draw program doesn't look any better **on the screen** than it does in paint, but it **prints** beautifully. And you can edit (change) it as often as you like.*

AppleWorks:
Presentation

AppleWorks includes a **presentation** module that makes it easy and fun to create professional-looking slideshow presentations. Make slideshows for your family and friends, for school, or for work. Then present the slideshows on a computer, or print them onto transparencies so you can display them on an overhead projector. If you make your presentation on a computer, you can include movies, sounds, and visual transitions between slides. To aid you in your presentation, print a copy of the slideshow and include notes to yourself. AppleWorks lets you set slideshow playing options so you can design the presentation to suit your needs.

You can present your slideshow on the computer, full screen, and use the arrow keys to go forward and back from slide to slide.

Get Ready to Create a Presentation

Now, you might be in one of four different situations, depending on whether you've been following along or not. Choose the situation you're in and follow the directions:

This is the Presentation icon.

A. **You just finished the drawing exercise and the drawing document is still on your screen.**

1. Save this drawing (if you want): press Command S.

2. Click the red Close button in the upper-left corner, or use the keyboard shortcut Command W (W for Window).

3. Go to the next page in this book.

B. **You finished the drawing exercise, saved and closed it, and didn't quit AppleWorks. You still see the Button Bar.**

✪ You are exactly where you need to be! Go to the next page.

C. **You finished the drawing exercise, saved and closed it, and didn't quit AppleWorks. BUT you don't see the Button Bar.**

1. Find the AppleWorks icon in the Dock. Single-click it.

2. After you click the AppleWorks icon, the "Starting Points" palette and the Button Bar will appear at the top of the screen.

3. Go to the next page of this book.

D. **You skipped the previous exercise, or you turned off your computer and came back later, and AppleWorks is not open on your Mac.**

1. Open AppleWorks just like you did the first time: Single-click its icon in the Dock.

   Or go to the Applications folder, then open the AppleWorks folder. The AppleWorks application is inside the AppleWorks folder! Double-click the AppleWorks application icon.

2. Click the "Presentation" icon in the "Starting Points" palette.

3. Go to the next page (of this book), but skip the first step because you just started a new document.

Open a New Slide Presentation Document

To open a new, blank presentation document, use the Button Bar: single-click on the button that has a "slide" image on it.

Take a minute to look at the new document window and the "Controls palette. If you don't see the Controls palette, click the "Show Controls" button in the Button Bar (shown circled, below). *Or* from the Window menu, choose "Show Presentation Controls."

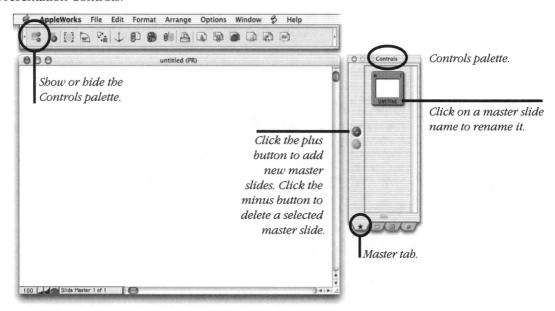

Show or hide the Controls palette.

Controls palette.

Click on a master slide name to rename it.

Click the plus button to add new master slides. Click the minus button to delete a selected master slide.

Master tab.

Master Slides and the Controls Palette

A **master slide** is a *template,* or reusable slide, that includes design elements that will appear on other slides. It's a lot easier and faster to create a good-looking presentation if you don't have to build every slide from scratch. And when you use master slides, your presentation has a consistent, professional look.

You can use more than one master slide in a presentation. For instance, you might have a collection of photographs from your European tour, so you could create separate master slides for the sets of photos from each country.

The "Master tab" at the bottom of the **Controls palette** (shown above) displays a panel of small, thumbnail versions of the "master slides" you will create (as described on the following page). From here you can choose which master to use as a background for each slide.

Make a Master Slide

The master slide will be a consistent background on which you'll place the other, changeable elements of your presentation. You can use a solid color, a pattern, a design created in AppleWorks or somewhere else, a photo, or a combination of all those things. Use the tools and techniques you learned earlier in this chapter to create shapes filled with colors and patterns, then add some text to the page.

Leave large areas of the layout empty so your individual slides can use that space for text, photos, clip art, or movies.

Draw a round cornered rectangle, add a border, and fill with a solid color.

Add a text headline

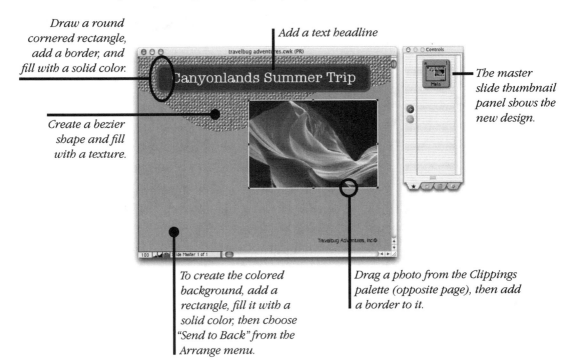

The master slide thumbnail panel shows the new design.

Create a bezier shape and fill with a texture.

To create the colored background, add a rectangle, fill it with a solid color, then choose "Send to Back" from the Arrange menu.

Drag a photo from the Clippings palette (opposite page), then add a border to it.

Add a Photo or Clipart to the Slide

Drag photos into the presentation window from any window on your Desktop. For instance, open your Pictures folder in which you have stored your photos. Make it a List View and resize it to tall and skinny over on the right side of your monitor. Then in AppleWorks, just drag a photo from your Pictures folder and drop it on the presentation window.

In the example presentation, I found the photo in the **Clippings palette,** provided by AppleWorks. The Clippings palette is a handy place to keep images, text, movies, and other items that you want to reuse in your documents. AppleWorks has provided lots of images already, but you can make your own collections (as separate panels) of art, logos, photos, or whatever. Almost anything that can be digitized can be dragged into the Clippings palette— photographs, movies, illustrations, scanned images, drawings and paintings you created in AppleWorks, etc.

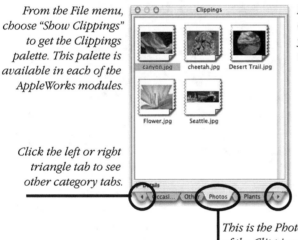

From the File menu, choose "Show Clippings" to get the Clippings palette. This palette is available in each of the AppleWorks modules.

Drag images from the Clippings palette into your presentation window.

Click the left or right triangle tab to see other category tabs.

This is the Photos panel of the Clippings palette.

Make the First Slides of the Presentation

Once you have a master slide, you can make a number of new slides using the master as a background.

1. Click the **Master tab** (the star) at the bottom of the Controls palette.

2. Single-click on the master slide thumbnail image you created.

3. Click the **Slide tab** (circled, below) at the bottom of the Controls palette.

4. Click the "plus" button to add a thumbnail of the master slide to the Slide panel. The new slide displays full-size in the document window, ready to be customized with your content.

5. Do something like add a new shape, fill it with a texture, then add text, as shown below.

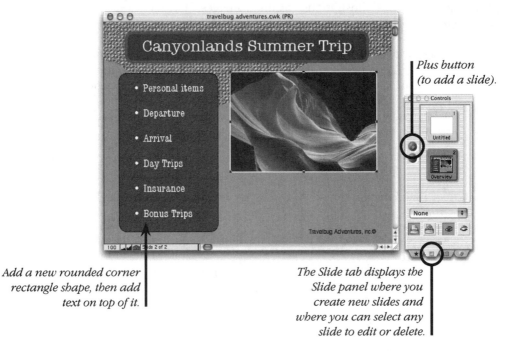

Plus button (to add a slide).

Add a new rounded corner rectangle shape, then add text on top of it.

The Slide tab displays the Slide panel where you create new slides and where you can select any slide to edit or delete.

Make More Slides from this Master

To create another new slide using the same master, click the plus button again. A new thumbnail appears in the Slide pane, and the new slide displays in the document window, ready to be modified. Continue this procedure until you've created as many slides as you need.

The Controls Palette Features

The bottom of the Controls palette has several useful buttons.

> **To mark a slide to print (or not),** select the slide in the panel, then click one of the printer buttons.

> **To hide or show a slide in a slideshow,** select the slide, then click the "Hide slide" or "Show slide" button.

The **Transitions** button is explained on the next page.

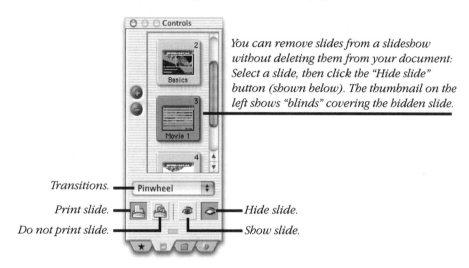

You can remove slides from a slideshow without deleting them from your document: Select a slide, then click the "Hide slide" button (shown below). The thumbnail on the left shows "blinds" covering the hidden slide.

Transitions.

Print slide.

Do not print slide.

Hide slide.

Show slide.

Add Transitions Between Slides

Add some visual interest to your slideshow by creating "transitions" between slides. AppleWorks includes a pop-up menu full of different effects that you can apply with a click of the mouse.

To create a visual transition:

1. Select a slide in the Slide panel to which you want to apply a transition. The effect will be applied between the selected slide and the following one.

2. Click the "Transition" pop-up menu in the Slide panel.

3. Choose one of the transitions in the list, as shown to the left.

When using master slides, some elements don't change from slide to slide, which makes some transitions look strange or minimizes their effect. In that case, I usually prefer the "Fade" transition—it creates the visual illusion that most of the content of the original slide stays on the screen as the changing elements fade out and in. Of course, the entire slide is actually changing, but since some elements of the slide are identical, they *appear* to stay on the screen. When you switch to slides that use master backgrounds that are completely different, any of the transitions provide a great dramatic effect to emphasize the new background.

Single-click the Transitions pop-up menu in the Slide panel to choose an effect.

Preview Your Slideshow

At any time you can play your slideshow to evaluate it. It's a good idea to check transitions to see if they add interest—or not. You may also realize you have too many slides that are similar (thus boring), or too few slides to communicate your message.

This is the "Start Show" button.

1. Click the "Start Show" button in the Button Bar.

2. The slideshow fills the entire screen as it plays.

   Press the Right arrow on your keyboard to advance to the next slide. Press the Left arrow to return to the previous slide.

3. To stop the show and return to your Desktop, press the Escape key (esc) on the top-left corner of your keyboard, or press Command Period (.).

Add a Movie to a Slide

If you think a slideshow presentation is fun, you haven't seen anything yet. You can even add QuickTime movies to a slide! Where do you get QuickTime movies? You can sometimes download them from other people's web sites (ask permission), and some digital cameras can make short QuickTime movies. Or if you're using iMovie on your iMac to edit home movies, you can export an iMovie as a QuickTime movie.

For this exercise, I have some QuickTime movies that I made with iMovie and that I placed in a Clippings panel.

To add a QuickTime movie to a slide:

1. Select the thumbnail slide (in the Slide panel of the Controls palette) in which you want to add a movie, as shown in the figure on page 410.

2. Locate a QuickTime movie on your computer. Drag the movie's QuickTime icon from its location to the open presentation window.

3. Resize the movie if it's too large: Click on the movie to select it, then hold down the Command and Shift keys and drag one of the corner "handles."

Tips: **To start playing a movie,** double-click it.

Stop play with a single click, even if the movie controls are not visible.

See below, left, to show the movie controls.

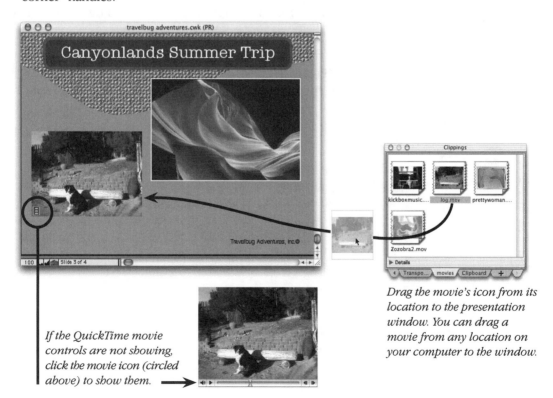

If the QuickTime movie controls are not showing, click the movie icon (circled above) to show them. ➝

Drag the movie's icon from its location to the presentation window. You can drag a movie from any location on your computer to the window.

More Movie Tidbits

You can put more than one movie on a slide. Drag the movies into any position and resize them to fit. Play each movie individually, or play them all at once. Your iMac is powerful enough to do everything.

Be careful when resizing movies in AppleWorks— smaller is okay, but if you resize a movie to a larger size, it looks bad (pixelated).

The Organize panel.

The Organize Panel

Click the "Organize" tab to group, rearrange, rename, or delete slides in your presentation.

To add a folder, click the "plus" button.

To delete a folder, select it and click the "minus" button.

To rearrange the slides and folders into any order, or to move slides from one folder to another, press-and-drag them. The slides will show or print in the order they appear in this window.

The Slideshow panel

Use the Slideshow panel to customize settings for slides, movies, and sounds.

To make movie playback controls visible, as in the example shown above, click the "Show controls" checkbox in the "Movies and Sounds" section of this panel.

Play button.

The Slideshow panel.

Make Slide Notes

You can include notes with your slides to help you plan what to include in the slide content, or to help plan your verbal presentation. Print your slide notes to aid you in your presentation.

To make slide notes:

1. Click the "Slide" tab at the bottom of the Controls palette.

2. Select a slide.

3. From the Window menu at the top of your screen, choose "Notes View."
   A checkmark will appear next to the item to indicate that Notes View is turned on.

4. Type your notes in the Notes "frame" that appears under the slide.

Tip: To return to a normal view of your presentation, go to the Window menu, then choose "Notes View" again to turn the notes off.

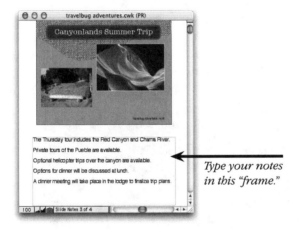

Type your notes in this "frame."

To print your notes:

1. From the File menu, choose "Print...."

2. In the Print window, choose "AppleWorks 6" from the pop-up menu.

3. Click the "Notes" button, then click "Print."

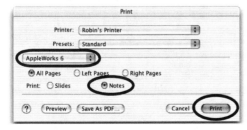

Notice you can also choose to print your slides from this dialog box.

Image Format and Size Recommendations

AppleWorks will accept most common image file formats, such as TIFF, JPEG, PDF, and EPS. These are some format recommendations to help make your presentation more efficient.

All slides in an AppleWorks presentation document are a standard **size** of 640 pixels wide by 480 pixels tall (about the size of most 14-inch monitors). Photos that you insert should be that size or smaller, although you can resize a photo by dragging it to a smaller size in the presentation window.

Photos should have a maximum **resolution** of 72 ppi, but AppleWorks will accept higher resolutions. Higher resolution images won't look any better on the screen, plus they take up more disk space.

The **color mode** of an image should be set to RGB (red, green, blue) to look its best. If you use an image whose color mode is CMYK (cyan, magenta, yellow, black), the color looks oversaturated and dark. Digital cameras create RGB images, and scanners usually scan in RGB mode by default.

Photo specifications: 640 by 480 pixels, 72 ppi resolution, RGB color mode.

These are clip art images from the Clippings window.

OmniGraffle

OmniGraffle

Some Macs include an application called **OmniGraffle,** a powerful diagramming and charting tool, used for visual organization of everything from fanciful ideas to corporate structures. With OmniGraffle you can create family trees, beautiful flow charts, organizational charts, and almost anything else. Use it to make finished projects or as a conceptual visualizing tool for brainstorming.

Basically, OmniGraffle uses boxes and lines as organization tools. But the variety and flexibility of these boxes and lines are what makes OmniGraffle both powerful and fun. It can be used on a basic, simplistic level, or as a sophisticated, professional tool. You can export an OmniGraffle document in a variety of image formats, including a web page format that can include hot links to web addresses and other actions.

If OmniGraffle wasn't bundled with other software on your Mac, you can go to **www.omnigroup.com/applications/omnigraffle/** and download one of three versions: a *Free Version* (you're limited to creating 20 items per document), a *Free Trial License* (it's in licensed mode, with an expiring one-day trial license), or as a *Licensed Version* (you buy a license to fully enable the application). As with other OmniGroup products, the license is reasonably priced and the program is very satisfying, both functionally and aesthetically.

The chart on the next page could have been created in lots of different drawing, word processing, or desktop publishing programs. But OmniGraffle goes beyond drawing shapes and adding text, letting you reorganize the elements, move them around without breaking the connections, or easily change the graphic attributes of any element. As you'll see from some of the templates that are included with OmniGraffle, this software was really designed for programmers and engineer types who need a powerful visualization tool for highly technical projects. While OmniGraffle's capabilities go far beyond what most of us need, it's a great tool on its most simplistic level.

The Document Window Overview

An OmniGraffle document window's toolbar provides a "Drawing Tools" bar that contains eight tools, three icons that hide or show special floating windows, a couple of icons to change the stacking order of elements, and icons to lock or unlock elements in a document.

The following pages explain each of the tools and windows you can use to create a chart such as the one below. As you become familiar with the tools, windows, and palettes, you can quickly and easily visualize your ideas and share them with others.

Hide/Show:
Info Viewer window.
Selection window.
Palettes window.

Drawing Tools.

Send to Front/Send to Back.

Drag shapes from a palette to a document, add text labels, then use the Line tool (the arrow icon) from the Drawing Tools bar to connect items. Drag a graphic anywhere in the document and the connections remain.

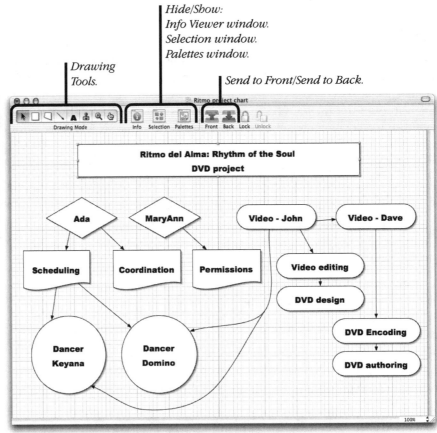

As I move these shapes, the lines follow along, one advantage of working with OmniGraffle as opposed to a regular drawing program.

The Drawing Tools

As in any application, click a tool to select it. However, some of these tools behave a little differently from what you may expect. Usually when you select a tool, you expect it to stay selected—but four of these tools (those shown in bold, below) revert back to the Selection tool after being used *unless* you select them with a double-click instead of a single click. Look for these visual clues: a tool highlighted with a *blue* color will stay selected indefinitely (until you select another tool). A tool highlighted with *gray* will revert back to the Selection tool after being used. If you double-click a tool that reverts, it highlights in *blue,* indicating it will stay selected indefinitely.

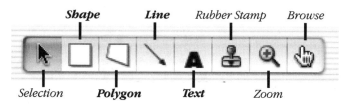

To modify the attributes of the Shape, Polygon, Line, Text, or Browse tool, select the tool, then click the "Show Info" icon in the toolbar to open the "Info" window. Learn about the Info window on page 424.

Selection tool

Use the Selection tool to select objects or lines in a document so you can move them around, modify their shape, or delete them.

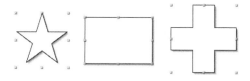

When selected with the Selection tool, objects display "knobs" you can drag to alter the size or shape. Shift-drag to maintain the original proportions.

Shape tool

The Shape tool lets you draw rectangular shapes. Click anywhere in a document and drag a rectangular shape of any size or shape. You can change the many attributes of a shape (fill, color, stroke, drop shadow, rotation, etc.) through the Info window (see page 424).

Polygon tool

The Polygon tool draws irregular shapes. Each click in a document wth the Polygon tool adds a "knob" to the shape. To close a polygon shape, click on the first knob you created, *or* double-click anywhere you want to finish the shape. To constrain the angles of the lines to multiples of 45 degrees, hold down the Shift key as you click.

A polygon can have any number of straight sides.

Line tool

The Line tool connects items and visually shows the relationship between them. Choose the line color, style, and weight, modify line heads and ends, and set other line attributes in the "Info" window (see page 424). There are three basic line styles, shown below, to choose from in the Info window.

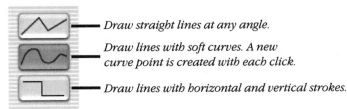

Draw straight lines at any angle.

Draw lines with soft curves. A new curve point is created with each click.

Draw lines with horizontal and vertical strokes.

- ▾ **To connect two shapes,** select the Line tool, then click inside a shape and drag to the inside of another shape. The start and end points of the line snap to the centers of the shapes, or to the nearest magnetic point, if there is one (see page 427 to learn about magnetic points).

- ▾ **To reshape a line,** drag any knob.

- ▾ **To add additional knobs,** Option–double-click on a line.

- ▾ **To delete an intermediate knob,** click it, then press Delete.

Tip: To change an existing line style, click it with the Selection tool, then click a Line Style button in the "Line Info" pane.

*The three basic line styles are shown above. Lines have **green knobs** at their head points, **red knobs** at their tail points, and **blue knobs** at intermediate points.*

Text tool

Use the Text tool to set type and create labels for shapes and lines. The Text tool icon displays the selected default font.

To set the default font:

1. Click once on the Text icon.

2. Open the Fonts panel. From the "Format" menu, choose "Font," then choose "Show Fonts."

3. Select a font family, typeface, and font size. You can also specify a text color.

Tip: With the text tool, click outside a shape to create a text box that autosizes to fit your text as you type.

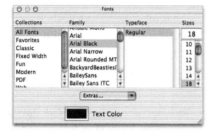

To add a label (text) to a line:

1. Click the Selection tool icon.

2. Double-click on a line.

3. Type in the text entry box that appears on the line. Set label alignment and other attributes in the "Line Info" window (page 425).

To add a label to a shape:

1. Click the Text icon.

2. Click inside a shape.

3. Type a label name in the text entry box that appears inside the shape.

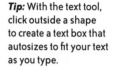

Rubber Stamp tool

When making a chart, you may want to repeat a particular shape in many different places on the chart. You can use the Rubber Stamp tool for this.

To make duplicate copies of an existing graphic:

1. Click the Rubber Stamp icon.

2. Option-click on a shape or graphic.

3. Click in the document where you want to place a duplicate.

Tip: The small triangle on the stamp turns white when you press the Option key, indicating it will load the item you click on next. After loading an item, the triangle turns black, ready to stamp the loaded item wherever you click.

Zoom tool

The Zoom tool lets you enlarge or reduce the document view.

▾ **To increase the document magnification:** Select the Zoom tool and click in the document. The document view magnifies by 100 percent increments with each click of the Zoom tool. The magnified view is automatically centered on the click location.

▾ **To reduce the document magnification:** Select the Zoom tool and Option-click in the document. The document view reduces by 100 percent increments with each click of the Zoom tool. The reduced-magnification view is automatically centered on the click location.

▾ **To zoom in without centering** the magnification on the click location: Select the Zoom tool and Shift-click in the document.

Browse tool

The Browse tool allows you to detect and activate "actions" that have been attached to graphics, such as opening an email form or a web page. If you plan to export your OmniGraffle document as an "HTML Image Map," the actions you attach will function on the web page in which the image is placed.

To attach an action to a graphic:

1. Click the Browse icon in the toolbar.

2. Open the "Action Info" window (click the Info icon in the toolbar, then, in the Info pane, choose "Action" from the pop-up menu).

3. Choose to "Open a URL" or "Run a Script."

   Open a URL requires that you enter a web address in the text box.

   Run a Script requires that you enter the name of an AppleScript that is in your "Scripts folder."

   Typically, scripts are stored in: YourHomeFolder/Library/Application Support/OmniGraffle/Scripts.

   AppleScripts are written in a simple (ha!) programming language that can control actions in applications that are AppleScript-enabled. This can be an efficient and powerful tool for performing repetitive tasks. You can often find great AppleScripts written for various applications on the Apple site, or you can search other places on the Internet.

   You can put an AppleScript icon in your OmniGraffle toolbar, then click that icon whenever you want to access the Scripts folder. See page 431.

The Selection Pane

Use the Selection pane to select all the instances of a shape in a document when there are lots of shapes to choose. If you decide to change all the round-cornered rectangles in a chart to square-cornered rectangles, you can instantly select them all and, using the "Shape Info" pane, pick another shape to replace them all. Any labels you created will remain in place.

Selection

To change all instances of a shape:

1. Click the "Selection" icon in the toolbar (shown above, right).

2. The "Selection" pane opens to show all shapes that occur in the document. Click a shape in the Selection pane to automatically select all matching shapes in the document.

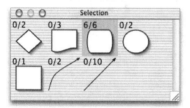 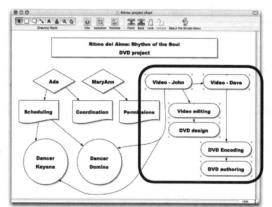

The Selection pane (above) shows all existing shapes in the document (right). The numbers next to a shape indicate how many instances of a shape are selected, and how many are in the document.

Select a shape in this pane and all matching shapes in the document are selected.

3. Click the "Show Info" icon (the one with the "**i**") in the document toolbar to open the "Info" pane.

4. From the "Info Panes" pop-up menu, choose "Shape."

5. In the "Shape Info" pane, choose a shape to replace the existing selected shapes.

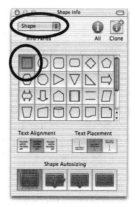 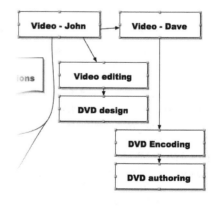

As soon as a new shape (circled above) is chosen, the selected shapes in the document change to that shape.

Info

The Info Viewer Window

To open the **Info Viewer** window, click the "Show Info Panel" icon in the OmniGraffle document toolbar. The Info Viewer window can show twelve different panes that are accessible from the "Info Panes" pop-up menu. Each pane contains settings to adjust or modify an OmniGraffle document, a drawing tool, or selected graphic items in a document.

All of the Info windows on the following pages are the same *window,* but show different *panes,* determined by the current pop-up menu selection.

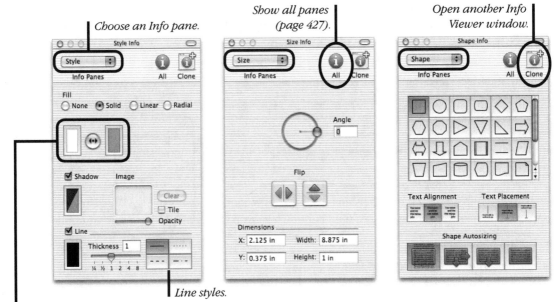

Choose an Info pane.

Show all panes
(page 427).

Open another Info
Viewer window.

Line styles.

Click a box to set
Fill (left) and Stroke
(right) colors. Click
the button between
them to switch colors.

In the **Style** pane, to fill
a shape with a photo
or other image, drag
the photo from your
Desktop and drop it
into the "Image" well
(above, left), then adjust
the opacity of the image
with the Opacity slider.
See an example on the
next page.

Style Info

From this pane, choose the fill style, color of a shape, and the style settings of a *selected* line, shape, or graphic.

Size Info

Select a graphic or a shape in a document, then modify its rotation angle, flip it horizontally or vertically, or enter precise dimensions for it.

Shape Info

Change the shape of an existing shape in a document, modify text alignment or placement, and set Shape autosizing attributes.

If you've created a label by double-clicking on a line, use the modifiers in the bottom half of the "Line Info" pane (below, left) to adjust the label's location and orientation of labels.

You can create interesting visual effects with graphics by filling shapes with images and adjusting the image transparency in the Style pane, as described on the previous page. For more information about adding images to shapes, see page 435.

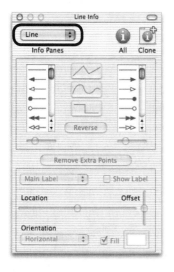

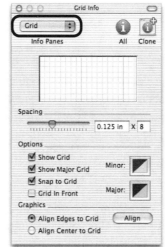

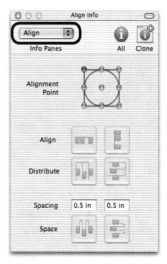

Line Info

The Line Info pane is where you set the style of start and end points of lines **To choose a line's start point,** select a graphic from the left box; **to choose a line's endpoint,** select a graphic from the right box. Click the Reverse button to reverse the line direction. The bottom controls let you control the label's visibility, location, and orientation.

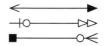

These are a few of the 25 different line ending styles.

Grid Info

The Grid Info pane lets you control the visibility, scaling, and color of a grid that aids in alignment of items in a document.

Align Info

The Align Info pane's tools align *selected* items in a document.

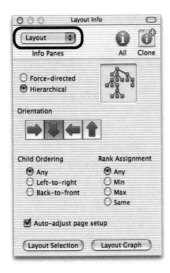

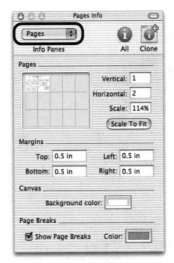

Layout Info

With the tools and options in this pane, you can rearrange and organize the graphics in your document based on two automatic layout styles: "Force-directed" and "Hierarchical." Select a style, choose behavior options, then click either "Layout Selection" or "Layout Graph." Unless you're experienced with these layout styles, they may be more confusing than useful.

Pages Info

This is where you control the size and orientation of your document, plus some other settings. To make your document two pages wide, click the second page in the Pages well (so that two white pages are showing). Or type a number of pages in the "Vertical" and "Horizontal" text boxes. If your chart is too large or small for the desired page size, click the "Scale To Fit" button. Select "Show Page Breaks" to make a line visible where pages meet. This is helpful in planning placement of graphics.

Layers Info

Use the Layers Info pane to create and manage layers in your document. Complex documents may benefit from using layers; variations of data (or different layout versions) can be placed on separate layers, then the layers can be turned on or off as the different data (or versions) are needed.

1. Click the "plus" button to create a new layer. Double-click the default layer name to type a new name.

2. Select items in a document to put on the new layer.

3. Click "Move Selected Graphics to Layer."

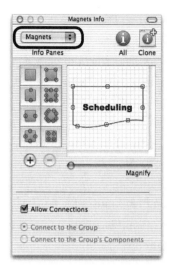

Magnets Info

In the Magnets pane you can determine where lines connect to a shape and if connections are turned on or off. When lines connect to *ordinary* shapes, the line points to the center of the shape; when lines connect to *magnetized* shapes, the line points to the nearest magnet.

To magnetize a shape:

1. Select a shape in a document to show it in the Magnets Info preview.
2. Click one of the magnet icons on the left to add magnets to the selected shape. Use the "Magnify" slider to enlarge the preview.

   Click the "plus" button to *manually* add a magnet to the shape.

   To delete a magnet, click the magnet point, then press Delete.

Magnetized   *Ordinary*
shape   *shape*

Action Info

You can attach two kinds of "actions" to graphics: **Open a URL** opens a designated web site when a user clicks a graphic with that action attached to it. **Run a Script** activates a designated AppleScript that can run various commands, such as opening a file in the Finder (see page 422).

All Info

This pane displays icons for all of the other panes. Instead of choosing a pane from the pop-up menu, you can click one of these icons to open a pane. **For extra-easy access to a frequently used Info pane,** drag its icon from this pane to the Info Viewer toolbar. Command-drag an icon off the toolbar to remove it.

The graphic above has an "Open a URL" action attached to it. When the "Browse" tool hovers over the graphic, the shape highlights and shows a blue lightning bolt on the side. Click to open an attached web site.

Palettes

Using Palettes: Prebuilt Graphics

OmniGraffle includes palettes of **prebuilt graphics** that are useful to programmers, information architects, engineers, and even people like us who just need a few basic shapes to work with. Some of these palettes are simple and self-explanatory, and others are so complex that if you need them you're probably not reading this book—you're probably writing the software.

The palettes you're most likely to use are shown below: **Basic, Magnetized,** and **OrgChart.** The other palettes are shown on the next page.

To open and use the Palettes window:

1. Click the "Palettes" icon (shown above, left) in the OmniGraffle toolbar.
2. From the pop-up menu, choose a palette you want to open.
3. Drag a shape from the palette to your document.

   Once the shape is placed in your document, you can resize or modify any way needed.

Click the "Edit" icon to make changes to existing shapes in the palette.

Click the "New" icon to create your own custom palette (page 430).

Select a palette from the pop-up menu.

To add another "Palettes" icon to the toolbar (next to "Basic"), Control-click on the toolbar. From the "Customize" sheet that drops down, drag the Palette icon of your choice to the toolbar.

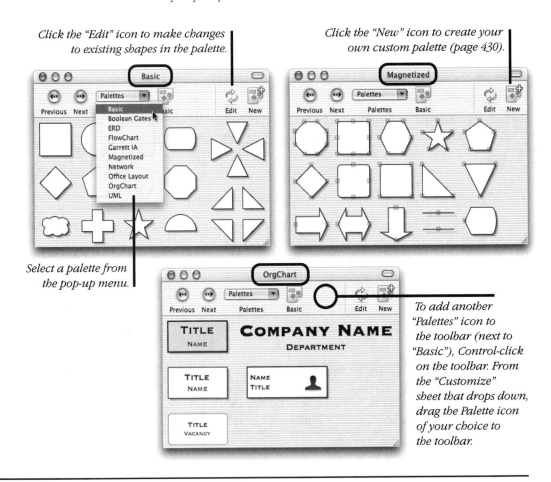

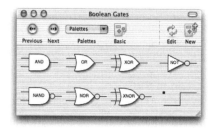

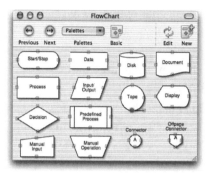

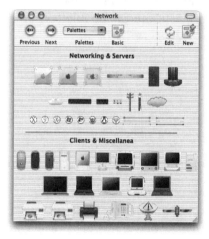

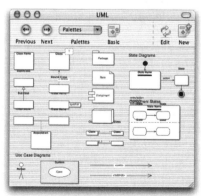

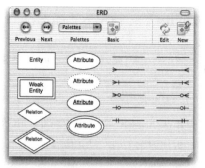

OmniGraffle also includes these collections of graphics in the "Palettes" window.

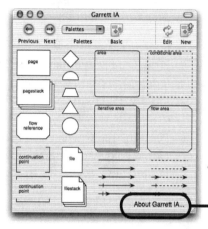

Tip: If you're interested in Information Architecture, or just curious, click "About Garrett IA…" to open a very informative web site.

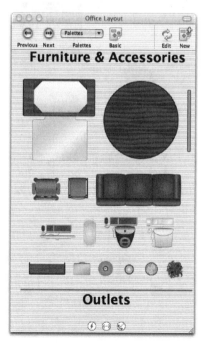

Create Your Own Palettes

If you have a collection images or shapes you plan to use a lot, you can create a new palette that contains just your custom graphics.

1. Click the "Palettes" icon in the toolbar to open the window of palettes.

2. Click the "New" icon in the Palettes window toolbar.

3. In the new "Untitled" palette editor window that opens, create custom shapes with the drawing tools, or drag images into the window from the Finder.

   Images and shapes you add immediately show up in an "Untitled" palette viewer window on your Desktop.

4. From the File menu, choose "Save." This makes the new palette *temporarily* available, until you close the palette. **To permanently add** the palette to your palette options, take one more step to *install* the palette.

5. Place the file you just saved into this folder: navigate inside your Home Folder to Library/Application Support/OmniGraffle/Palettes. Put the new palette file in the "Palettes" folder.

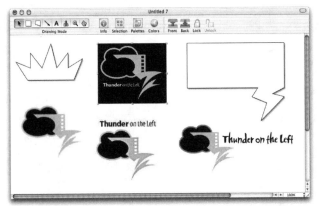

The palette viewer shows items as you add them to the palette editor window on the right.

Add shapes to the palette editor window by creating them with the drawing tools, or drag images into the window from the Finder.

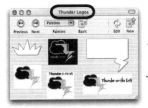

After you save the new palette, it's ready for you to drag items from it to a document window.

Customize the Toolbar

As you become familiar with OmniGraffle, you'll find yourself using favorite tools that aren't in the toolbar. And some of the items in the toolbar may be taking up space without being used. You can customize the toolbars of the document window, the Info Viewer, and the Palettes pane.

1. Control-click on a toolbar, then from the contextual menu that appears, choose "Customize toolbar...."

2. From the "Customize" sheet, drag your favorite items to the toolbar. The example below shows the "Colors" icon dragged to the toolbar.

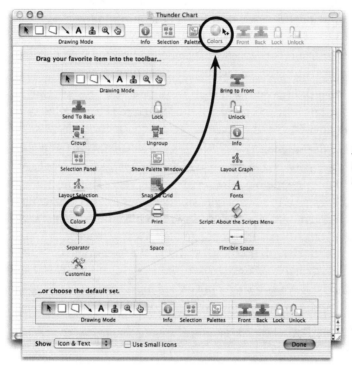

Drag any icon from the "Customize" sheet to the toolbar.

3. From the "Show" pop-up menu at the bottom of the window, choose to display items in the toolbar as "Icon & Text," "Icon Only," or "Text Only."

4. Check the "Use Small Icons" box if you prefer that style or if you have a lot of icons in your toolbar. The difference between large and small icons is not very dramatic, but you still can choose.

   To remove an icon from the toolbar, Command-drag it from the toolbar to the Desktop. It will disappear in a poof of smoke.

Set Your Preferences

Open the Preferences window and check the seven different panes to see if there are any settings or options you want to change.

To open the Preferences window, from the OmniGraffle application menu, choose "Preferences." They're grouped into seven categories. Most of the options are self-explanatory; those that may not be are explained on the following pages.

General preferences

Tip: When entering a number in a text box for conversion to the units chosen in the General Preferences, valid unit abbreviations are:

in for inches
cm for centimeters
pt for points
p for picas

▼ **Measurement units:** Choose a unit of measurement from the pop-up menu that will be used in rulers, in the Info window, and in some text boxes used for entering measurements. You can type a number in some text boxes, followed by a unit abbreviation (see sidebar tip), and it will be converted to the units of measurement chosen here.

▼ **On Startup:** Choose if you want to automatically re-open any documents that were open the last time you quit OmniGraffle, or to remember and re-open palettes that were open.

▼ **Saving documents:** The default is **Save as single file,** but if a document contains images or image fills, the images are "serialized" and saved in the same file. The serialization process inflates the data size of images, and the overall file size becomes inflated. If the file size is a problem, you can choose **Save as a file wrapper.** This saves the OmniGraffle data and a separate file for each image into a folder, but the "file wrapper" shows in the Finder as a single file icon. File wrappers can be awkward to work with, so an alternative would be to choose **Save as a single file unless there are images.** This option creates a file wrapper only when the document contains images.

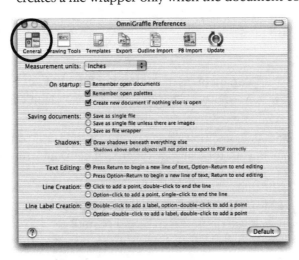

Drawing Tools preferences

Choose which tools appear in the Drawing Mode bar that appears in a document's toolbar.

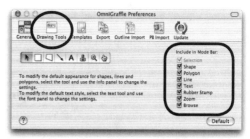

Templates preferences

Set a default "New Document Template" that opens when you create a new document. To add a new location for OmniGraffle to search for templates, click the "New Path" button (the plus sign), then enter a path name. To remove a path name, select it, then click the "minus" button.

Export preferences

▼ **Export with room around graphics**

Adds padding around your exported document rather than letting the outside extremities of graphics determine the outside edge of the exported file. If the exported file is to be used in another sort of document, this may or may not be good. For instance, if you design a web graphic or chart to be an *exact* size, 600 x 400 pixels for instance, you wouldn't want extra room placed around the graphics. But then there are times when you might want extra breathing room around a file.

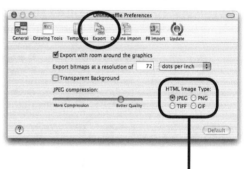

If you plan to export your document as an HTML Image Map (one of the options in the "Export" menu), this setting determines the file format that will be used.

▼ **Export bitmaps at a resolution of 72 dots per inch**

If your exported file is to be shown on a monitor, 72 dots per inch is the proper setting. If you're going to export a file to be printed on a high-resolution printer, you should set the resolution higher; *300 dots per inch* is a common resolution for commercial printing.

▼ **Transparent background**

Some web graphics, such as PNG or GIF files, can show transparency to allow background images or colors to show through parts of the image. If you're exporting the document for such a use, check the Transparent Background box.

▼ **JPEG compression:**

If exporting as a JPEG file, use the slider to choose a compromise between smaller file size (more compression) and better quality.

Outline Import preferences

This pane lets you set options for formatting imported **OmniOutliner** documents. OmniOutliner is an application also developed by OmniGroup, the developers of OmniGraffle.

▼ **Graphic Style**

The selected *Style Group* is used to set graphics and line styles when you import an OmniOutliner document. Each of the items in the *Style Groups column* displays a list of Level Styles in the *Level Styles column*. Each Level Style displays a preview in the *Preview* column. Items in the Level Styles column determine the line style used and the style of graphic that will be applied to each level of an imported outline.

▼ **Layout Type**

Choose one of the automatic layout styles: "Force-directed" or "Hierarchical." "Hierarchical" usually works best for most simple projects.

To add new graphic styles, click the "plus" button. **To remove a style,** click the "minus" button.

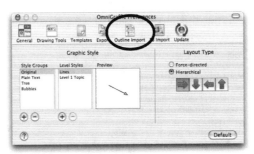

PB Import preferences

This pane is for programmers who want to import *Project Builder* (PB) files, Apple's integrated development environment for Mac OS X.

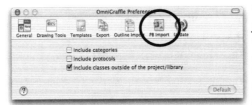

When importing a PB file, OmniGraffle uses the Objective-C header from the Project Builder framework to construct a diagram of the inheritance, protocol, and category relationships.

Update preferences

The Update pane lets you set how (manually or automatically) and when your computer checks for OmniGraffle updates.

More Information about Adding Photographs or Images

There are several different ways to add an image to a document or to a shape within a document.

To add photographs or other images:

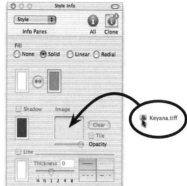

▼ *Drag and drop* an image file icon from anywhere on your computer into an existing graphic shape. The image stretches as necessary to fill the shape.

▼ *Drag and drop* an image file icon onto the background of a document. The image is placed on the background as its own shape, undistorted.

▼ *Cut and paste* an image from another document into an OmniGraffle document background or into a shape on the OmniGraffle page.

▼ *Drop an image onto the "Image" well* in the Style Info pane, as shown on the right. First select a shape, click the "Info" icon in the document toolbar, then drag an image from the Finder onto the "Image" well.

The image stretches as necessary to fill the shape. Check the "Tile" box to place the image in the shape undistorted. The image will "tile" (repeat), if necessary, to fill the shape area. The tiling may not be visible unless you drag the shape knobs to make the shape larger.

OmniGraffle image file formats

OmniGraffle can use almost any format that other applications use. The most popular formats are PDF, TIFF, JPEG, PNG, GIF, and PICT.

Lock Items to Prevent Accidents

Lock items to prevent any accidental clicks from changing their shape or position as you work in a document.

▼ **To lock an item,** select one or more items, then click the Lock icon in the toolbar.

▼ **To unlock an item,** select it, then click the Unlock icon.

Export Your Files

Export your OmniGraffle document in a variety of formats so you can share it with others.

1. From the File menu, choose "Export...."

2. In the Export sheet that drops down, enter a name in the "Save as" box. From the "Where" pop-up menu, choose a location in which to save the exported file.

3. From the "File Format" menu, choose one of six image formats:

   PDF, JPEG, GIF, or PNG: Formats most suited for viewing on computers and web pages.

   TIFF, EPS, PDF: Formats best for printing.

   PDF: Format suited for web pages and for printing.

   HTML Image Map: A web page format that defines "hot spots" that link to other web pages when you click on them. If you plan to use this format and place the exported file on a web page, you can assign "actions" to selected shapes in your document; the action will automatically open a web address when someone clicks the shape (see "Action Info pane" on page 427).

4. Select other Export options, then click "Save."

For information about these options, see "Export Preferences" on page 433.

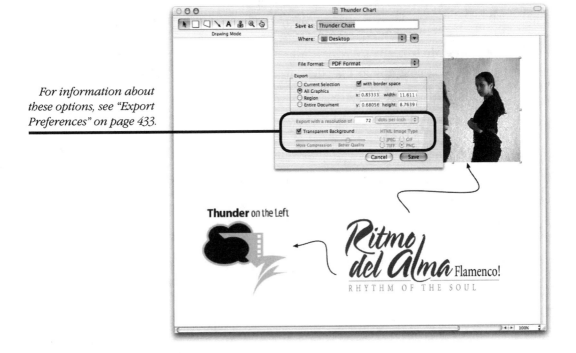

FAXstf

On your Mac you might have the software called **FAXstf X.** With this software you can create a letter in any application of your choice and fax it right from the screen. And you can also receive faxes into your computer (your M must be turned on), then print the fax on your own printer—or just read i on the screen and never print it at all. It's great and it's easy. In this chapter I'll walk you through sending a fax page, and I'll also show you how to set things up so your Mac will receive faxes.

This is the monster drawing from the AppleWorks tutorial (Chapter 17). You can fax it to your friends and loved ones. They'll be so impressed.

FAXstf X

FAXstf™ X makes it possible to send and receive faxes straight from your Mac. FAXstf works with the Address Book application to address faxes, and uses the Apple internal modem to send and receive faxes. If you have an AirPort wireless network, DSL, or cable modem connection, you must physically connect a **phone line** to the modem connection on the back of the Mac (and plug the other end into a phone jack) to use FAXstf.

Install and Set Up FAXstf X

Before you can use FAXstf, you need to install the application and perform a few basic setup steps.

FAXstf X 10.0 Installer

To install FAXstf X:

1. To find the FAXstf installer, click on the Applications button in any window Toolbar to open the Applications folder.

2. In the Applications folder, double-click the **Installers** folder to open it.

3. Double-click the "FAXstf X 10.0 Installer" icon and follow the simple installation directions.

FAXstf is actually two small applications, the **Fax Browser** and the **Modem Center.** These two applications, plus the Mac OS X **Print Center,** need to be set up before you send a fax.

First, set up the Print Center

Print Center

1. Open the Applications window, then open the "Utilities" folder and find the **Print Center** application.

   Double-click the Print Center icon to open the "Printer List" window, as shown below.

   (If the "Printer List" window does not automatically appear, go to the Printers menu and choose "View Printer List.")

2. You will get either the Printer List window or an alert message, both shown below. Click the "Add Printer…" or "Add…" button because you need to add the Apple modem printer to this list.

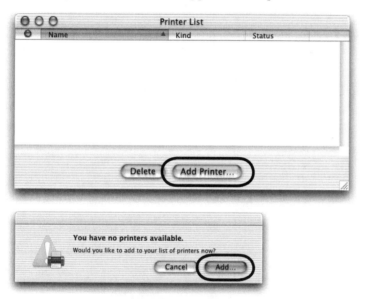

—*continued*

3. A "sheet" drops down in front of the list, and the sheet has a pop-up menu on it. From that menu, choose "FAXstf," as shown below.

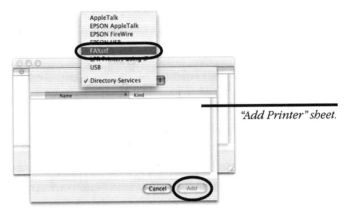

"Add Printer" sheet.

4. "Apple Internal Modem" will appear in the sheet below the menu; click on that name to select it, then click the "Add" button. The Apple Internal Modem will appear in the Printer List, as shown below.

This is what the Printer List looks like after
adding "Apple Internal Modem."

5. Now that "Apple Internal Modem" is added to the Printer List, FAXstf can fax from any application that is capable of printing.

6. You can **Quit** the Print Center now.

Second, set up the Fax Browser Preferences

The contact information you specify in the Fax Browser "Preferences" window appears on your fax cover sheet to identify you as the sender.

Fax Browser

1. Open (double-click) the Fax Browser application that's located in the FAXstf X folder.

2. From the Fax Browser menu, choose "Preferences...."
   Click the "Identity" tab to show the Identity pane, as shown below.

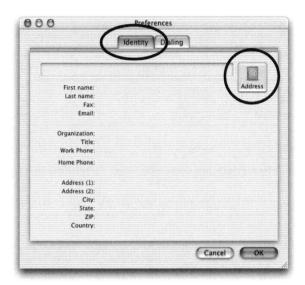

3. Single-click the "Address" button, circled above, to open the Address Book, shown below. If you don't already have one, you need to create a contact information card for yourself.

   Each card in Address Book is called a **vCard**, or virtual card. **To create a card,** click the "New" button in the toolbar, then enter the information. You don't have to fill in every field, but you must enter a first name, last name, and fax number for the Fax Browser Preferences to accept it.

For all the details about the Address Book that comes with Mac OS X, see Chapter 5.

Click the "New" button to create a vCard for yourself.

While you're here, you might as well add cards for everyone you know.

—continued

4. Drag your personal vCard from the Address Book list and drop it in the text field at the top of the Identity panel.

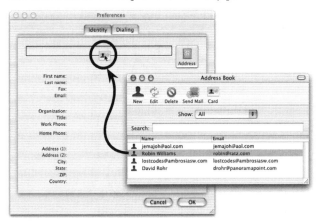

5. If you need a **prefix** before you call out from your phone line, such as a code for an outside line or a credit card number, click the **Dialing** tab.

Click the "Use prefix" checkbox and enter the number in the prefix field.

Sometimes you need a comma after a number or between a series of numbers to slow down the dialing operation—each comma makes the phone wait a few seconds before continuing. By default, a comma in FAXstf creates a two-second delay, but you can change that, if necessary; see the opposite page.

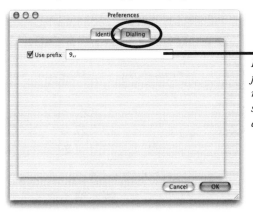

In this example, the fax software will dial a nine, then will wait four seconds before it dials the actual fax number.

6. Click OK.

Third, set up the Modem Center

Modem Center

1. Double-click the Modem Center application in the FAXstf X folder. Notice "Apple Internal Modem" appears as a result of setting up the Print Center.

   The current "Status" is "Idle," but when you send a fax, the changing states of the modem display in this window (dialing, connecting, sending, handshaking, etc.).

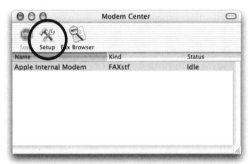

2. Click the "Setup" button, circled above, to show the setup sheet.

3. Click the **General tab,** if it's not selected, to show the General options.

   Name: Should already say "Apple Internal Modem."

   Station Message: Enter your fax number. This number is used to identify yourself to another fax device.

   Dialing: Select your type of phone service.

   Volume: Choose a volume for your modem speaker.

   On: Choose when you want the modem speaker turned on.

   Comma pauses: Specify a time delay that applies to commas in a number or prefix, as shown on the opposite page.

—continued

4. Click the **Sending** tab.

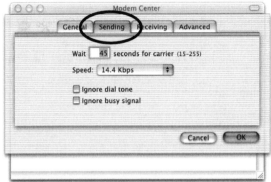

Wait: Specify the length of time to wait for a fax machine to answer.

Speed: Select a baud rate for the modem. Choose the highest option available, 14.4Kbps. This is the fastest speed that a fax can be sent.

Ignore dial tone: Forces FAXstf to dial a fax number even if it can't detect a dial tone, as when going through a hotel PBX switchboard.

Ignore busy signal: Forces FAXstf to continue trying to connect when it detects a busy signal.

5. Click the **Receiving** tab.

Answer after: Set how many rings before FAXstf answers an incoming fax call. If you don't want FAXstf to automatically answer incoming calls, set this number to 0. (See page 448 for more info on this.)

Speed: Set the modem's baud rate for receiving faxes—choose the fastest option, 14.4Kbps. If you have trouble receiving faxes, try a slower baud rate.

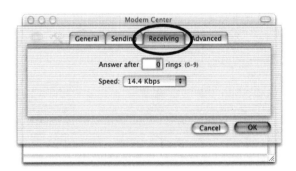

6. Ignore the **Advanced** tab. Click OK.

Send a Fax

Now that you've set up FAXstf, you can finally send a fax. You can fax from any application on your Mac that ordinarily has a print option.

If you haven't followed the steps on the previous seven pages, you need to do so before you send a fax.

1. Open the document on your computer that you want to fax.

2. From the File menu, choose "Print...."

3. In the Print window, choose "Apple Internal Modem" from the Printer pop-up menu (as shown below).

4. From the lower pop-up menu, choose "Addresses" to show the Addresses pane of the Print window, as shown below.

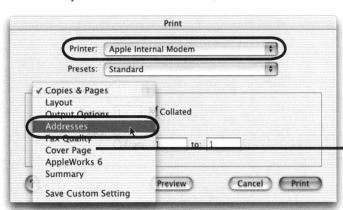

Notice from this pop-up menu you can also choose to add a "Cover Page" message, as well as adjust the quality of the fax.

5. In the Addresses pane, below, click the "Address" button on the right to open the Address Book, which is shown on the following page.

—continued

6. In the Address Book, find the vCard of a person to whom you want to send a fax. If there isn't one, click the "New" button and make one for that person. Make sure the vCard contains a fax number in the "Fax" field.

Drag the vCard and drop it in the Addresses pane of the Print window, as shown below. You can fax the document to more than one person at a time—just drag over a vCard for each recipient.

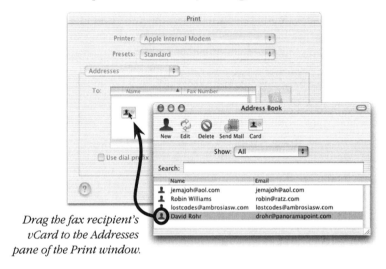

Drag the fax recipient's vCard to the Addresses pane of the Print window.

7. If you want to put a short message on the fax cover page, choose "Cover Page" from the lower pop-up menu (shown on the previous page).

In the Cover Page pane that appears, type a short message that will automatically print on a fax cover page.

8. Click the "Print" button in the lower-right corner of the Print window to send the fax.

FAXstf Animated Dock Icons

During a fax transmission, watch the FAXstf icon in the Dock. The inside of the circle will change and animate to illustrate the various stages of the fax operation.

Idle

Pulsing green dot: You're ready to send or receive a fax.

Dialing

Animated number keys: The modem is dialing a fax number.

Ringing

Animated sound waves: The modem detects an incoming call.

Connecting

Two buckles connect: The modem is connecting to another device.

Sending

Data rising from a document icon: A fax is being sent.

Receiving

Data falling into a document icon: A fax is being received.

Handshaking

A page being torn away: The modem is "shaking hands," something that occurs during the transmission of pages.

Hanging up

Two buckles moving apart: The connection is terminating.

Error

Pulsing red dot: An error occurred during the fax transmission.

During a fax transmission, the Modem Center window automatically opens on the Desktop to display the modem status.

Receive a Fax

You cannot receive a fax unless you have instructed FAXstf to automatically answer telephone calls, as described on page 444. I'll explain how to do this again because this is the one setting you might have to change regularly, depending on your phone line situation. How many rings you tell FAXstf to wait before it picks up depends on whether you have a dedicated fax line or whether your fax line is also the only phone line in the house.

If your Mac is connected to a **dedicated fax (phone) line,** set the value to **1** so FAXstf will answer as quickly as possible.

If you have an Internet connection that uses your modem, you cannot send or receive faxes while you are online, nor can you get online while you are sending or receiving a fax.

If your Mac is connected to a **phone line that is also used for phone calls,** set the value to 3, 4, or a higher number that gives you time to answer the phone, if you choose, *before* FAXstf automatically picks it up. Then when you are expecting a fax, let the phone ring until FAXstf picks it up.

If you have an **answering machine,** you'll have to set the number of rings to 0 (zero) while you're away from your desk so you can get messages. When you are back, change the rings to pick up.

To change the number of rings before FAXstf picks up to take a fax, or to **turn off FAXstf** altogether:

1. Open the Modem Center.
2. Click the "Setup" button in the toolbar.
3. Click the "Receiving" tab.

   Set the "Answer after" value to **0** rings to make sure FAXstf does *not* answer the phone (this effectively turns off FAXstf).

   Change the value to between **1** and **9** rings and FAXstf will answer any phone call that comes in (unless you leap for the phone and grab it first).

When a fax comes in, the Fax Browser automatically opens on your screen so you'll know what has arrived.

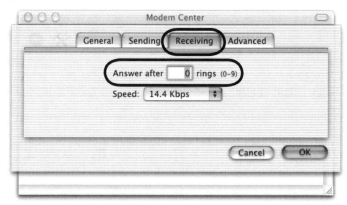

The Fax Browser Window

Fax Browser

Use the **Fax Browser** to view your fax documents. You can also choose a fax to print, delete faxes that you don't want to keep, and archive (save in another place) faxes that you need to keep. **To open the Fax Browser,** double-click the Fax Browser icon in the FAXstf folder.

The Fax Browser window features a collapsible "Drawer"—click the **Trays** button in the toolbar (circled, below) to open and close the Drawer. This Drawer contains several "Trays" in which you can store and organize your faxes: Just drag any fax from the list area and drop it in a Tray.

Archive selected faxes by dragging them from the list area to the Archive Tray in the drawer.

Click to open and close the Drawer.

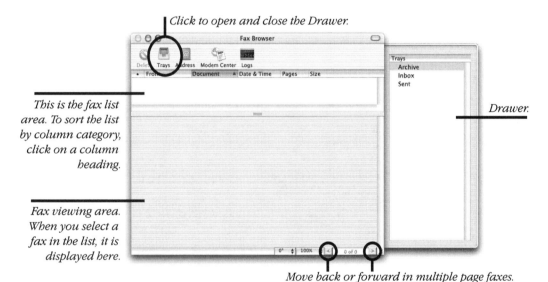

This is the fax list area. To sort the list by column category, click on a column heading.

Fax viewing area. When you select a fax in the list, it is displayed here.

Drawer.

Move back or forward in multiple page faxes.

The Fax Browser toolbar

> **Delete:** Deletes the currently selected faxes in the fax list.
>
> **Trays:** Opens and closes the collapsible Drawer that contains your fax Trays.
>
> **Address:** Opens the Address Book application.
>
> **Modem Center:** Opens the Modem Center where you can change your modem settings.
>
> **Logs:** Opens the Activity Log file that contains a record of your fax activities.

Fax Browser

View a Fax

All faxes you receive are placed in the "Inbox" tray that appears in the Fax Browser Drawer, as shown below. Click on the "Inbox" tray to show a list of received faxes. A blue dot next to a fax in the list indicates that it has not been viewed.

Single-click on a fax in the list to display it in the viewing area of the Fax Browser window, as shown below. The controls at the bottom of the window let you rotate the selected fax, zoom in or out, and jump to specific pages of a multiple-page fax.

If you've used the Mail program, you'll find this browser window very similar.

Print a Fax

Select a fax in the Fax Browser list (single-click on it), then from the File menu, choose "Print...." Make sure your printer (not the "Apple Internal Modem") is chosen in the Printer pop-up menu, as shown below.

Fax Browser

Select a fax in the Fax Browser list, then choose "Print...."

Make sure the printer chosen here is your actual printer, not "Apple Internal Modem"!

Modem Center

Modem Center Preferences

There are a couple of other settings you can customize, if you like, as shown below. To get the preferences, open the Modem Center, then go to the Modem Center menu (next to the Apple), and choose "Preferences…."

Windows

Click the "Windows" tab to choose if the Main Window and Active Modems will show when the Modem Center application launches. These settings don't really affect how you use FAXstf, and the Modem Center opens automatically when you send a fax. I prefer to leave the default settings alone.

Logging

Click the "Logging" tab to determine how often a New Activity Log is created. For most people, looking at a fax log file once is enough to satisfy their curiosity forever. Unless your life revolves around faxing, the "Never" option is probably sufficient.

Inkwell

Inkwell is Apple's handwriting recognition technology. It converts your hand-written words to text which you can then insert into any open document. You can also draw in Inkwell, then place that drawing into a document.

To use Inkwell, you must have a **graphics tablet** connected to your computer. If you haven't connected a graphics tablet or installed its software, you won't see the Ink icon in your System Preferences window, as shown on the next page.

You may notice in the System Preferences window that Inkwell is called Ink. They are the same thing, and this chapter uses the name Inkwell.

What's a graphics tablet?

A graphics tablet is a device used for drawing. A pressure-sensitive stylus (like a pen with no ink) uses radio waves to draw on a special tablet. Any place you touch the stylus to the graphics tablet, a stylus icon or cursor appears on your computer screen in a relative position. The tablet simulates natural-media tools (pens and brushes) by varying the appearance of strokes according to how hard you press the stylus against the tablet. The tablet's own software lets you adjust the sensitivity of the stylus and define certain functions.

A variety of graphics tablets are available with varying price ranges, but I've been very happy with the low-priced Wacom Graphire2 USB tablet, having used it with Inkwell, Adobe Illustrator, Adobe Photoshop, and Corel Painter.

Open the Ink Preferences

Once you've installed the graphics tablet software, the **Ink** icon will appear in the Hardware section of the System Preferences window.

You won't see this icon until you've connected a graphics tablet and installed its latest software.

To turn on Inkwell:

1. Click the System Preferences icon in the Dock.

2. Click the Ink icon, circled above, to open the Inkwell preferences.

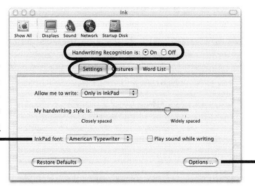

Choose a font for InkPad (shown on the opposite page) to use when it converts your handwriting into text.

See page 458 for information about the "Options…" button.

3. At the top of the Ink window (above) are "On" and "Off" buttons. Click "On" to start Inkwell and to make the **InkBar** visible, shown below.

Zoom button.

The InkBar is always visible while Inkwell is running.

To make the InkBar go away, *click the "Off" button, shown above.*

To shrink the InkBar *down to one button (shown above right), click the green Zoom button. To expand the InkBar, click the Zoom button again.*

Make Your Setting Choices

The **Settings** tab shown on the previous page shows various Inkwell settings that you can adjust.

The "Allow me to write" pop-up menu lets you choose where on the screen you can create a handwritten message.

▼ Choose **Only in InkPad** if you want to always place your handwriting on the built-in InkPad (an on-screen tablet for writing, shown below). When this option is chosen, the Wacom stylus behaves like a mouse *until* it's positioned on top of the open InkPad, and *then* it becomes a drawing/writing tool.

The InkBar.

The InkPad.

Tips:

Inkwell recognizes print-style handwriting, not cursive-style.

Write in a straight line.

Try looking at the graphics tablet instead of at the screen.

Put a sheet of ruled paper on top of your Wacom tablet (or under its plastic flap) and concentrate on following the guides on the paper. The Wacom stylus and tablet use radio waves that can go through any paper you place on top of the tablet.

▼ Choose **Anywhere** from the pop-up menu and wherever your stylus cursor is positioned on the screen, a yellow notepad appears under it so you can start writing. Each word you write is inserted at the insertion point of an open document. In the example below, the text is being placed in the "Untitled" TextEdit document.

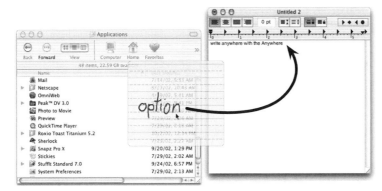

The "Allow me to write Anywhere" option creates a yellow notepad wherever the tablet stylus touches the Desktop.

Tools in the InkBar

The **InkBar** holds the tools that you use in Inkwell. The InkBar is always visible if Handwriting Recognition is turned "on" in the Ink Preferences. If the "Help" icon and the "Open Ink Preferences" icon are hidden, click on the double arrows to show them in a pop-up menu.

Arrow/Stylus icons

Click the Arrow icon in the InkBar to toggle between it and the Stylus icon.

▼ When the **Arrow icon** is visible, it's the same as choosing **Only in InkPad,** as explained on the previous page. Your cursor becomes an arrow except when it is positioned on top of the InkPad, and then it becomes a stylus for handwriting.

▼ When the **Stylus icon** is visible, it's the same as choosing to **write Anywhere,** as explained on the previous page. A yellow writing pad appears under the cursor anywhere you touch the stylus to the screen so you can handwrite text that will be inserted in an open document.

Command, Shift, Option, and Control icons

The InkBar displays symbols for the modifier keys on your keyboard: Command, Shift, Option, and Control (in that order). These allow you to perform basic Mac commands with your stylus instead of having to press these keyboard keys—when you click any of these modifier icons with your stylus, it's the same as pressing that key on your keyboard.

For instance, if you click the Command icon in the InkBar, then press the letter O on your keyboard (with your finger), the Open dialog box appears on your screen. If you're experienced using a graphics tablet, this may be an attractive feature, but it may seem more awkward than useful.

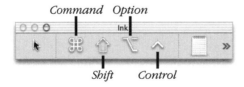

Now Try It

Here is a quick little practice exercise to show you how Inkwell actually works. Make sure you followed the steps on page 454 to turn it on. For this exercise, use the "Anywhere" option as described on page 455.

To write in Inkwell:

1. Click the "Show InkPad" icon in the InkBar to open InkPad, the on-screen writing tablet. (Skip to Step 2 if the InkPad is already open).

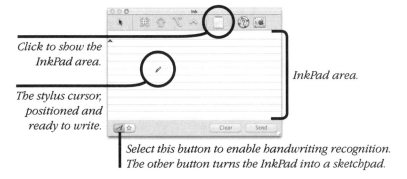

Click to show the InkPad area.

The stylus cursor, positioned and ready to write.

InkPad area.

Select this button to enable handwriting recognition. The other button turns the InkPad into a sketchpad.

2. With a tablet stylus, write the word "hello."

*Until you've practiced a little, handwriting with a stylus can be awkward. **To erase everything and start over,** click the "Clear" button beneath the InkPad.*

3. When you stop writing, Inkwell identifies the word and converts it to text on the InkPad.

Move the Inkwell text to another document

When you're ready to place your handwritten text into a document, make sure the document is open and the insertion point is flashing where you want to insert the text. Click the "Send" button in the bottom-right corner of InkPad. The converted text is placed in the document at the flashing insertion point. Amazing.

More Handwriting Preferences

There are several options in the Preferences you might want to check out.

Adjust the Settings Options

If Inkwell **works too fast** for you and converts a word before you can finish writing it, go back to the Ink Preferences and adjust the Settings Options.

1. Click the "Open Ink Preferences" icon in the InkBar, circled below.

2. In the Ink Preferences window, click the "Settings" tab, then click the "Options" button.

3. From the drop-down panel that appears, choose settings for handwriting recognition. Click OK.

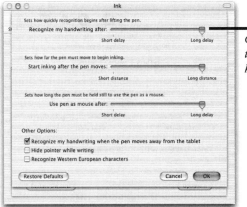

Choose "Long delay" to slow down Inkwell's handwriting recognition.

The animation window shows how to draw a Gesture.

Gestures

Gestures are text-editing commands to Undo, Cut, Copy, Paste, etc., with the stylus. Learn the actions in this panel, then use them while you're writing with Inkwell.

To learn an action, click on the name of an action to select it, then watch the stroke animate in the box on the right. A description of the gesture appears below it. Practice drawing the gestures by duplicating the animation stroke movements.

Word List

If you frequently use words that Inkwell doesn't recognize, add them to this list to help Inkwell identify them.

To add words to Inkwell:

1. Click the "Open Ink Preferences" icon in the InkBar.
2. Click the "Word List" tab.

3. Click the "Add…" button.
4. Type a word in the "New word for Word List" panel that drops down.
5. Click OK to enter the word in the list.

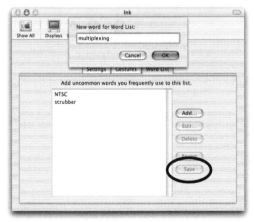

To delete a word from the list, select it, then click the "Delete" button.

To edit a word, select it, then click the "Edit…" button.

6. Click the "Save" button.

Use InkPad as a Sketchpad

The InkPad can also be used as a **sketchpad.** You can send quick sketches, simple maps, or rough schematics to another document, such as an email message that you're composing or a word processing document.

To sketch with Inkwell:

1. Click the InkPad icon in the InkBar to open Inkwell's writing tablet.

2. Click the "Star" icon in the bottom-left corner to convert the writing tablet to a sketchpad.

3. Using the graphics tablet and stylus, draw something.

4. When finished, click the "Send" button to place the sketch in an open document of your choice. The location of the flashing insertion point determines where the sketch gets placed.

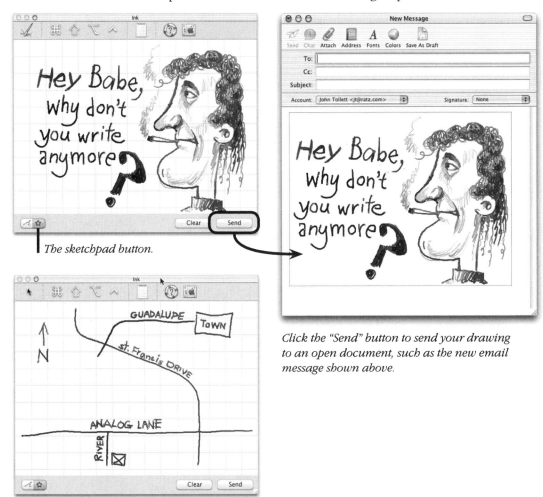

The sketchpad button.

Click the "Send" button to send your drawing to an open document, such as the new email message shown above.

Section five

Index

Symbols

A

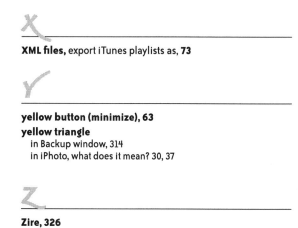